Retail Geography

T0295757

The retail sector is an integral part of a national economy. From the political economy perspective, all consumer goods have surplus values locked up in them; the surplus values are not realized until the consumer goods are purchased by consumers through various distribution channels. As such, retailing is the essential link between production and consumption.

The success of a retail business depends on two general factors: the location of the retail outlet, and management of the business. Both factors are equally important. If the business is located in the wrong place with the wrong customer base, it will not generate expected sales. Similarly, if the business is poorly managed and operated, it will not perform well even if the location is right. Influenced by both traditional and new location theories, *Retail Geography* is conceptualized and organized using the retail planning process as the framework. The technical and methodological chapters help guide the reader with detailed descriptions of the techniques and are supported with practical examples to reflect the latest software development.

Retail Geography provides a state-of-the-art summary and will act as a core textbook for undergraduate and graduate students of economic geography interested in specializing in retail and business geography. The practical examples also make it a valuable handbook for practitioners in the field, as well as students of retail management and commercial real estate management.

Shuguang Wang is Professor of Geography at Ryerson University, Canada. He has taught retail geography for 20 years and is well versed in the various theories and methods. He has published widely on retailing topics and has presented multiple papers at international conferences. His research on this subject culminated with the publication of *China's New Retail Economy: A Geographic Perspective* (Routledge, 2014).

Paul Du is an experienced spatial analyst. After obtaining a Master of Spatial Analysis degree in 2005, he worked as a GIS Analyst at Ryerson University's Centre for the Study of Commercial Activity, Canada, for seven and a half years, where he completed many retail-related research projects. In the recent past, he collaborated with Shuguang Wang to develop and test several major retail geography labs.

Retail Geography

Shuguang Wang and Paul Du

Routledge
Taylor & Francis Group

NEW YORK AND LONDON

First published 2021
by Routledge
52 Vanderbilt Avenue, New York, NY 10017

and by Routledge
2 Park Square, Milton Park, Abingdon, Oxon, OX14 4RN

Routledge is an imprint of the Taylor & Francis Group, an informa business

Library of Congress Cataloging-in-Publication Data
Names: Wang, Shuguang, 1956- author. | Du, Paul, author.
Title: Retail geography / Shuguang Wang and Paul Du.
Description: New York, NY : Routledge, 2020. | Includes bibliographical references and index.
Identifiers: LCCN 2020004554 (print) | LCCN 2020004555 (ebook) | ISBN 9780815358589 (hardback) | ISBN 9780367435110 (paperback) | ISBN 9781003003762 (ebook)
Subjects: LCSH: Retail trade–Location. | Industrial location.
Classification: LCC HF5429 .W333 2020 (print) | LCC HF5429 (ebook) | DDC 381/.1–dc23
LC record available at https://lccn.loc.gov/2020004554
LC ebook record available at https://lccn.loc.gov/2020004555

ISBN: 978-0-8153-5858-9 (hbk)
ISBN: 978-0-367-43511-0 (pbk)
ISBN: 978-1-003-00376-2 (ebk)

Typeset in New Baskerville
by Wearset Ltd, Boldon, Tyne and Wear

Visit the eResources: www.routledge.com/9780367435110

This book is dedicated to Feng and Wenfei.

Contents

Figures

Tables

Preface

This book is written as a text for senior undergraduate and graduate students who are interested in specializing in retail/business geography. Courses for which this textbook is suitable include Geography of Retailing, Business Geography, Marketing Geography, and Spatial Analysis of Commercial Activity. It can also serve as a supplementary text for students in retail management, marketing, and real estate management, who take retail geography as a professionally related subject. Ideally, users of this text should have acquired familiarity with introductory statistics and geographical information systems (GIS).

A survey of the existing books (ten or so, published in the last 30 years) reveals that while each of them served the students and instructors very well at the time of their publication and for a period of time thereafter, there is a need for an updated text that covers and blends the essence of both the orthodox retail geography and the new geography of retailing to reflect the recent changes in the retail industry as well as the advancement in geotechnologies. Recently, the major developers and venders of business location intelligence software have all been actively offering free webinars to promote their computer-based analytical platforms. However, the webinars and the online manuals mostly focus on operational instructions for the software, and are not intended to provide an understanding of the theories and the theoretical conceptualizations on the basis of which the software has been developed. This current book intends to fill the gap by blending theory and practice in one single volume.

For continuity in the development of retail geography, this book includes the core topics covered in the various existing books, but with a new organizational framework. Specifically, the current book is presented with three distinctive features. First, it is guided by both the traditional location theories and the theory of the new geography of retailing. Second, the component chapters are conceptualized and organized using the retail planning process as the framework. Third, the methodological chapters are presented with detailed descriptions of the techniques, and are also supported with practical examples to reflect the latest software development. While some examples and case studies are selected from published works, the book is rich in original research conducted by the authors of this text. These features also make the textbook a worthwhile reference for students to keep after graduation from the university and while they work in the profession of retail/business location analysis. Outside universities, there is a large number of business/retail consulting professionals who may find this book a useful handbook for their practical work.

With 20 years of teaching and research experience in the field of retail geography, I took on the task of writing the entire book. Accordingly, I am responsible for any errors that might exist in it. My co-author Paul Du contributed to the design and test of the case studies and created all the graphic and cartographic work with professional quality.

The 11 component chapters are written in language suitable for undergraduate and master's students, and are kept short and concise for a one-semester course. Suggested teaching format is a two-hour lecture plus a one-hour lab or tutorial. Instructors are advised to design labs and assignments using data that are "local" and "relevant" to students to stimulate their interest and curiosity. Experiential learning through local case studies also enhances employment opportunities for the students who choose retail geography and location research as a specialization. The delivery sequence of the topical chapters (Chapters 2–10) can be altered to suit the needs of the course. For example, Chapters 7–10 may be introduced before Chapters 5–6. This will prepare students for doing technique-based labs and assignments in the middle of the semester, rather than as they near the end of the semester.

Some may question the relevance of publishing such a book in the era of e-commerce and online retailing, which has contributed to the closure of many bricks-and-mortar stores. Despite the trend that online retailing is taking increasing market shares, it accounts for less than 10 percent of the total retail sales in most countries. Not only will bricks-and-mortar stores continue to stay for a long time, but online retailers (including Amazon) themselves are moving towards a business model of multichannel or omnichannel retailing by building physical stores of their own. In other words, retail geography still matters and store location analysis is still needed. So, such a textbook is still relevant. As Birkin et al. (2002: 1) argue, [even in the era of e-commerce and online retailing] "location issues in retailing have never faded away, and indeed, ... have never been as important as they are today."

Retail geographers do need to develop more sophisticated and intelligent spatial analysis techniques that are capable of dealing with omnichannel networks, and the big spatial data offer opportunities for such development. Collaboration between academic researchers, company in-house practitioners, and data scientists is most likely to lead to breakthroughs in searching for improved or innovative methods. Hopefully, the next generation of retail geography textbooks will feature and incorporate such techniques.

Shuguang Wang
Department of Geography and Environmental Studies
Ryerson University
January 1, 2020

REFERENCES

Birkin, M., Clarke, G. & Clarke, M. (2002). *Retail Geography and Intelligent Network Planning*. Chichester, England: John Wiley & Sons, Ltd.

1 Introduction

The retail sector is an integral part of a national economy. From the political economy point of view, all consumer goods have surplus values locked up in them, and the surplus values are not realized until the consumer goods are purchased by consumers through various distribution channels (Blomley, 1996). As such, retailing is the pivotal link between production and consumption; and the accumulation of retail capital is achieved through "repeated acts of exchange" between consumers and retailers (Ducatel & Blomley, 1990: 218).

In a typical capitalist market economy, the retail sector consists of diverse types of retailers. Some of them are corporate retailers, which operate multiple stores in the form of a chain and with a complex organizational structure. Others are independent retailers with a single store location. In terms of ownership, corporate retailers can be further differentiated as publicly traded companies and privately owned chains. Relative to independent retailers, corporate retailers are small in number, but they command the largest share of the consumer market.

The success of a retail business depends on two general factors: the location of the retail outlets, and management of the business. Both factors are equally important. If the business is located in the wrong place with the wrong customer base, it will not generate expected sales. Similarly, if the business is poorly managed and operated, it will not perform well, even if the location is right.

Retailing is a subject of study for two groups of scholars and students—business management and geography—but they approach the subject from different perspectives. The former are concerned with consumer behavior and business organizations, including logistics, merchandising, marketing, in-store display, and supply chain; whereas the latter focus on selection and determination of business locations and delimitation of trade areas in localized markets. Despite being enrolled in different programs, students of geography and business management often take courses from "the other" school for professional development. For many students, retail geography has been a popular subject, as it frequently leads to rewarding professional jobs in retail corporations, banks, commercial real estate companies, and business consulting firms.

ADVANCEMENT OF RETAIL GEOGRAPHY AS A SUBJECT OF STUDY

Retail geography, which originated as *marketing geography*, but has lately been called by some *business geography*, was created as a separate field of study in the mid-1950s in the United States. William Applebaum is widely regarded as the chief architect of this field of study. He emphasized that marketing geography should be viewed essentially as an applied, rather than a purely academic subject (Applebaum, 1954). He also considered that the best place to develop the field of marketing geography was in business itself. Marketing geography was further developed and advanced by such leading geographers as Brian Berry and David Huff. In its first 40 years, retail geography was primarily concerned with the identification of the demand for various goods and services (i.e., areal expression of demand), and with the spatial arrangements for the supply of them (i.e., areal structure of the system of supply) through an efficient distribution network (Davis, 1976). In general, this orthodox retail geography (as it is being called by some contemporary retail geographers) was founded on a predictive and instrumentalist epistemology, and most of its ontological presumptions are linked to the neo-classical economic view of the world, such as the *central place theory*, *gravity model*, and *distance decay function*, which conceive of space as a neutral container, at most affecting transportation costs. Further, it maintained a focus primarily on the retailer rather than on the supply chain as a whole, and was restricted to concentrating on the geography of stores but neglecting the geography of such important trends as the centralization of retail distribution operations. The traditional maxim of "location, location, location" was well reflected in the orthodox retail geography as a study focus (Jones & Simmons, 1993).

The early 1990s witnessed a major paradigm shift in the study of retail geography. The orthodox retail geography was re-theorized and reconstructed by Wrigley, Lowe and a few other European economic geographers, and a new geography of retailing was advocated to reflect the series of important changes in the global economy. The new geography of retailing has three important characteristics in comparison with the orthodox retail geography (Lowe & Wrigley, 1996).

First, it takes a political economy approach, seeing retail capital as a component part of a larger system of production and consumption (Blomley, 1996). As such, its study scope extends to include production spheres in the system of circulation activities, particularly the production–commerce interface, namely the changing relations between retailers and suppliers. Aided by advanced technologies, retailers have developed logistically efficient stock-control systems and centrally controlled warehouse-to-store distribution networks. These systems permit shorter and more predictable lead time, with important implications for configuration of new retail spaces as well as reconfiguration of existing retail spaces.

Second, it is concerned with the geography of retail restructuring and the grounding of global flows of retail capital (i.e., sinking of retail capital into physical assets in overseas markets) and its spatial outcomes in the form of retail facilities of different formats. Innovative retailers, teamed up with developers, create differentiated spaces of retailing in the same market or different markets, and premeditate them to induce consumption (Ducatel & Blomley, 1990).

Third, it calls for much more serious treatment of regulations because the regulatory state is an important force influencing both corporate strategies and geographical market structures. In the view of Lowe and Wrigley (1996), the orthodox retail geography was remarkably silent about regulation and the complex and contradictory relations of retail capital with the regulatory state. With the exception of a discussion concerning the constraining influence of land use planning regulations, the transformation of retail capital appeared to take place in a world devoid of the macro-regulatory environment that shapes competition between firms and the governance of investment. In the context of the new retail geography, regulations include both public-interest and private-interest interventions, with the former concerning the relations between retailers and consumers, and the latter concerning relationships between retailers and suppliers (including producers).

While the new geography of retailing advanced the theoretical development and expanded the study scope of the subject, there is no place in its agenda for traditional concerns with store location research, GIS, and models that are commonly used to address such strategic issues as evaluating existing branch performance, impacts of new store openings/store closures/store relocations, and finding the optimal location for a new outlet (Birkin et al., 2002). Even Wrigley and Lowe (2002: 17) themselves acknowledge that "we are conscious that some of our readers may feel that we have moved a long way away from what they might regard as the heart of geographical perspectives on retailing." There is clearly a need to integrate both the orthodox retail geography and the new geography of retailing.

THE RETAIL PLANNING PROCESS AS THE ORGANIZATIONAL FRAMEWORK OF THIS BOOK

The success of a retail corporation depends on a well-defined planning process, in which retail geographers have an important role to play.

As illustrated in Figure 1.1, the retail planning process starts with the retail company setting up its development goals and objectives on the basis of the company's market strength and the resources it possesses (see Box 1 in Figure 1.1) The goal of resource-rich companies is

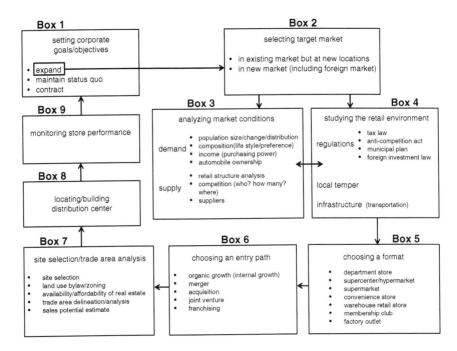

Figure 1.1 The Retail Planning Process.

usually to *grow* or *expand*. There are two general types of growth strategies: non-spatial and spatial. The former refers to driving sales from the existing stores, often by reducing prices, increasing merchandise offerings, and improving service and store environments (Epstein, 1984). The latter refers to store network expansion by adding more retail outlets at more locations. For companies that are mediocre performers, the goal is often to *defend and maintain market share while improving performance of the existing stores*. The weak retailers are most likely to choose to divest, either *reducing operation scales* by closing unprofitable stores, or *closing the operation entirely*.

If a company decides to expand, the next step is to select a target market. (Box 2). A market can be as large as a country or region, and can be as small as a city or town. Alternative strategies range from expanding in the same market to entering a new market. A suitable market is selected based not only on an extensive analysis of the market conditions but also on a careful examination of the holistic retail environment. This is particularly important when a new market is being considered by a corporate retailer. At the international level, some countries are defined as *developed markets* with well-established trading rules and regulations, while others are described as *emerging markets*, which are converging towards the developed markets in advanced economies. While having not yet reached the level of market efficiency with strict standards in accounting and securities regulation to be on par with advanced economies, emerging markets are nonetheless sought after by multinational retailers for the prospect of high returns, as they often experience faster economic growth as measured by gross domestic product (GDP), though investments in these markets are often also accompanied by higher risks due to political instability, domestic infrastructure problems, and currency volatility.

Market conditions are assessed for both demand for and supply of consumer goods (Box 3). Typically, the level of demand is estimated with three fundamental factors—population size, population composition, and disposable income—which in combination determine demand quantity and purchasing powers. In some cases, the level of automobile ownership is also considered because it affects consumer mobility and hence shopping behaviors. Projected population change (either increase or decrease) is an important consideration in market condition analysis as well, as it facilitates decision making with regard to the scale of retail development so as to meet future demand while also minimizing investment risks and potential sunk costs.

On the supply side, market condition assessment includes both retail structure analysis and competition analysis. This helps to gauge the level of market saturation or "crowdedness", the strengths and weaknesses of competitors, and "the market space" left for new entrants. Walmart introduced its Sam's Club to Canada in 2006. In the next three years, it opened six outlets in southern Ontario, where Costco had already established a strong presence with a large base of loyal customers. Apparently due to underestimation of the competitiveness of Costco in Canada and southern Ontario in its planning process, the six Sam's Clubs could not make a profit and had to be closed three years later, in 2009.

The holistic retail environment includes regulations, public attitude (i.e., "local temper"), and infrastructures (Box 4). Different countries, or even different provinces and municipalities, can have different regulations, such as tax laws, an anti-competition act, land use bylaws, and even foreign investment policies. In capitalist market economies, governments rarely own or operate retail stores, except for a few selected consumer goods (such as the non-merit goods of alcoholic beverages, cigarettes, and cannabis). While retailers enjoy a high degree of freedom in business decision making, governments do intervene in the retail industry with regulatory measures, often in the form of public policies, to mitigate negative impacts. In turn, these policies, which are supposed to reflect the values of the society, impose limits on the retailer's freedom to deal with competitors and conduct business with suppliers and consumers, thus affecting retail operations and the overall market structure. The importance of regulations is appropriately recognized in the new geography of retailing.

In the Western democracies, the public attitude towards certain retailers is also an important consideration in retail planning. In the United States, anti-Walmart sentiments in some communities have derailed the retailer's plans to enter a number of local markets. The opposition is more than against the big box format; it has also been against the way Walmart conducts business, including its anti-union corporate culture, low wages, and heavy-handed treatment of suppliers. Walmart now operates 4,800 outlets across the United States. Yet, it has not been able to enter New York City—the largest metropolitan market in the United States—due to strong opposition mounted by the city's anti-Walmart activists.

Once a market is chosen, the retailer needs to decide what format of retailing is the most appropriate and profitable in that market (Box 5). Alternatives are the convenience store, department store, supermarket, supercenter (or hypermarket, as it is known in Europe), membership club, warehouse retail store, and factory outlet. The suitability of a particular format is dependent on the market conditions. Some retailers operate stores in more than one format. Walmart entered Canada in 1994, choosing the discount department store format. Because that format was not as profitable as expected, Walmart later introduced both supercenters and Sam's Clubs to Canada. While its supercenters have been flourishing, the Sam's Clubs did not and had to be closed. When Walmart entered China in the mid-1990s, it introduced and experimented with three formats simultaneously: supercenter, Sam's Club, and neighborhood supermarket. Likewise, the supercenters are the most successful, but the Sam's Clubs grew very slowly. In the last 20 or so years, Walmart has opened 362 supercenters in China, but only ten Sam's Clubs. Neighborhood supermarkets are a failure, still with only two stores.

Consideration of retail formats and selection of market entry paths often go hand in hand (Box 6). Alternative paths include organic growth (also known as internal growth), merger/acquisition, joint ventures, and franchising. Each entry path has its own merits and limitations, as described in Chapter 6.

For the purpose of organic growth with new store development, detailed location analysis along with trade area analysis is necessary (Box 7). This is usually done after approval is obtained from the relevant government authorities: central or federal government in the case of foreign markets; or local governments in the event of domestic market. The tasks include:

- site selection
- market condition analysis at the store level
- search for suitable and affordable real estate
- review of zoning bylaws
- trade area analysis
- pro forma analysis
- estimation of sales potential

Retail chains often also conduct location-allocation analysis, which is concerned with the selection of sites for a set of stores simultaneously to serve a spatially dispersed population: that is, to allocate a given spatial distribution of demand to a specific number of retail outlets. The questions to be answered with location-allocation modeling are: how many stores are needed in the target market? how many can be supported? where should they be located?

Spatial expansion of a store network must be supported by a network of distribution centers. For retailers operating large chains, deployment and construction of distribution centers is also an important part of retail planning (Box 8). A distribution center operated by a corporate retailer is a specialized warehouse stocked with goods to be redistributed to the retail outlets in the same regional market. It constitutes a principal part of the entire order fulfillment process and allows a single location to stock a vast number of products.

After the business goes into operation, store performance is monitored continually (Box 9). Depending on the ongoing performance, corporate goals/objectives are revisited and adjusted. Again, the strong performers and profitable retailers are most likely to reinvest—to *grow* and *expand*; the mediocre performers may decide to *maintain status quo* and focus on improving performance of the existing stores; and the poor performing retailers are forced to *contract* by closing stores or selling off the entire operation to others (back to Box 1 in Figure 1.1).

As illustrated in Figure 1.1, the retail planning process is complex, requiring knowledge from multiple disciplines and involving the participation of experts with different professional backgrounds. Retail geographers with training in spatial analysis are equipped with the techniques and tools to play an important role in market condition analysis and location analyses, as highlighted in Boxes 3 and 7 of Figure 1.1. These tasks reflect the typical concerns of the orthodox retail geography, but their conceptualization is now informed and improved by the theorizations in the new geography of retailing. In addition, the analytical methods and tools have been automated with the use of GIS. For example, ESRI's *Business Analyst* now offers a comprehensive suite of tools including the calibrated Huff Model and the various location-allocation models that are based on different criteria in response to different constraints. Caliper has been adding these tools incrementally to its *Maptitude* software.

THE NEED FOR AN UPDATED RETAIL GEOGRAPHY TEXTBOOK

Despite retail geography being an interesting, important, and career-relevant subject of study, there are only a handful of textbooks available for adoption by university instructors and students, and the books are all in need of update to reflect the recent changes in the retail economy, the recent development in geotechnologies, and the re-theorized retail geography. The currently available books are:

- Jones, K. & Simmons, J. (1993). *Location, Location, Location: Analyzing the Retail Environment.* Toronto, Canada: Nelson Canada.
- Clarke, G. & Longley, P. (1995). *GIS for Business and Service Planning.* New York, NY: Wiley & Sons, Inc.
- Wrigley, N. & Lowe, M. (1996). *Retailing, Consumption and Capital: towards the New Retail Geography.* Essex, England: Longman Group Ltd.
- Wrigley, N. & Lowe, M. (2002). *Reading Retail: A Geographical Perspective on Retailing and Consumption Spaces.* London, England: Arnold.
- Thrall, G. I. (2002). *Business Geography and New Real Estate Market Analysis.* New York, NY: Oxford University Press.
- Birkin, M., Clarke, G. & Clarke, M. (2002). *Retail Geography and Intelligent Network Planning.* Chichester, England: John Wiley & Sons, Ltd.
- Church, R. L. & Murray, A. T. (2009). *Business Site Selection, Location Analysis, and GIS.* Hoboken, NJ: John Wiley & Sons, Inc.
- Leventhal, B. (2016). *Geodemographics for Marketers: Using Location Analysis for Marketers.* London, England: Kogan Page Ltd.

Location, Location, Location was one of the earliest and most comprehensive texts in the field of retail geography. It covers all aspects of retail geography, and was widely adopted in Canadian universities, as well as in American universities with a different edition titled *The Retail Environment* (published by Routledge in 1990). However, this book has not been revised and updated since 1993.

GIS for Business and Service Planning is an edited volume, consisting of 12 chapters. While this book provides a comprehensive coverage of GIS application in business and service planning (including retailing), its focus is limited to only certain aspects of the retail planning process. Moreover, the book has not been updated since its publication in 1995, since which time considerable advancements have been made in GIS technologies.

The book **Retailing, Consumption and Capital** was revolutionary in advancing the study of retail geography. It re-theorizes the orthodox retail geography and makes close links to consumption, production, retail capital, and regulations. Since the purpose of the book is to

advocate and illustrate a paradigm shift in retail geography, it contains
no discussion of retail location analysis at all.

Reading Retail is essentially a companion of *Retailing, Consumption
and Capital*. In a combination of selected academic readings from a
variety of sources and interpretation of the readings by the book
authors, this textbook is written and organized as a "guide" for an audi-
ence of undergraduate students to appreciate the nature of academic
writing and to critically review the contemporary debates on the geography of retailing and consumption spaces. Like *Retailing, Consumption and Capital*, it contains no discussion of retail location analysis.

Business Geography and New Real Estate Market Analysis provides rich
examples of business location analysis, but with a heavy focus on real
estate market analysis. Of the ten chapters in it, only one concerns
retailing. So, its suitability as a textbook for retail geography is very
limited.

Retail Geography and Intelligent Network Planning is another comprehensive textbook of retail geography. It not only covers aspects of the
new retail geography but also includes extensive treatment of retail site
selection and trade area analysis. It is a pity that there has been no
update since its publication in 2002, and most examples in the book
are British case studies, lacking North American contents.

Business Site Selection, Location Analysis, and GIS is a highly specialized
textbook with a heavy focus on business site selection and location analysis. It is rooted richly in location theories and complex mathematical
modeling, and also incorporates a variety of GIS applications in its
chapters. Yet, this 12-chapter book includes no discussion of the other
side of the fundamentals of retail geography—market condition analysis and the geography of demand. Nor does it link to the theoretical
debates advanced in the new geography of retailing.

Published in 2016, *Geodemographics for Marketers* is the most recent
of the eight books described here. But this book is also limited
in scope: it deals with only one component in the retail planning
process—application of geodemographics in trade area analysis and
marketing.

The above survey of the existing books (published in the last 30
years) reveals that while each of them served the students and instructors very well at the time of their publication and for a period of time
thereafter, there is a need for a new textbook that covers and blends
the essence of both the orthodox retail geography and the new geography of retailing, with updated case studies to reflect recent changes
in the retail economy and industry, as well as recent advancement in

geotechnologies. This current book is written to fill the gap and meet the need. For continuity in the development of retail geography, the current book includes some of the topics covered in the various existing books, but with a new organizational framework.

ORGANIZATION OF THE CURRENT BOOK AND CHAPTER SYNOPSIS

Using the retail planning process as the conceptual framework, this book is organized into 11 chapters.

Chapter 1 Introduction

The Introduction starts with an explanation of the importance of retailing in the national economy and of the paradigm shift that has led to the re-theorization of the geography of retailing. This is followed by a detailed description of the retail planning process to establish the conceptual framework and set up the context for the entire book. It illustrates where in the planning process retail location analysis is situated, and how location analysis relates to the other components of the planning process. Through a survey of the existing textbooks, this chapter also explains why a new textbook is needed.

Chapter 2 The Contemporary Retail Economy

Retailing was the oldest form of economic activity, but it has always been changing and evolving. In particular, a series of revolutionary changes have taken place in the retail industry worldwide in the last three decades, amid the globalization of the world economy and the advancement of logistic and information technologies. These changes have thrown the retail industry into upheaval, resulting in what industry commentators call an "unforgiving retail environment" or a "volatile retail ecosystem". These changes have not only given rise to new retail formats and new delivery channels, but also altered the traditional store location requirements and opened new areas of research for retail geographers. A good understanding of these changes and the forces behind them is therefore essential for retail geographers to participate effectively in retail planning and analysis. This chapter provides a condensed discussion of the recent changes that are the

characteristics of the contemporary retail industry. These include
(1) significant restructuring and reshuffling in the retail industry;
(2) the emergence of big box stores and power centers to become new
leading retail formats; (3) the new retailer–supplier relationship
tipping towards retailers; (4) intensification of retail internationalization; and (5) the rise of e-retailing and the diversification of retail
distribution channels.

Chapter 3 *The Geography of Demand, Expenditure Patterns, and Market Segmentation*

A good knowledge of the geography of demand for consumer goods
and services and expenditure patterns is fundamental to location
research for retail businesses. In market condition analysis (Box 3 in
Figure 1.1), retail geographers and market analysts not only consider
the current population size, but also forecast population changes
within the planning horizon. This chapter explains why demand for
consumer goods varies in different markets and what factors influence
the level of demand (including population size and composition, disposable income, and consumption patterns by income groups). In
addition to explaining the sources of data, this chapter describes such
techniques as geodemographic analysis, market segmentation, and
population projection.

Chapter 4 *Retail Structure Analysis*

On the supply side, market condition assessment includes retail structure analysis. This helps retailers to gauge the level of market saturation, the strengths and weaknesses of the potential competitors, and
the market space left for new entrants. Retail structure refers to the
mix of different types of retail activity (i.e., stores/facilities) in a given
area of geography. It can be analyzed according to four aspects: ownership structure, business structure, format structure, and geographical
structure. The chapter explains how retail structure analysis can assist
retailers, commercial real estate developers, and municipal planners in
business decision making and in control of excessive supply of certain
types of retail activity. It also describes the type of data that are needed
for retail structure analysis. Three case studies are presented to illustrate how retail structure analysis is conducted and interpreted for
both macro-level and micro-level geographies.

Chapter 5 The External Retail Environment: Role of Regulations and Community Attitude

This chapter accounts for the retail environment, which includes government regulations and local attitudes toward certain retailers and formats, as illustrated in Box 4 of Figure 1.1. Different countries, but also provinces and municipalities, can have different regulations, such as foreign investment policies, business tax law, anti-competition law, and land use bylaws. Within the capitalist market economy, where retailers enjoy a high degree of freedom in business decision making, governments still intervene in the retail industry with regulatory measures, often in the form of public policies, to mitigate negative impacts. In turn, these policies, which are supposed to reflect a society's values, impose limits on retailers' freedom to deal with competitors and to conduct business with suppliers and consumers, affecting retail operations and the overall market structure. In this chapter, the various types of public intervention, which are often imposed by different levels of government and implemented at different spatial scales, are described and expounded with various examples.

Chapter 6 Spatial Growth Strategies

Once a market is chosen (on the basis of market condition analysis and retail environment assessment), the retailer considers a suitable entry path, which is an important part of corporate spatial strategies (see Box 6 in Figure 1.1). Alternative entry paths include organic (or internal) growth, merger, acquisition, joint ventures, and franchising. Each entry path has its own merits and limitations. This chapter compares the different entry paths with particular emphasis on their geographical implications. For example, while organic growth gives the retailer more control over the pace of store development and operation, its spatial growth can be slow because of the lengthy process of store location selection and the difficulty of acquiring properties, particularly in foreign markets. Merger and acquisition can produce fast network expansion and rapid geographic growth in markets where the retailer is currently un- or under-represented. Through merger and acquisition, the retailer can also eliminate competition from the target market. However, buying an existing chain requires a large upfront investment, and achieving organizational and cultural fit in the stage of implementation and integration can also be very costly. Franchising can produce fast store network expansion with less capital investment and therefore lower risks. However, the level of profit is low, and the franchisor's control over the operation of the franchisees can be weak.

Chapter 7 Market Screening, Retail Location Analysis, and Site Evaluation

For the purpose of organic growth, detailed location analysis is necessary (Box 7 in Figure 1.1), usually after approval has been obtained from the relevant government authorities: nation-states in the case of foreign markets, and local governments in domestic markets. Location analysis starts from submarket screening, and includes site selection, market condition analysis at the store level, a search for suitable and affordable real estate, and review of zoning bylaws. This chapter covers the various methods of business site selection and evaluation, with an emphasis on cluster analysis, multi criteria ranking, and regression analysis.

Chapter 8 Trade Area Delineation and Analysis

Trade area delineation and analysis often goes hand in hand with business site selection (Box 7 in Figure 1.1). Given that it uses a different set of techniques, trade area delineation and analysis is treated in a separate chapter from store site selection. Two groups of techniques are reviewed and elaborated in this chapter. The first group deals with the techniques used to define the trade area of a single store, including the circular and driving distance/time methods. The second group includes techniques used to delineate the trade areas of a set of stores, including Thiessen Polygon, Reilly's Law, and the Huff Model. The application of these methods is demonstrated with examples using different statistical and GIS software. The sales potential estimate method is also explained because knowing sales potential is the ultimate purpose of trade area analysis for retailers.

Chapter 9 Store Network Planning and Location-allocation Modeling

Retail chains are often concerned with the selection of multiple store locations simultaneously to serve a spatially dispersed population: that is, to allocate a given spatial distribution of demand to a specific number of outlets. This is achieved using location-allocation modeling.

When used in retail planning and location analysis, this technique assists in determining how many stores are needed in the target market, how many can be supported, and where they should be located. Although location-allocation overlaps with site selection and trade area delineation in the same process, given its complexity and uniqueness in its approach, it warrants treatment in a single and separate chapter. Four location-allocation models are discussed in this chapter: *minimum impedance, maximum coverage, maximum market share,* and *target market share.* Their operations are illustrated in ESRI's *Network Analyst* environment.

Chapter 10 Location Analysis and Site Selection of Distribution Centers

Spatial expansion of a store network must be supported by a network of distribution centers. For retailers operating large chains, the deployment and construction of distribution centers is also an important part of retail planning (Box 8 in Figure 1.1). A distribution center operated by a corporate retailer is a specialized warehouse stocked with goods to be redistributed to the retail outlets in the same regional market. It is a vital part of the entire order fulfillment process, enabling a single location to stock a vast number of products. Even online retailers, such as Amazon, need distribution centers, from which merchandise is delivered to consumers. Unlike retail stores, distribution centers do not interact directly with consumers. Besides, they are much larger in size and generate different traffic patterns. They therefore have different location and space requirements. This chapter explains the three general location selection criteria and the specific factors that need to be examined and investigated closely when making a decision on geographic positioning of a distribution center. Three methods that are familiar to geographers are also described.

Chapter 11 Conclusions

In this final chapter, connections between and among the various chapters are highlighted, and the role of geography and spatial analysis in retail planning is reiterated. Readers are also reminded that the retail planning process is complex, and requires the participation of experts with different professional backgrounds. What retail geographers contribute to the retail planning process is to provide decision support to the high-level corporate management team. Through communication of results, retail geographers serve as liaison people between management and the new technology, methods, and data. While e-commerce will not mean the death of the importance of distance and geography, and big data do not necessarily make the existing location research methods obsolete, they will lead to better choices of variables to improve simulation and prediction accuracy through model calibration. In the meantime, retail geographers need to develop more sophisticated and intelligent spatial analysis techniques, capable of dealing with omnichannel networks.

KEY POINTS OF THE CHAPTER

- The retail sector is an integral part of a national economy. All consumer goods have surplus values locked up in them, and the surplus values are not realized until the consumer goods are purchased by consumers through various distribution channels. As such, retailing is the essential link between production and consumption.
- The success of a retail business depends on two general factors: the location of the retail outlets, and management of the business. Both factors are equally important.
- Accordingly, retailing is a subject of study by two groups of scholars and students—business management and geography—but they approach the subject from different perspectives.
- A long-established subject of study, retail geography is concerned primarily with store location research and trade area analysis. New models and geotechnologies have been developed progressively to advance the study of retail geography. For many students, retail geography has been a popular subject, as it frequently leads to rewarding professional jobs in retail corporations, banks, commercial real estate companies, and business consulting firms.
- The early 1990s witnessed a major paradigm shift in the study of retail geography, and a new geography of retailing was advocated. Taking a political economy approach, the new geography of retailing extends the study scope to include the changing relations between retailers and suppliers and the grounding of capital in the form of retail facilities. It also calls for serious treatment of regulations because the regulatory state is an important force influencing both corporate strategies and geographical market structures.

- There is clearly a need to integrate both the orthodox retail geography and the new geography of retailing, a gap that the current book aims to fill.
- The retail planning process is complex, requiring knowledge from multiple disciplines and involving the participation of experts with different professional backgrounds. Retail geographers with training in spatial analysis are equipped with the techniques and tools to play an important role in market condition analysis and location analyses. These tasks reflect the typical concerns of the orthodox retail geography, but their conceptualization is now informed and improved by the theorizations in the new geography of retailing.

REFERENCES

Applebaum, W. (1954). Marketing geography. In P. E. James & C. F. Jones (Eds.), *American Geography: Inventory and Prospect* (pp. 240–257). Syracuse, NY: Syracuse University Press.

Birkin, M., Clarke, G. & Clarke, M. (2002). *Retail Geography and Intelligent Network Planning*. Chichester, England: John Wiley & Sons, Ltd.

Blomley, N. (1996). "I'd like to dress her all over": masculinity, power and retail space. In N. Wrigley and M. Lowe (Eds.), *Retailing, Consumption and Capital: towards the New Retail Geography* (pp. 238–256). Essex, England: Longman Group Ltd.

Church, R. L. & Murray, A. T. (2009). *Business Site Selection, Location Analysis, and GIS*. Hoboken, NJ: John Wiley & Sons, Inc.

Clarke, G. & Longley, P. (1995). *GIS for Business and Service Planning*. New York, NY: Wiley & Sons, Inc.

Davis, R. L. (1976). *Marketing Geography: with Special Reference to Retailing*. London, England: Methuen.

Ducatel, K. & Blomley, N. (1990). Re-thinking retail capital. *International Journal of Urban and Regional Research, 14*(2), 207–227.

Epstein, B. J. (1984). Market appraisals. In R. L. Davis & D. S. Rogers (Eds.), *Store Location and Store Assessment Research* (pp. 195–214). Chichester, England: John Wiley & Sons, Ltd.

Jones, K. & Simmons, J. (1993). *Location, Location, Location: Analyzing the Retail Environment*. Toronto, Canada: Nelson Canada.

Leventhal, B. (2016). *Geodemographics for Marketers: Using Location Analysis for Marketers*. London, England: Kogan Page Ltd.

Lowe, M. & Wrigley, N. (1996). Towards the new retail geography. In N. Wrigley and M. Lowe (Eds.), *Retailing, Consumption and Capital: towards the New Retail Geography* (pp. 3–30). Essex, England: Longman Group Ltd.

Thrall, G. I. (2002). *Business Geography and New Real Estate Market Analysis.* New York, NY: Oxford University Press.

Wrigley, N. & Lowe, M. (1996). *Retailing, Consumption and Capital: towards the New Retail Geography.* Essex, England: Longman Group Ltd.

Wrigley, N. & Lowe, M. (2002). *Reading Retail: A Geographical Perspective on Retailing and Consumption Spaces.* London, England: Arnold.

2 The Contemporary Retail Economy

Retailing was the oldest form of economic activity, but it has always been changing and evolving. In the last three decades, a series of revolutionary changes have taken place in the retail industry worldwide, amid the globalization of the world economy and the advancement of logistic and information technologies. A good understanding of these changes and the forces behind them is essential for retail geographers to participate effectively in retail planning and analysis. This chapter provides a condensed discussion of the recent trends in the contemporary retail industry.

RETAIL CHAINS CONTINUE TO BE THE MOST IMPORTANT FORM OF RETAIL CONCENTRATION, BUT SIGNIFICANT RESTRUCTURING AND RESHUFFLING HAVE TAKEN PLACE

With no exceptions, all corporate retailers are chain operators, which provides a way of introducing scale economies while avoiding the restrictions of market fragmentations. Retail chains often account for 70 percent or more of the total retail sales in a metropolitan market. The 1990s and the 2000s witnessed significant restructuring of retail chains, leading to further concentration of retail capital into the hands of a few "super leagues" (Marsden & Wrigley, 1996). Some chains sought to acquire, or merge with, others to consolidate resources, and rose to the status of global corporations.

Concentration of retail capital began in the 1980s, but accelerated in the 1990s, and was reinforced in the new millennium. In the United Kingdom, the top five food retailers (Sainsbury's, Tesco, Argyll, Asda, and Dee) held 43 percent of the national market share in 1985; their share rose to 61 percent in 1990 (Wrigley, 1993). In 1991, the French firm Carrefour took over two other domestic hypermarket chains: Euromarche and Montlaur. In 1999, it merged with Promodes to create the largest European food retailing group and the second largest worldwide (at that time).

One sector in the U.S. retail industry where the trend towards concentration and the emergence of mega chains was the most evident in the 1990s was drug store retailing (Wrigley & Lowe, 2002). A wave of mergers and acquisitions in the sector resulted in the disappearance a large number of smaller chains and independents, and the emergence of a few mega chains. The major firms also began to acquire each other. For example, CVS and Revco, previously the fourth and fifth largest drug store chains in the U.S., merged to form the second largest national chain; Rite Aid (previously the second largest) acquired Thrifty Payless (the seventh largest); and J. C. Penney's drug store division (the eighth largest) acquired Eckerd (the third largest). Throughout the 1990s, smaller chains and independents were disappearing at the rate of 2,000 stores per year, and the largest five mega chains dominated the national market, accounting for 53 percent of the total drug store sales in 1997, compared with only 28 percent in 1990 (Wrigley & Lowe, 2002).

Table 2.1 lists the top 30 corporate retailers in the world in 2017. With one exception—JD.com of China—all of them are based in the Western advanced economies of the United States (12), Germany (5), France (3), the United Kingdom (2), the Netherlands (2), Australia (2), Japan (2), and Canada (1), where most retail capital concentrates and most retail innovations are made. Large corporate retailers are better able to invest in information technology and centralized distribution systems, which enables them to more effectively perform their competitive functions by reducing the turnover time of commodities (Hughes, 1996), and create and maintain their "competitive space" (Wrigley & Lowe, 2002).

Shuffling in ranks also occurred among the top 30 retailers themselves. Seven of the 12 U.S.-based and four of the five Germany-based corporations had improved their rank since 2012 (see the first column in Table 2.1). Albertsons Companies climbed from position 240 in 2012 to fifteenth place in 2017, after a series of acquisitions of other firms including Safeway, Inc.—the twenty-fifth largest retailer in 2012. Most impressively, Amazon.com, the world's largest non-store general merchandise retailer, doubled its revenue in the five-year period

2012–2017, rising to the fourth largest retailer in the world. Its rapid expansion has been achieved at the expense of many other retailers. In 2017, Amazon acquired Whole Foods Market, Inc., a multinational supermarket chain headquartered in Austin, Texas, for US$13.9 billion. There have been rumors that it is attempting to purchase Target and a bank (Mellor & Boyle, 2018). However, those retailers based in France and the UK have slid down the ladder. In particular, Tesco slid from the second largest in 2012 to the tenth in 2017, with a 27 percent decrease in retail revenue. The French Auchan, Casino, and Centers Distributeurs slid down by two, three, and one places, respectively.[1] JD.com is a non-store merchandise retailer in China. Its rank jumped from 142 in 2012 to 20 in 2017. In contrast with Amazon, which has operations in 30 countries, JD.com generates all of its revenue from its home country.

Many other retail chains were not as fortunate, and subsequently went under. In recent decades, there have been unprecedented numbers of retailer failures, including dominant brands. The department store shuffle in Canada is a case in point.

As of 1994, Canada had six department store chains serving the national market. These were Woolco, Eaton's, Kmart, Zellers, Sears, and The Bay. Today, only The Bay still exists, while all the others have disappeared. Woolco was a wholly owned subsidiary of the U.S.-based F. W. Woolworth Company. It first entered the Canadian market in 1967, and by the early 1990s had almost 150 stores. In 1994, it was acquired by Walmart, which turned 122 of the Woolco stores into Walmart department stores. Kmart was a wholly owned subsidiary of the S. S. Kresge Co. in the United States, and also came to Canada in 1967 (Doucet, 2001). It later expanded to operate 112 stores in Canada. As a result of Kmart's ongoing financial difficulties, its Canadian division was sold to competitor Zellers in 1998. The Kmart stores were either closed or absorbed into the Zellers brand. Eaton's, the oldest department store chain in Canada, which once had more than 80 outlets and dominated most of the downtown shopping centers in the Canadian cities, went bankrupt and folded its entire operation in 1999, withdrawing from the national market it had served for 130 years.

The trend continued in the new millennium. Zellers, a major Canadian discount department store retailer, was founded in 1931; it was acquired by Hudson's Bay Company (HBC) in 1978. Subsequently, a series of acquisitions and expansions (including the acquisition of Kmart) allowed Zellers to reach its peak with 350 stores in 1999.

Table 2.1 The Top 30 Corporate Retailers in the World by Retail Revenue, 2017

Rank (with 2012 rank)	Company	Home country	Dominant format	Retail revenue (US$M)	Retail revenue change 2012–2017 (%)	# Countries of operation
1 (1)	Wal-Mart Stores, Inc.	U.S.	Hypermarket/Supercenter/Superstore	500,343	6.6	29
2 (3)	Costco Wholesale Corporation	U.S.	Cash & Carry/Warehouse Club	129,025	30.1	12
3 (5)	The Kroger Co.	U.S.	Supermarket	118,982	23.0	1
4 (16)	Amazon.Com, Inc.	U.S.	Non-store general merchandise	118,573	102.4	14
5 (6)	Schwarz Unternehmens Treuhand KG	Germany	Discount Store	111,766	28.1	30
6 (8)	The Home Depot, Inc.	U.S.	Home Improvement	100,904	35.0	4
7 (11)	Walgreens Boots Alliance Co.	U.S.	Drug Store/Pharmacy	99,115	38.4	10
8 (9)	Aldi Einkauf GmbH & Co. oHG	Germany	Discount Store	98,287	34.6	18
9 (12)	CVS Health Corporation	U.S.	Drug Store/Pharmacy	79,398	24.7	3
10 (2)	Tesco PLC	UK	Hypermarket/Supercenter/Superstore	73,961	−27.0	8
11 (26)	Ahold Delhaize (formerly Koninklijke Ahold N.V.)	Netherlands	Supermarket	72,312	71.2	10
12 (10)	Target Corporation	U.S.	Discount Department Store	71,879	−0.1	1
13 (13)	Aeon Co., Ltd.	Japan	Hypermarket/Supercenter/Superstore	70,072	11.0	11
14 (21)	Lowe's Companies, Inc.	U.S.	Home Improvement	68,619	35.8	3

	Company	Country	Type			
15 (240)	Albertsons Companies, Inc.	U.S.	Supermarket	59,925	1436.5	1
16 (14)	Auchan Holding SA	France	Hypermarket/Supercenter/Superstore	58,614	–0.7	14
17 (18)	Edeka Zentrale AG & Co. KG	Germany	Supermarket	57,484	2.8	1
18 (17)	Seven & I Holdings Co., Ltd.	Japan	Convenience Store	51,889	–11.0	19
19 (22)	REWE Combine	Germany	Supermarket	49,713	1.5	11
20 (–)	JD.com, Inc	China	Non-store general merchandise	49,088	636.7	1
21 (19)	Wesfarmers Limited	Australia	Supermarket	48,748	–10.1	4
22 (15)	Woolworths Limited	Australia	Supermarket	42,891	–26.8	3
23 (20)	Casino Guichard-Perrachon S.A.	France	Hypermarket/Supercenter/Superstore	42,631	–20.1	27
24 (23)	Best Buy Co., Inc.	U.S.	Electronics Specialty	42,151	–6.5	4
25 (24)	Centres Distributeurs E. Leclerc	France	Hypermarket/Supercenter/Superstore	41,535	–7.3	6
26 (7)	Metro AG	Germany	Cash & Carry/Warehouse Club	40,961	–52.3	15
27 (30)	The IKEA Group (INGKA Holding B.V.)	Netherlands	Furniture	37,426	3.6	29
28 (28)	J Sainsbury plc	UK	Supermarket	36,611	–0.6	2
29 (–)	The TJX Companies, Inc.	U.S.	Apparel/Footwear	35,865	38.6	10
30 (–)	Loblaw Companies Limited	Canada	Hypermarket/Supercenter/Superstore	35,147	13.5	6

Source: adapted from Deloitte Touche Tohmatsu Limited (DTTL) and Stores Media, 2019.

However, fierce competition from Walmart and an inability to adjust to the increasingly volatile retailing industry resulted in Zellers losing significant ground in the 2000s. In January 2011, HBC announced it was to sell the lease agreements for up to 220 Zellers stores to the U.S.-based retailer Target. In 2013, HBC closed all remaining Zellers stores. In a short period of two years, 2013–2015, Target opened 133 stores in Canada at the former Zellers locations. Sadly, Target also missed the mark: unable to achieve its goal and objectives in the Canadian market, it had to close its entire Canadian operation in 2015 (Lang, 2015). Termed a "spectacular failure", the short-lived Target Canada became "a gold standard case study for what retailers should not do when they enter a new market" (Shaw, 2016).

Sears Canada was the Canadian subsidiary of the U.S.-based Sears department store chain. Starting as a joint venture between the Canadian Simpsons department store chain and the American Sears in 1953, it became a fully owned company in 1984 and was renamed Sears Canada Inc. When Eaton's folded its operation in 1999, Sears Canada acquired its remaining assets and locations. By 2016, Sears Canada still had a store network with 140 corporate stores. In June 2017, it filed for creditor protection and subsequently closed all of its branches in Canada.

After successive waves of industry shuffling in the past 25 years, only two department store retailers are left to serve the Canadian consumers—HBC, an upscale and fashion-oriented retailer; and Walmart, a discount retailer—each occupying a different segment of the consumer market with minimal competition. The demise of the other department stores is attributed to many factors, such as competition from the various specialty stores; but they were all also victimized by the ongoing crusade of Walmartization. Even HBC is now owned by the U.S.-based NRDC Equity Partners, meaning that Canada has no Canadian-owned department stores any more—a loss of national identity in this retail subsector.

Retailer failures are of course not limited to Canada; they are happening in the U.S. and other countries as well. For example, Toys 'R' Us dominated the toy store business in the 1980s and the early 1990s, when it was one of the first "category killers". It later expanded to Canada, the UK, and several Asian countries. In the new millennium, its business went downhill. Saddled with five billion dollars in debt, and able neither to return to profitability after a period of bankruptcy protection, nor to find a buyer, Toys 'R' Us had to shut down its entire U.S. division and close all 735 domestic toy stores and Babies 'R' Us stores in 2017, after 60 years in business (Kopun,

2018a, 2018b). Its international divisions in Canada, the UK, and Asia are still in operation because they are under the ownership of different investors. The massive U.S. closures have affected not only thousands of retail jobs, but also the big toymakers in the supply chain including Mattel and Hasbro.

THE DOMINANCE OF MALLS HAS DECLINED SIGNIFICANTLY, AND BIG BOX STORES AND POWER CENTERS HAVE EMERGED TO BECOME NEW LEADING RETAIL FORMATS

The shopping center was the most successful land use, real estate, and retail business concept of the twentieth century (Beyard & O'Mara, 1999). It dominated the retail landscape in U.S. and Canadian cities for nearly 40 years from the 1950s to the late 1980s, during which there were more shopping centers than movie theaters and more enclosed malls than cities (Kowinski, 1985). Shopping centers were so pervasive that they served the entire metropolitan city in a hierarchical system, consisting of neighborhood, community, regional, and superregional centers, spatially distributed in a fashion analogous to central places in Christaller's Central Place Model. Each type of shopping center had a clearly prescribed tenant mix, trade area size, and even physical form (Urban Land Institute, 1985). Historically, the large shopping centers, or malls as they are commonly called, were anchored by department stores. They not only served as shopping destinations, but also offered a wide range of dining, entertainment, and recreation experiences under one roof, becoming the new "palace of consumption". Typical examples are the West Edmonton Mall in Canada (493,000 m²; once had four national brand and one regional brand department stores[2]) and the Mall of America in the United States (466,000 m²; anchored by four department stores[3]). At the same time, this booming development created an industry of shopping center developers and real estate investment trusts (REITs), responsible for developing and managing most of the large shopping centers.

Beginning in the late 1980s, major technological innovations took place in the distribution system. These innovations included highly computerized goods-tracking systems and inventory control, enabling the generation of instant databases and direct communications with manufacturers (Hughes & Seneca, 1997). This has led to the emergence of a new retail format, known as "big box" stores, including membership clubs, warehouse retail stores, and supercenters (known as hypermarkets in Europe). They are highly specialized, concentrating on specific subsectors of retailing. Within the subsector, they provide a wide selection of brand-name products at substantially lower prices, because face-to-face service is reduced, interior decoration is minimal, and they often sell in bulk packages. They are much larger in size than conventional stores in the same retail subsector, hence dubbed as category-dominant retailers or "category killers". They often serve a whole region or even the whole country in the form of a chain, with multiple branches at various locations, contributing to retail decentralization in North American cities in a big way. They are mostly located at highway intersections, accessible only by car (Jones & Doucet, 1998)

At first, such stores were freestanding outside shopping centers. Gradually, several big box stores began to cluster together, along with some ancillary service activities, at one location in the form of a planned plaza, commonly called a "power center" (also known as a "warehouse retail park" in Europe). Where two or more power centers have developed adjacent to each other within 1-km distance, or where big box stores are added to the parking pad of an existing regional or superregional shopping center, the conglomeration is called a power node or power cluster (Hernandez & Simmons, 2006; Yeates, 2011). The major differences between power centers and regional/superregional shopping centers are summarized in Table 2.2.

Table 2.2 Differences between Regional/Superregional Shopping Centers and Power Centers

Characteristics	Shopping center	Power center
Physical form	enclosed	open air
Tenant type and mix	a few anchor stores (traditionally department stores), plus a bunch of smaller, specialty stores	big box, new format stores plus a few ancillary service outlets (such as coffee shops and quick service restaurants)
Interior decoration	elaborate and esthetically appealing	moderate to bare
Cost	expensive to build and maintain; property tax high	much less expensive to build and maintain; lower property tax
Location and accessibility	in both inner city and suburbs; auto-oriented, but can be accessed by public transit	almost all in suburbs and completely auto dependent

In less than ten years, this new format was adopted by a variety of retail businesses. For example, the number of big box stores in one regional market in Canada, the Greater Toronto Area (GTA), increased from fewer than 200 in 1990 to 1,500 in 2010, providing about one-third of the retail space in the GTA (Yeates, 2011). The big box stores and power centers have become leading retailers and destination shopping locations in the Western retail system to draw the masses. These new retail spaces have been created and manipulated by the innovative retailers and commercial real estate developers to induce consumption, and have been widely blamed as the cause of the "graying" of regional and superregional shopping centers and the demise of department stores in North American cities. In a nutshell, big box retailing has impacted malls in two major ways: it has absorbed most of the new market capacity, and cut into the markets of existing malls, thus fracturing mall business strategy (Yeates, 2011).

Before the emergence of big box stores, department stores were entrenched anchors in most regional and superregional shopping centers. They have now become a relic of a bygone shopping era. The Hudson Valley Mall in Kingston, New York, with 765,000 square feet of floor space, was appraised at a value of US$87 million in 2010, but was sold for only US$9.4 million in 2017 after its two anchors—J. C. Penney and Macy's—were closed in 2016 (Clark, 2017). J. C. Penney in 2017 announced a plan to close up to 140 stores. Macy's also planned to close about 100 stores, or 14 percent of its total stores (D'Innocenzio, 2016). Many other mall regulars, such as Gymboree and Payless Shoe-Source are closing stores (Heath, 2017). In Canada, the closure of Zellers, Targets, and Sears also left many big holes in the shopping centers that once hosted them. Many mall owners are struggling to find replacements to fill the void spaces and maintain rent income. Unable to backfill the vast retail space vacated by Target, the owner of Five Points Mall in Oshawa of Ontario had to sell the empty space to a self-storage company and plans to demolish the enclosed part of the mall, turning it into an open-air plaza.

The result is a decline in investment opportunities and suppressed investment for many shopping center developers and REITs (Lowe & Wrigley, 1996). As observed by Mary Mowbray, Senior Vice President, Retail Canada at Colliers International, the shopping center market is being bifurcated: higher-end and premier malls with newer tenants are doing better than local shopping centers (Kopun, 2017). In response to the trend, the three major Canadian REITS—Cadillac Fairview Corp., Oxford Properties Group, and Ivanhoe Cambridge—all pared down their portfolios to focus on top-tier malls. In the last ten years, Cadillac Fairview shrank the number of its mall properties from 40 to 20, Oxford Properties down to fewer than a dozen, and Ivanhoe Cambridge from 48 to 28.

In response to the changing competitive environment, mall owners have to devise new business strategies to cope with the declining shopping traffic and sales. One such strategy is to embrace certain big box retailers and (re)introduce supermarkets as new anchors. Because grocery consists of low-order goods purchased on a frequent basis, a supermarket can be a big draw for shoppers to shopping centers. Another strategy is to add experience-driven tenants that face less competition from online retailers, such as upscale restaurants, premier movie theaters, medical services, entertainment, and fitness clubs (Veiga, 2017). Some shopping centers have also designated some retail space as popup stores to rotate tenants. While monthly rent is not necessarily low, the popup retailer (also nicknamed retail Airbnb or guerrilla retailer) pays the higher rent only for a short period of time, and sale and profit in that period can be quite high, especially for popular seasonal products. Other shopping centers are experimenting with hosting events on their parking lots, such as carnivals, concerts, and food-truck festivals, with the hope that some attendees also visit the stores inside the mall (Perlburg, 2017). Many low-quality shopping centers are in danger, because lenders have stopped financing them and they cannot get a new loan. Those centers that could not be revived simply by re-tenanting have been converted to other uses, or have been redeveloped with a mix of smaller and less costly open-air "lifestyle centers" and condo towers on the same property to create a vertical trade area and bring shoppers closer to the shops.

All retail format has a life cycle. The big box store and power center are no exception. In more recent years, growth and expansion of big box stores and power centers have slowed down, partly because of over-supply of retail spaces in the power centers, but also because of the closure of the underperforming retailers, leaving many "ghost boxes" in the host power centers. They are also losing appeal to some shoppers, particularly seniors who perceive big box stores as being too cavernous and unpleasant to shop in and often accessible by car only. Despite the doom-and-gloom predictions of some commentators, big box retailers are not down for the count yet. Some of them have begun to move into city centers with a scaled-down footprint, to "right size" the store platform to fit customer needs (Kulp, 2017). Some suburban big boxes (such as Staples) have been downsizing their bricks-and-mortar presence and sublet part of the store space to complementary businesses.

THE RETAILER–SUPPLIER RELATIONSHIP HAS TIPPED TOWARDS RETAILERS

For many years, producers of consumer goods dictated brands, types, and price of products being sold in the retail market. Since the late 1980s, retailing has been shifting from being the sales agent for manufacturing and agriculture to being the production agent for consumers; and the balance of the retailer–supplier relationship has tipped towards the large retail chains. This power shift has accelerated with the ongoing process of retail capital consolidation. While still mediating between consumers and producers, the mega chains are no longer neutral mediators, nor are they passive receivers of consumer goods supplied to them by producers. Instead, they induce consumers to select goods with larger profit margins, and erode manufacturers' share of the surplus value by influencing patterns of consumption in their own favor and by using their bargaining power to demand discriminatory discount and lock manufacturers into retailer-led supply situations (Hughes, 1996: 99). They also aggressively develop "own-label" (or private-label) products as a competitive strategy. These are products made by one manufacturer for sale under a retailer's brand by a contract between the two parties. The retailer specifies everything about the product—what goes in it, how it is packaged, what the label looks like—and pays the manufacturer to have it produced and delivered to its distribution centers or to its stores directly. For example, Kenmore is Sears' private label for home appliances (refrigerator, stove/oven, dishwasher, washer and drier), and is a familiar brand to many households in the U.S. and Canada. However, Sears does not manufacture appliances; most Kenmore appliances are made by such well-known manufacturers as Whirlpool, LG, and Frigidaire. Another example of private label is Costco's Kirkland signature. Retailer-brand products are often positioned as lower-cost alternatives to national or international brands; but recently, some private-label brands have been positioned as "premium" brands to compete with existing "name" brands. Such brands are generally less expensive than national brands, as the retailer can optimize the production to suit consumer demand and reduce advertising costs. As such, a link is established between these brands, the retailer's corporate identity, and consumer trust in the retailer's reputation (Wrigley & Lowe, 2002). Equipped with this new power, retailers can either reduce selling spaces for manufacturers' brands in their stores or, at an extreme, delist the manufacturers' brands.

With their significant purchasing and bargaining power, large retailers manage to exploit *negative working-capital cycles* by negotiating for an extended credit payment period, to reduce circulation costs and accelerate accumulation of retail capital (Marsden & Wrigley, 1996). Pressure is often placed on suppliers to develop just-in-time production programs and factory-to-warehouse distribution systems to match the demands of the retailers, thus reducing inventory holdings on the side of the retailers. As a sarcastic saying goes, "The second-worst thing for a manufacturer to do is sign a Walmart contract, so stringent are its cost demands. The worst thing is failing to do so, given the importance of Walmart's shelf space" (Olive, 2003), reflecting the hate-and-love relationship between suppliers and powerful retailers. In July 1998, the Office of Fair Trading (OFT) of the United Kingdom announced its first full investigation of the increasing power and market dominance of the major British food retailers, triggered by ongoing complaints from suppliers about the detrimental impact of retailer concentration and market dominance (Wrigley & Lowe, 2002). Overtly, the complaints were that food retailers were not passing on to consumers the lower prices they were obtaining from the producers. The subtext of the complaints must also include their resentment of the excessive returns obtained by the retailers at the expense of the suppliers.

INTERNATIONALIZATION OF RETAILING HAS INTENSIFIED

Retail internationalization is not new, but it has intensified significantly since the 1990s, becoming a powerful driver of changes in retail geography. In the most fundamental sense, international operation of retailers is motivated by either or both of the following factors or drivers: saturation of domestic market, and a strategic need to explore new markets and secure first-mover advantages (Yip, 1992; Alexander, 1993; Akehurst & Alexander, 1995; Simpson & Thorpe, 1999). Elango (1998) concludes that low domestic growth rates, strong import competition, and high global market growth rates motivate the industry to seek international expansion; but only those firms that have adequate resources in administration and R&D (research and development) and have achieved high operational efficiency are likely to succeed in expanding into foreign markets. Indeed, the most successful international retailers are those based in the U.S., Western Europe, and Japan.

With reference to another model developed by Vida and Fairhurst (1998), the direction and pace of the retail internationalization process is influenced by both firm characteristics and the external retail environment. The key characteristics internal to the firm are resource availability and commitment, and its differential advantages. The external retail environment factors include market conditions, consumer affluence and cultural preference, competition, and regulation. They serve as promoters or inhibitors for whether a firm will initiate international retail activities, maintain a constant level of involvement, increase or decrease its involvement, or completely withdraw from the international market (Vida & Fairhurst, 1998: 145).

As Dawson (1994: 268) correctly points out, "any move towards multi-store operation has to acknowledge that culture varies through space". Initially, international retailers chose markets that had the least physical and psychic distances in order to minimize cost and the degree of uncertainty about sourcing and operation (Whitehead, 1992). For example, most U.S.-based multinational retailers have used Canada as the convenient experimental ground to test their internationalization strategies and business models. As a firm gains more experience, it enters markets with greater physical or psychic distances but also great potential profitability (Erramilli, 1991). In recent decades, the major multinational retailers have increasingly turned their attentions to the *emerging markets* in Asia and Latin America (Wrigley, 2000), which offer the attractions of rapid economic development and rising levels of affluence and consumer spending, combined with extremely low levels of penetration of Western forms of retailing and associated distribution systems. They seek to expand in foreign countries using a variety of entry paths ranging from licensing and franchising to joint ventures and direct investment in wholly owned subsidiaries.

The retail internationalization process is complex. Dawson (2003: 4) proposed a four-phase model to describe the complex process: stability, consolidation, control, and dominance. Initially, there is considerable fluidity as the firm gains understanding about the new market. In the second phase, the firm adjusts to new conditions, consolidating its position. After that, it begins to try to exert control over vertical and horizontal channel relationships. When the retailer becomes established in the market, mature strategies seeking market dominance, and similar to those used in the home country, are applied. Dawson (2003) also points out that few firms pass through the complete model. Many firms fail to achieve their objectives and therefore decide to withdraw from the market at some stage. The failures of four high-profile international retailers in Chile (namely, Home Depot and J. C. Penney of the U.S., Carrefour of France, and Royal Ahold of Holland) and their subsequent withdrawal from that country are testimony to the challenges of retail internationalization ("Globalization's winners and losers", 2006). The reasons for their failures vary, and the "standardization versus adaptation" debate continues in the study of internationalization of retailing.

As shown in Table 2.1, 25 of the top 30 retailers in the world have operations in multiple countries. Walmart became an international company in 1991. By 2017, it had more than 11,200 stores under 55 banners in 29 countries. It continues to expand its international operations in response to the switching of consumer interest towards online retailing. In 2016, Walmart signed a strategic agreement with China's JD.com to expand delivery services in Chinese cities to compete with Alibaba (Walmart, 2016; Sun, 2018). In 2018, Walmart acquired a 77 percent ownership of India's Flipkart—an online retailer founded by two former Amazon employees in 2007 (Associated Press, 2018). Currently, Flipkart's supply chain arm, eKart, serves customers in 800 cities and makes 500,000 deliveries daily. The French Carrefour went international in the 1970s, and has also intensified its overseas operations since the late 1980s. As of 2019, it operates 12,000 stores in 30 countries. For many multinational retailers, revenue from their overseas operations has become an increasingly important part of business success, or even of survival.

Associated with the process of retail internationalization have been spatial switching of retail capital across national borders and creation of retail spaces in foreign landscapes of consumption (Lowe & Wrigley, 1996), but the benefits for the capital-receiving countries are mixed. Since opening up to foreign retail capital in 1992, China has become the largest emerging market that all major international firms have desired to penetrate. Table 2.3 shows the presence and market penetration of the major international retailers in China as of 2010. For example, in the first 15 years, Walmart opened 219 supercenters in 95 Chinese cities; Carrefour opened 182 hypermarkets in 58 cities in China. The international retailers not only brought about direct

Table 2.3 Major Foreign Retailers in China, 2010

Retailer	Year of first store opening	Category*	Format	Market penetration	
				No. of stores	No. of cities
Isetan (Japan)	1993	department store	department store	4	4
Carrefour (France)	1995	G.M. & food	hypermarket	182	58
Walmart (U.S.)	1996	G.M. & food	hypermarket	219	95
Jusco (Japan)	1996	G.M. & food	department store	27	14
Metro (Germany)	1996	G.M. & food	warehouse/membership	48	34
Ikea (Netherlands)	1998	furniture	warehouse	8	8
Ito Yokado (Japan)	1998	G.M. & food	supermarket	12	2
Auchan (France)	1999	G.M. & food	hypermarket	41	21
B&Q (UK)	1999	home improvement	warehouse	40	17
Uniqlo (Japan)**	2002	apparel	specialty store	170	41
Tesco (UK)	2004	G.M. & food	hypermarket	109	38
Zara (Spain)**	2006	apparel	specialty store	60	31
Home Depot (U.S.)	2006	home improvement	warehouse	7	3
Best Buy (U.S.)	2006	electronics	big box/specialty store	277	36
H&M (Sweden)**	2007	apparel	specialty store	114	47

Source: China Chain Store Associations, 2011; various corporate annual reports and websites.

Notes
* G.M. = general merchandise.
** 2012 data.

investment to the country, but also introduced new retail formats and transferred advanced logistic technologies to their local partners, which helped to nurture a national team of domestic retailers (Wang, 2014). Of the top 250 retailers in the world, ten of them are mainland China-based, though none of them has achieved multinational status yet.[4] The domestic retailers are now able to counter-compete with the international heavyweights to gain market shares.

In Canada, the impacts of retail internationalization have been more pronounced. It contributed to the demise of many long-established domestic retailers, as accounted for earlier in this chapter. Today, most subsectors of retailing are dominated by U.S.-based multi-nationals: Walmart and The Hudson's Bay in general merchandise; Home Depot and Lowe's in building materials and home improvement; Staples in stationery and office supplies; Best Buy in consumer electronics; and Costco in membership clubs. The only subsector where the domestic retailers are able to resist foreign competition and hold their market share is food retailing.

There are two widely varying viewpoints about the growing role of foreign retailers in Canada (Simmons & Kamikihara, 1999). National-ists tend to focus on the cultural impacts: the replacement of Canadian companies and banners by American firms and brands, and the loss of national identity in the retail industry. A contrasting viewpoint is that opposition to American retailers is more emotional, concerning social, instead of economic, issues. Canadian consumers actually benefit from increased choice of consumer goods at lower prices brought about by the major international retailers. Competition from international retailers also motivates domestic retailers to improve their operational efficiency by adopting retail innovations and investing in new information and distribution technologies. While there are some job losses, most foreign-owned stores are still staffed with Canadian employees, except a small number of high-rank executives.

International retailers constantly monitor their business perform-ance and adjust their global portfolios accordingly. When and where they underperform, or their performance deteriorates, they divest from the market: they either scale down their operations or leave the market entirely. Walmart acquired the British Asda in 1999. After nearly 20 years, its operation in the UK has not been going as well as it anticipated. In 2018, Walmart announced its intention to sell its majority ownership of Asda to J. Sainsbury plc., the UK's second largest supermarket chain, reducing its control of Asda to 42 percent. This is part of Walmart's refined growth strategy: to exit underperforming markcts (cvcn if these are mature markels) and focus on pursuing faster-growth international markets such as China and India (Sasso et al., 2018). Similarly, Carrefour China in 2019 sold 80 percent of its ownership to the domestic retailer Suning, reducing its China stakes to 20 percent (Shi, 2019).

E-RETAILING HAS BEEN GAINING INCREASED MARKET SHARE AND RETAIL DISTRIBUTION CHANNELS HAVE BEEN DIVERSIFIED

In the early 1990s, a new agent of retailing and a new form of retail space—online shopping and the web store—came into being, whereby consumers purchase goods or services from a seller over the internet, without having to visit a bricks-and-mortar store. Initially, shoppers needed to have access to a computer connected to the internet and a method of electronic payment—typically a credit card. Once a payment was received (usually through a third-party e-commerce business that facilitates online money transfer between consumers and retailers, such as PayPal), the goods were shipped to a prescribed address via post or courier services, or they could be picked up by the consumer from a nearby store. This format of electronic commerce began to be used for business-to-consumer (B2C) transactions and mail order, and led to the creation of the famous Amazon in 1995 and eBay in 1996.

At the beginning of online retailing, shoppers were deterred by fraud and privacy concerns, such as the risk of cyber theft of their credit card number and identity. Over time, such risks have been greatly reduced by the use of secure sockets layer (SSL) encryption and firewalls, and e-retailers have improved their refund policies. As a result, more and more consumers are encouraged to shop online for the benefits of convenience and saving, as the web stores are open all year round with no after-business hours and with no restrictions by location and distance.

The increased popularity of online retailing has led to another assault on, and brought about another disruption to, bricks-and-mortar stores. Shopping online is frictionless, and shoppers can get almost unlimited information about the merchandise they are buying. It therefore recalibrates what people think what shopping should be (Kopun, 2017). In the new world order of retail, shoppers have become more tech savvy. Many of them now use mobile devices (mainly smartphones and tablets) to shop, order, and pay; or they go to a store to look at and feel a product, and then buy it online from Amazon, turning the bricks-and-mortar stores into showrooms. Dubbed the biggest "big box" store with unmatched product offerings, Amazon has expanded its merchandise offerings to also include a wide assortment of products sold by third-party sellers. More than 100 million paying customers have signed up for Amazon Prime for a membership fee of $99 per year (Weise, 2018), receiving free, two-day shipping. According to Consumer Intelligence Research Partners, Prime subscribers spend significantly more on Amazon: US$1,300 per year on average, compared with US$700 for non-Prime shoppers. This means that the paying members alone would divert US$13 billion sales from various bricks-and-mortar stores. Amazon continues to be on the march, successfully moving into merchandise that Walmart and other retailers traditionally have sold. Not all categories of merchandise have the same level of suitability for sale online. Standardized merchandise, such as books, music, video games, computers, and consumer electronics, have much higher levels of suitability than furniture and grocery (see Table 2.4). For many years, fast fashion drove shoppers into malls, creating the mentality that there should always be something new in the specialty stores in malls. This is not so any more. As reported by Coresite Research (Rupp, 2018), Amazon Fashion has become the second most-shopped apparel retailer, behind only Walmart but tied with Target, as measured by number of shoppers. The 2017 PwC Total Retail Survey (Maxwell, 2017) reveals that 40 percent of the participating consumers intend to purchase clothes online (also see Table 2.4).

Any retail that is not Amazon-proof is now in danger. More and more retailers responded to the new shopping patterns by offering both multichannel retailing (selling both in store and online, but separately) and omnichannel retailing (order online but pick up in store or have the merchandise delivered to home; or purchase in store but have the merchandise delivered to home). All major retailers now do business through omnichannels. Those that are not adapting to the digital shift fast enough are mostly struggling with maintaining market share, or even with survival. One of the reasons for the bankruptcy of Toys 'R' Us is that instead of developing its own e-commerce platform, it opted to enter a ten-year agreement with Amazon in 2000 to create a co-branded online toy store. However, the partnership soon collapsed in a dueling lawsuit, resulting in Toys 'R' Us missing "early move" opportunities to enter e-commerce. In its bankruptcy filing, Toys 'R' Us acknowledged that Amazon's low prices were tough to match.

Table 2.4 Percentage of Consumers Who Intend to Purchase Online by Merchandise Category

Merchandise category	Percentage of consumers
Book, music, movies, video games	60
Consumer electronics and computers	43
Clothing and footwear	40
Toys	39
Health and beauty	37
Sports equipment and outdoor	36
Household appliances	33
Jewelry and watches	32
Do-it-yourself home improvement	30
Furniture and hardware	30
Grocery	23

Source: PwC Total Retail Survey (Maxwell, 2017).

After Amazon purchased Whole Foods Market (including its 13 stores in Canada) in 2017, and launched free two-hour Whole Foods home delivery in six cities for its Prime members, it has raised the stakes in the highly competitive grocery delivery wars in both the U.S. and Canada. Walmart is expanding its same-day grocery delivery service in ten metropolitan areas in the U.S., for a flat fee of $9.95 and minimum spending of $30 per order (D'Innocenzio, 2018). It is also testing a home delivery service using its store workers to drop off merchandise to customers' homes after they finish work (Soper, 2017). Equipped with its 4,700 stores as "fulfillment centers" and armed with one million workers as potential delivery persons, Walmart is poised and determined to win this new retail war.

In Canada, the three largest supermarket chains—Loblaws, Sobeys, and Metro—also responded quickly by starting to focus on e-commerce offerings. Loblaws began to offer home delivery services in late 2017 in Toronto and Vancouver, and planned to expand the service to five other urban markets in 2018, including Montreal, Halifax, and Regina. To speed up the process, it teamed up with Instacart—a California-based grocery startup—that processes online orders and provides delivery services. In addition, it planned to expand its "Click-and-Collect" program, which enables shoppers to order online and pick up from a nearby store, by adding 500 new pickup sites in 2018 (Sagan, 2018). Sobeys plans to roll out its own online grocery business in 2020, in partnership with the British firm

Ocado Group plc. The latter will use its advanced robotic technology to create an e-commerce platform and run an automated warehouse and a fleet of delivery vans (Chambers, 2018; Deschamps, 2018).

Before e-commerce came into play, goods were distributed to consumers in a linear channel: manufacturers sold large quantities of products to wholesalers; wholesalers sold the products to retailers, who in turn sold the products to consumers. In the age of e-commerce, the distribution system has become much more complex, and distribution routes have been shortened, including both multichannel and omnichannel retailing. In many cases, producers now sell products directly to consumers through their own online channels, bypassing wholesalers and retailers.

The ongoing development of e-retailing will continue to reduce foot traffic to bricks-and-mortar stores, and home delivery will be the next big business improvement. Amazon has been experimenting with a number of innovations, one of which is the Amazon Key (Fowler, 2017). An internet connected smart lock, the Amazon Key allows a delivery worker to get into people's homes using a one-time access code, and only Amazon employees are allowed to deliver merchandise inside a home for safety and security. The purchaser does not need to be home; he/she will get a phone notification of when the delivery will arrive at his/her house. Once the door is unlocked, a camera sends a live stream to the homeowner, and records the whole event.

Despite its rapid expansion, retail e-commerce sales are still less than 15 percent of the total retail sales in all countries. In 2019, the share is 11 percent in the U.S. and 9 percent in Canada (Statisca, 2019). While e-commerce offers great convenience, many shoppers still prefer to go into a store for shopping experience and for good bargains. Further, people still go to malls to participate in the social aspect of shopping, especially in suburban or exurban places where few large gathering places are available (Clark, 2017). For this reason, bricks-and-mortar stores will not disappear, and store location research is still relevant and still matters. Even online retailers are now opening physical stores for consumer experience and for those consumers who do not want to pay a shipping fee, but prefer to pick up their orders from a nearby store. The Amazon Go, a cashierless store, is such an experiment. In an Amazon Go store, shoppers mill around pushing a smart shopping cart that has a barcode scanner, a scale, and a payment system for self-service.

KEY POINTS OF THE CHAPTER

- The retail industry has always been changing and evolving. Several revolutionary changes have taken place simultaneously in the last three decades:
  - retail chains continue to be the most important form of retail concentration, but significant restructuring and reshuffling have occurred;
  - the dominance of malls has declined, and big box stores and power centers have emerged to become new leading retail formats;
  - the retailer–supplier relationship has tipped towards retailers;
  - internationalization of retailing has intensified;
  - e-retailing has been gaining traction and increased market shares, and retail distribution channels have been diversified.
- These changes have given rise to new retail formats and new delivery channels; they have also changed the traditional store location requirements and opened new areas of research for retail geographers. A good understanding of these changes and the forces behind them is essential for retail geographers to participate effectively in retail planning and analysis.
- Bricks-and-mortar retailers will continue to lose market shares to e-retailers, and more of them may close for good. However, many stronger ones will emerge after repositioning themselves and after further industry shuffling and rationalization. Most corporate retailers will be seen doing business in omnichannel. One new area of research for retail geographers is distribution of retail facilities (both physical stores and fulfillment centers) for merchandise pickup and home delivery.

NOTES

1 The French Carrefour was listed as the fourth largest retailer in the world in 2012, but it is missing in the 2017 list for unknown reasons.
2 The four national brand department stores were Eaton's, The Bay, Sears, and Zeller's; the regional brand department store was Woodward's.
3 Nordstrom, Macy's, Bloomingdale's, and Sears.
4 The only exception is Suning. Ranked the thirty-sixth among the top 250 retailers in the world in 2017, Suning has a limited presence in Japan after it acquired a small Japanese electronics retail, Laox, in 2009 and turned the Laox stores into tourist-focused duty-free shops.

THE CONTEMPORARY RETAIL ECONOMY

REFERENCES

Akehurst, G. & Alexander, N. (1995). Developing a framework for the study of the internationalisation of retailing. *The Service Industries Journal*, 15(4), 204–210.

Alexander, N. (1993). Internationalisation: interpreting the motives. *International Issues in Retailing, ESRC Seminars: Research Themes in Retailing*, Manchester Business School/Manchester School of Management, March 15.

Associated Press. (2018). Walmart buys stake in India's Flipkart. *Toronto Star*, May 10, B6.

Beyard M. & O'Mara. W. (1999). *Shopping Centre Development Handbook* (3rd edition). Washington, DC: ULI–the Urban Land Institute.

Chambers, S. (2018). Sobeys joins online-delivery battle. *Toronto Star*, January 23, GT1.

China Chain Store Association. (2011). *China Chain Store Almanac*. Beijing: China Commerce Publishing House.

Clark, P. (2017). How to bring a struggling mall back to life. *Toronto Star*, March 4, B13.

Dawson, J. A. (1994). Internationalization of retailing operations. *Journal of Marketing Management*, 10(4), 267–282.

Dawson, J. A. (2003). Introduction. In J. Dawson et al. (Eds.), *The Internationalization of Retailing in Asia* (pp. 1–5). London, England: Routledge Curzon.

Deloitte Touche Tohmatsu Limited (DTTL) and Stores Media. (2019). *The 22nd Annual Global Powers of Retailing Report*. www2.deloitte.com/content/dam/Deloitte/global/Documents/Consumer-Business/cons-global-powers-retailing-2019.pdf.

Deschamps, T. (2018). Sobeys plans ahead in supermarket wars. *Toronto Star*, March 15, B1.

D'Innocenzio, A. (2016). Macy's shuts 14% of stores in the U.S. *Toronto Star*, August 12, B1.

D'Innocenzio, A. (2018). Walmart to expand grocery delivery. *Toronto Star*, March 15, B1.

Doucet, M. (2001). *The Department Store Shuffle: Rationalization and Change to the Greater Toronto Area*. (Research Report 2001–05). Toronto, Canada: Center for the Study of Commercial Activity, Ryerson University.

Elango, B. (1998). An empirical examination of the influence of industry and firm drives on the rate of internationalization by firms. *Journal of International Management*, 4(3), 201–221.

Erramilli, M. K. (1991). The experience factor in foreign market entry behaviour of service firms. *Journal of International Business Studies*, 3(22), 479–501.

Fowler, G. A. (2017). Amazon is the gust that won't go away. *Toronto Star*, December 8, B1.

"Globalization's winners and losers: lessons from retailers J. C. Penny, Home depot, Carrefour, Ikea and others". (2006). *Strategic Direction*, 22(9), 27–29.

Heath, T. (2017). Grocers: the new mall anchors? *Toronto Star*, March 13, B6.

Hernandez, T. & Simmons, J. (2006). Evolving retail landscapes: power retail in Canada. *The Canadian Geographer*, *50*(4), 465–486.

Hughes, A. (1996). Forging new cultures of food retailer-manufacturer relations. In N. Wrigley and M. Lowe (Eds.), *Retailing, Consumption and Capital: towards the New Retail Geography* (pp. 90–115). Essex, England: Longman Group Ltd.

Hughes, J. & Seneca, J. (1997). Two business revolutions at work. *Business News New Jersey*, February 3, 9.

Jones, K. & Doucet, M. (1998). *The Big Box, The Big Screen, The Flagship and Beyond.* (Research Report 1998–7). Toronto, Canada: Center for the Study of Commercial Activity, Ryerson University.

Kopun, F. (2017). Lights out at the local mall. *Toronto Star*, May 6, B1.

Kopun, F. (2018a). "Business as usual" up north. *Toronto Star*, March 10, B1.

Kopun, F. (2018b). Toys "R" Us to sell off stores. *Toronto Star*, March 16, B1

Kowinski, W. S. (1985). *The Malling of America: an Inside Look at the Great Consumer Paradise.* New York, NY: William Morrow and Company Inc.

Kulp, K. (2017). Big-box retailers not down for count yet. *CNBC*, November 28. www.cnbc.com/2017/11/28/big-box-retailers-not-down-for-count-yet-analysts.html.

Lang, A. (2015). Target admits it missed the mark, but what does it mean for Canadian retail? *CBC News*, January 15. www.cbc.ca/news/business/target-admits-it-missed-the-mark-but-what-does-it-mean-for-canadian-retail-1.2906830.

Lowe, M. & Wrigley, N. (1996). Towards the new retail geography. In N. Wrigley and M. Lowe (Eds.), *Retailing, Consumption and Capital: towards the New Retail Geography* (pp. 3–30). Essex, England: Longman Group Ltd.

Marsden, T. & Wrigley, N. (1996). Retailing, the food system and the regulatory state. In N. Wrigley and M. Lowe (Eds.), *Retailing, Consumption and Capital: towards the New Retail Geography* (pp. 33–47). Essex, England: Longman Group Ltd.

Maxwell, J. (2017). Ten retailer investments for an uncertain future. *PwC Total Retail.* www.pwc.com/gx/en/industries/assets/total-retail-2017.pdf.

Mellor, B. & Boyle, M. (2018). Amazon may buy Target this year, analyst says. *Toronto Star*, January 3, B3.

Olive, D. (2003). Values outsourced: what are the social costs of the Walmart economy? *Toronto Star*, October 18. (Page number missing).

Perlburg, H. (2017). Mall fight back against web rivals. *Toronto Star*, April 24, B6.

Rupp, L. (2018). Amazon apparel puts the fear in Target, Macy's, J. C. Penney. *Toronto Star*, February 20, B3.

Sagan, A. (2018). Loblaw wants its services to "blanket the country". *Toronto Star*, May 3, B1.

Sasso, M., Ponczek, S. & Chambers, S. (2018). Walmart refines growth strategy. *Toronto Star*, May 1, GT9.

Shaw, H. (2016). Target Corp's spectacular Canada flop: a gold standard case study for what retailers shouldn't do. *Financial Post*, January 15. https://business.financialpost.com/news/retail-marketing/target-corps-spectacular-canada-flop-a-gold-standard-case-study-for-what-retailers-shouldnt-do.

Shi, C. (2019). Suning.com acquire shares of Carrefour China. *People's Daily* (overseas edition), June 24, p. 3.

Simmons, J. & Kamikihara, S. (1999). *The Internationalization of Commercial Activity in Canada*. (Research Report 1999–7). Toronto: Center for the Study of Commercial Activity, Ryerson University.

Simpson, E. & Thorpe, D. I. (1999). A specialty store's perspective on retail internationalization: a case study. *Journal of Retailing and Consumer Services*, 6(1), 45–53.

Soper, S. (2017). Walmart workers tapped for deliveries. *Toronto Star*, June 2, B4.

Statisca. (2019). E-commerce share of total retail sales in United States from 2013 to 2021. www.statista.com/statistics/379112/e-commerce-share-of-retail-sales-in-us/.

Sun, L. (2018). Walmart and JD.com tighten their alliance with a $500 million investment. www.fool.com/investing/2018/08/12/walmart-jdcom-tighten-alliance-500-million-invest.aspx.

Urban Land Institute. (1985). *Shopping Center Development Handbook* (2nd edition). Washington, DC: Urban Land Institute.

Veiga, A. (2017). Mall beef up options to boost shoppers. *Toronto Star*, December 20, B4.

Vida, I. & Fairhurst, A. (1998). International expansion of retail firms: a theoretical approach for future investigations. *Journal of Retailing and Consumer Services*, 5(3), 143–151.

Walmart. (2016). Walmart and J.D.com announce strategic alliance to serve consumers across China. https://corporate.walmart.com/newsroom/2016/06/20/walmart-and-jd-com-announce-strategic-alliance-to-serve-consumers-across-china.

Wang, S. (2014). *China's New Retail Economy: a Geographic Perspective*. New York, NY: Routledge.

Weise, E. (2018). Amazon Prime tops 100M subscribers. *Toronto Star*, April 20, B2.

Whitehead, M. B. (1992). Internationalisation of retailing: developing new perspectives. *European Journal of Marketing*, 26(8/9), 74–79.

Wrigley, N. (1993). Retail concentration and the internationalization of British grocery retailing. In R. D. F. Bromley & C. J. Thomas (Eds.), *Retail Change: Contemporary Issues* (pp. 41–68). London, England: UCL Press Ltd.

Wrigley, N. (2000). The globalisation of retail capital: themes for economic geography. In G. Clark, M. Gertler, & M. Feldman (Eds.), *Handbook of Economic Geography*. London, England: Oxford University.

Wrigley, N. & Lowe, M. (2002). *Reading Retail: A Geographical Perspective on Retailing and Consumption Spaces.* London, England: Arnold.

Yeates, M. (2011). *Charting the GTA: The Dynamics of Changes in the Commercial Structure of the Greater Toronto Area.* (Research Report 2011–6). Toronto, Canada: Center for the Study of Commercial Activity, Ryerson University.

Yip, G. S. (1992). *Total Global Strategy: Managing for Worldwide Competitive Advantage.* Englewood Cliffs, NJ: Prentice Hall.

3 The Geography of Demand, Expenditure Patterns, and Market Segmentation

Consumers are the lifeblood of the retail industry. Their preference, choice and shopping behavior fundamentally influence the way in which retailers conduct business, including where to set up stores and what merchandise to offer in the stores (Birkin et al., 2002). Furthermore, consumers are differentiated by income, gender, age, and ethnicity, and they tend to cluster in different parts of the city. Essentially, the spatial variation in demand governs the type, size and locations of retail stores (Jones & Simmons, 1993). Therefore, understanding the geography of demand for consumer goods and services and expenditure patterns is the first and fundamental step in market condition analysis, as illustrated in Figure 1.1 (Box 3). In market condition analysis, market analysts not only consider the current population size, but also forecast population change within a planning horizon. This chapter explains what factors influence the level of demand and why demand for consumer goods and services varies in different markets. In addition, the chapter describes such techniques as geodemographic analysis, market segmentation, and population projection.

FACTORS OF DEMAND

A market refers to a geographical area with a population of consumers who have demand for consumer goods/services and have disposable income to purchase them. A market also has a spatial dimension and boundaries, though the boundaries can be fuzzy and arbitrary.

Many factors affect demand for consumer goods and services in a market. Population size, population composition, and disposable income are the most fundamental. Additional factors include family formation, price of goods and services, inflation rate, consumer expectation of the economic future, and government regulations. They affect demand in various ways. Moreover, in different places, the degree of effects of these factors varies, and so does the level of demand. This forms the basis for understanding the geography of demand.

All members of the population are end consumers of many types of goods and services. Population size is therefore the foremost factor of demand, especially for such necessities as food, clothes, and shelter. Typically, the larger the population, the higher the demand.

Also important is the population composition on the lines of gender, age, and ethnicity, which separates the population into different segments of consumers, who often have different tastes or preferences for consumer goods. It is common sense that consumers of different genders and ages purchase different types of products. For example, a population with a high proportion of children and youths may have a high demand for toys, baby clothes, and school supplies, whereas a population with a high proportion of seniors may have a high demand for health care–related products and services. It is well documented that the older population has been growing faster than the population of children and youths across all developed countries. The 2016 Canadian census shows that for the first time in history, there are as many seniors as children 14 years and younger in Canada (Press, 2017). Even in China, the population is aging rapidly, resulting from 35 years of the restrictive one-child policy. The aging populations have created a "gray market" of considerable size, consisting mainly of baby boomers. Some of them enjoy a decent pension, supplemented with a large pot of savings. Others live on a meager fixed income topped up by *old age security* and *low-income supplements*—two types of government benefits for senior citizens. There is perhaps one thing in common among the gray consumers: their mobility is greatly reduced, which affects their shopping behavior and patterns. Many of them shun big box stores and power centers in the suburbs, but prefer convenience shopping near the location of their residence.

Today's younger consumers consist of Gen Y and Gen Z. The former group were born between the early 1980s and the mid-1990s; the latter group were born between the mid-1990s and the early 2000s, constituting the generation of millennials. They make up 25 percent of the U.S.

population and 27 percent of the Canadian population. These younger consumers tend to be tech savvy, and are more likely to do online shopping; or they shop in store but buy online (Black, 2019).

Consumers of varying ethnicity also exhibit different consumption patterns, resulting from their varying cultural and religious backgrounds. From a business point of view, ethnic minority groups collectively represent a large consumer market worthy of serious marketing considerations (Omar et al., 2004.) In both Canada and the U.S., the ethnic consumer market has been expanding rapidly, a result of not only increased immigration but also the expansion of the second and third generations of immigrants through new family formation. At the same time, the ethnic market has become more fragmented than ever, due to the diversification of immigrant origins. This is especially true in the immigrant-receiving metropolitan areas, where ethnic minorities now constitute a large segment of the consumer market. This market is no longer represented by low and unstable demand to be met by specialist businesses of low economies of scale. Population diversification has created new opportunities for ethnic entrepreneurs, and ethnic retailing has become an increasingly visible component of the retail landscape and the broader retail economy (Wang & Hernandez, 2018). Among all ethnic consumer goods, food is perhaps the most closely tied to ethnic identity and is the most frequently consumed. According to a report by Perry Caicco of CIBC World Markets (Condon, 2013), ethnic retailers in metropolitan Toronto take in $4–5 billion a year in food sales, as much as the total sales of Walmart's food division in the Toronto Census Metropolitan Area. Mainstream corporate retailers have realized that supermarkets cannot be a melting pot providing generic products to everyone, and that merely running ads in ethnic media at occasions of ethnic festivals is not enough to capture the new market growth. They need to engage in ethnic retailing in a variety of new ways, ranging from acquiring ethnic business operations to hosting ethnic retailers as co-tenants on their business premises (Wang & Hernandez, 2018).

Another crucial factor that combines with population to determine the level of demand and market size is disposable income. While most countries have seen an overall increase in disposable income over the last few decades, there has been increasing social polarization with widening gaps between the upper and the lower classes (Birkin et al., 2002). Consumers with high disposable income tend to not only buy higher-quality (and also more expensive) products, but also buy replacement more often. Therefore, disposable income affects demand through influencing lifestyle and preference for consumer goods and services. Studies also show that income affects demand for different types of goods. Essential or basic consumer goods (i.e., the necessities that are consumed by all people) are not sensitive to income. However, as income increases, demand for inferior (i.e., lower quality) goods decreases, because consumers shift to better quality goods. For normal goods, and particularly luxury goods that are used for pleasure and esteem, demand increases as income increases. High-income households are also associated with high automobile ownership and therefore a higher level of mobility. They have more choices for shopping destinations too.

Level of income is also the most important differentiator of market segments in geography. High-income and lower-income households often live in different quarters of a city. To match the demands and maximize market shares, many corporate food retailers run two classes of grocery stores: one as premium and full-service supermarkets, the other as discount supermarkets. They are located in different communities and neighborhoods to target different income groups. Discount supermarkets in a low-income area may stock lower-quality produce and meat, including groceries with a closer best-before date.

In most Western economies (North America, Western Europe, Australia, New Zealand, and Japan), family and household size has been steadily declining, now with more DINK (double income with no kids) households or same-sex unions, as well as more single-person households. Typically, larger households and families have a larger shopping basket. The more persons in the family or household, the more likely the consumers are to seek out cost-effective pricing, which is regularly offered at large format discount stores and membership clubs in bulk packages. Because there are more individuals to provide for in their households, it makes sense for them to be budget-conscious in all of their purchases (Tripathi & Sinha, 2006; Bruce, 2017). Smaller households with similar income are less price sensitive. They often also buy smaller packages of food and household supplies, and stay away from membership clubs such as Costco and Sam's Club. Overall, the demand for household appliances has been on the rise due to the increase in total number of households, because smaller condos also need to be equipped with basic home appliances.

Price of goods and services affects demand through the effect on purchasing power. For most consumers, higher prices reduce their purchasing power; so, as the price of a good increases, fewer units of that good will be purchased. While consumers maintain the usual level of demand for necessities (food, clothes, shelter, and medication), they shun discretionary purchases and reduce replacement frequency for high-price goods. The effect of price is also influenced by fluctuation in inflation rates. When inflation increases, demand decreases. Research also finds that consumer expectation of the economic future, such as a foreseen recession, may delay purchase decisions for big items and therefore suppress demand for the present time. Prices of related goods or services, which are either complementary or substitutes, affect demand as well. The complementary goods are those that are purchased along with another good. An example is gasoline and automobile. When the price of gasoline increases for an extended period of time, the demand for automobiles, especially large horsepower automobiles, declines. Substitutes are those that are purchased instead of a certain good. The opposite reaction occurs when the price of a substitute rises: consumers will want to buy more of the good and less of its substitute.

Retailers cannot raise people's income, but they often manipulate demand through promotion and adverting. Promotion works by periodically reducing prices of certain goods within a limited time period. Advertising influences demand in three ways, by: (1) drawing consumer attention and informing them of the availability of a product; (2) "educating" consumers by demonstrating the features of the product; (3) persuading them to purchase the product for the feature, price, and quality of the products, even by taking a loan from lenders (Karlan et al., 2009). Research reveals that consumers are highly sensitive to advertisements, as they sometimes get attached to the advertisements endorsed by their favorite celebrities. This results in an increase in demand for a product.

Government policies and regulations affect demand in a combination of two ways: limiting supply of, and imposing high sales tax on, certain goods (such as the demerit goods of cigarettes, cannabis, and alcohol) to safeguard social well-being; and restricting price increases on essentials (such as food and medicine) to assist low-income consumers.

HOUSEHOLD EXPENDITURE PATTERNS

Business geographers and market analysts often use the two most fundamental factors to estimate the overall size of a consumer market:

- number of consumers (or population size) * per capita disposable income; or
- number of households * average household disposable income

For retailers of a specific category of merchandise (such as food retailers), the above formula can be extended as:

- number of households * average household disposable income * percentage of household income spent on that category of merchandise

Market analysts often use the household expenditure data to develop profiles of purchasing patterns in different parts of a market. Some marketing firms create such profiles through their own consumer survey (via telephone survey or questionnaire survey). In most countries, relevant government agencies collect and disseminate household expenditure data for various levels of geography.

In the United States, consumer expenditure data are collected by the Census Bureau in two surveys: the Interview Survey for major and/ or recurring items, and the Diary Survey for more minor or frequently purchased items. Similarly, Statistics Canada conducts a national Survey of House Spending (SHS) annually in the ten provinces, and every other year in the three sparsely populated territories (Statistics Canada, 2018). Since 2010, SHS has combined the use of a questionnaire and an expenditure diary. The questionnaire collects, during a computer assisted personal interview, regular and less frequent expenditures on clothing, furniture, transportation, household equipment, etc., with recall periods based on the type of expenditure. The diary collects frequent expenditures (such as grocery and gasoline), which are difficult to recall during a retrospective interview. Selected households complete a daily expenditure diary for two weeks following an interview. The data are collected on a continuous basis from January to December of the survey year, from a sample of households spread over 12 monthly collection cycles. Longer reference periods are used for goods and services that are more expensive or are purchased infrequently or irregularly (known as high-order goods). Shorter reference periods are used for goods and services that are of less value or purchased frequently or at regular intervals (known as low-order goods).

The target population of the 2017 SHS was the population of Canada's ten provinces plus the three territorial capitals (Whitehorse, Yellowknife, and Iqaluit). Residents of institutions (e.g., inmates in prisons), members of the Canadian Forces living in military camps, and people living on Indian reserves were excluded, but these exclusions account for only 2 percent of the national population (Statistics Canada, 2018). The 2017 SHS sample consisted of 17,792 households

throughout the ten provinces and 929 households in the three territorial capitals. It was a stratified, multi-stage sample selected from the
Labor Force Survey (LFS) sampling frame. Sample selection com-
prised two main steps: (1) selection of clusters (small geographic
areas) from the LFS frame;[1] and (2) the selection of households within
each of these selected clusters.

SHS collects the following information pursuant to consumption
patterns:

- household expenditure on different things
- annual income of household members (collected from personal
  tax returns)
- demographic characteristics of the household
- dwelling characteristics (type, age, and tenure)
- household equipment (e.g., electronics; heating/air conditioning;
  and entertainment, recreation, and communications equipment)

The survey results are disseminated in a variety of dimensions. The
most useful ones are by geography (province and metropolitan area)
and household income, which reveal the geography of demand and
expenditure variations by household income. Table 3.1 shows the
expenditure profiles by aggregated categories of consumption and by
household income quintiles for Canada in 2017. The table reports
both *total expenditure* and *total current consumption.* Total expenditure
refers to the sum of total current consumption, income taxes, personal
insurance payments, pension contributions, gifts of money, alimony,
and contributions to charity. Total current consumption excludes
income taxes, personal insurance payments, pension contributions,
and contributions to charity.

This table reinforces the explanation of the effects of income on
demand and consumption patterns. Both total expenditure and total
current consumption vary greatly with levels of household income.
While the households in the highest income quartile spend three
times as much money in total current consumption as do those in
the lowest income quartile ($105,493 vs. $33,764), it accounts for
only 62.6 percent of their total expenditure, compared with 95
percent for the lowest income households. This means that the rich
households pay more income taxes and insurance premiums and
spend more on big ticket durables (as well as accumulating savings),
while the low-income households allocate most of their income on
current consumptions.

Table 3.1 Household Spending Profiles by Household Income Quintile, Canada, 2017

Aggregated categories	All $	All %	Lowest $	Lowest %	Second $	Second %	Third $	Third %	Fourth $	Fourth %	Highest $	Highest %
Total expenditure	86,070		35,556		52,887		73,272		100,120		168,398	
Total current consumption	63,723	74.0	33,764	95.0	46,075	87.1	59,439	81.1	73,744	73.7	105,493	62.6
Food	8,527	13.4	4,839	14.3	6,502	14.1	8,455	14.2	9,927	13.5	12,873	12.2
Shelter	18,637	29.2	11,733	34.8	14,539	31.6	16,991	28.6	20,994	28.5	28,921	27.4
Household operations	4,827	7.6	2,575	7.6	3,606	7.8	4,662	7.8	5,533	7.5	7,750	7.3
Household furnishings and equipment	2,314	3.6	1,050	3.1	1,632	3.5	2,168	3.6	2,577	3.5	4,139	3.9
Clothing and accessories	3,430	5.4	1,559	4.6	2,383	5.2	3,044	5.1	3,904	5.3	6,256	5.9
Transportation	12,707	19.9	5,103	15.1	8,675	18.8	12,239	20.6	15,267	20.7	22,230	21.1
Health care	2,579	4.0	1,299	3.8	2,080	4.5	2,743	4.6	3,161	4.3	3,612	3.4
Personal care	1,300	2.0	548	1.6	950	2.1	1,216	2.0	1,409	1.9	2,373	2.2
Recreation	3,986	6.3	1,573	4.7	2,211	4.8	3,382	5.7	4,959	6.7	7,797	7.4
Education	1,777	2.8	584	4.7	943	2.0	1,238	2.1	1,789	2.4	3,333	3.2
Reading materials and other printed matter	158	0.2	78	0.2	124	0.3	149	0.3	173	0.2	266	0.3
Tobacco products and alcoholic beverages	1,497	2.3	855	2.5	1,069	2.3	1,362	2.3	1,794	2.4	2,403	2.3
Games of chance	200	0.3	123	0.4	204	0.4	213	0.4	171	0.2	285	0.3
Miscellaneous expenditures	1,785	2.8	844	2.5	1,158	2.5	1,579	2.7	2,086	2.8	3,254	3.1
Income taxes	14,993	17.4	544	1.5	3,418	6.5	8,180	11.2	16,694	16.7	46,114	27.4
Personal insurance payments and pension contributions	5,137	6.0	511	1.4	1,929	3.6	3,987	5.4	7,203	7.2	12,050	7.2
Gifts of money, support payments and charitable contributions	2,218	2.6	736	2.1	1,465	2.8	1,566	2.3	2,478	2.5	4,741	2.8

Source: Statistics Canada, 2019.

For households of all levels of income, the highest proportions of consumption go to shelter (29 percent), transportation (20 percent), and food (13.4 percent). The low-income households spend much higher shares of their income on these necessities than do the high-income households. For instance, expenditure on shelter, transportation, and food account for 35, 15, and 14 percent of the total current consumption for the households in the lowest income quartile, but for only 27, 21, and 12 percent for the households in the highest income quartile. The fact that high-income households spend many more dollars on shelter, transportation, and food means that they live in bigger houses, use and maintain expensive (newer and luxury) vehicles, and consume high-quality food without heavy economic burdens.

Since paying for necessities is the top priority for the lower-income households, they often reduce their spending on other categories of merchandise. For instance, the households in the lowest income quartile spend the lowest proportions of their consumption dollars, among all households, on household furnishings and equipment (3.1 percent), clothing and accessories (4.6 percent), personal care (1.6 percent), and recreation (4.7 percent). When these percentages are converted into dollars, their consumption of these categories of merchandise is much less than what is spent by the higher-income households.

Most consumer goods are of marginal utility, which quantifies the added satisfaction that a consumer garners from consuming additional units of a good or service. The concept of marginal utility is used by economists to determine how much of an item consumers are willing to purchase. *Positive marginal utility* occurs when the consumption of an additional item increases the total utility, while *negative marginal utility* occurs when the consumption of an additional item decreases the total utility (Samuelson & Nordhaus, 1983). This suggests that there is a limit to merchandise consumption by quantity. Once a certain quality is reached, consumers with different income are differentiated by consumption quality: that is, high-income consumers shift to buying better quality products and also income elastic (or luxury) goods, but do not necessarily buy more of the same type of goods in quantity. On the other hand, low-income households have less money to spend on any kind of products, so their choices are restricted to a small number of cheap brands. For this reason, the amount of dollars of consumption should be more useful than the percentage of consumption in assisting retailers in making business decisions.

For retailers, expenditure data disseminated by smaller geographies are more useful than the national average. Statistics Canada disseminates the SHS data for public use for the ten provinces and the three territories. The data at Census Metropolitan Area (CMA) level of geography are available by custom requests only and for a fee. While the data are rich in content, there are limitations in representativeness for smaller geographies due to two factors. First, the sample size of the survey is small. For the largest province of Ontario with 5.17 million households (2016 census), only 2,562 were selected for interview in the 2017 SHS. Second, due to the voluntary nature of the survey, 672 selected households chose not to participate in the survey for various reasons. This reduced the number of usable responses to 1,637 for the entire province of Ontario.

Environics Analytics, Canada's leading marketing and analytical services company, provides current estimates of annual expenditures for almost 500 variables, spanning 18 categories of goods and services purchased and consumed by Canadian households. The database, titled *HouseholdSpend*, enables users to analyze potential expenditures by both average dollars per household and total dollars spent for any geographic level, from all of Canada to a small trade area. The database is produced using data from DemoStats, PRIZM and the Survey of Household Spending administered by Statistics Canada (https://environicsanalytics.com/en-ca/data/financial-databases/householdspend).

Some business analytics software is packaged with demographic and socioeconomic data along with household expenditure data. Both ESRI's *Business Analyst* and Caliper's *Maptitude* include a comprehensive suite of (estimated) household spending data at census tract level of geography for the major U.S. and Canadian cities.

MARKET SEGMENTATION

It has been established earlier in this chapter that demand for goods and services varies not only among, but also within, metropolitan regions. Since few companies are big enough to supply the needs of an entire market, most retailers and service providers need to break down the total demand into segments and choose those segments that the company is best equipped to handle. Therefore, identifying spatial clusters of similar consumers is important for any type of retailer and service provider in order to select the "right" locations for retail outlets. This is known as *market segmentation*, which is the process of defining and subdividing a large market into identifiable segments that have similar needs, wants, or demand characteristics. Its objective is to create more effective marketing strategies by designing a marketing mix that matches the expectations of customers in the targeted segment.

Market segmentation is based on the "science" of geodemographics, which is defined as the analysis of people by where they live (Sleight, 2004). It brings together "geo", implying geography, and "demographics" of households or individuals, into a single term. Neighborhoods are stratified by social class and ethnicity. Two principles underpin the use of geodemographics (Leventhal, 2016: 6). First, people who live in the same neighborhood are more likely to have similar characteristics than those who live in a different neighborhood. Second, neighborhoods can be categorized according to the characteristics of their residents. Two neighborhoods belonging to the same category are likely to contain similar types of people, even though they may be geographically far apart.

Population census is the primary source of data for geodemographics, and neighborhood classification is at the heart of geodemographics. The principal method of geodemographics is cluster analysis—a multivariate statistical procedure. The key to the application of cluster analysis is to choose the appropriate set of classification variables, also called discriminators.

The usefulness of geodemographics lies in its ability to pinpoint geographical locations of each segment (Leventhal, 2016). These segments can be communicated either on maps or as lists of spatial clusters. In the geodemographics literature, the term neighborhood is often used to refer to the spatial clusters of market segments. While neighborhood is a clearly delineated physical unit in the city planning literature, it is not a standard geography for census data aggregation and dissemination. In geodemographic analysis, such convenient data aggregation units as census tract and postcode are frequently used to identify and delineate market segments. In the era of e-commerce with reduced number of stores, geodemographic analysis is more important to bricks-and-mortar retailers than before, Users of the market segmentation products should also be aware of the two principal limitations of them: first, not every household is the same in the same spatial cluster, and there are always internal differences and outliers, known as ecological fallacy; second, cluster (or segment) profiles may change or degrade over time, and new classifications are necessary to update the market segmentation system.

Some leading business consulting firms offer off-the-shelf commercial segmentation systems, The best-known system is *Claritas PRIZM Premier* (Claritas, 2019). This system is a set of geodemographic segments for the United States, and is a widely used segmentation system in marketing to help America companies find customers. Combining demographics, consumer behavior, and geographic data, *PRIZM Premier* classifies every U.S. household into one of 68 consumer segments based on the household's purchasing preferences. It offers a complete set of ancillary databases and links to third-party data, allowing marketers to use data outside of their own customer files to pinpoint products and services that their best customers are most likely to use, as well as to locate their best customers on the ground.

PRIZM Premier segments are created according to socioeconomic ranks, which takes into account characteristics such as income, education, occupation, and home value. They are grouped into 11 *Lifestage Groups* and 14 *Social Groups*.

The Lifestage Groups are based on household age, affluence, and the presence of children at home. Within the three Lifestage Classes— Younger Years, Family Life, and Mature Years, the 68 segments are further grouped into 11 Lifestage Groups; each group's combination of the three variables—affluence, householder age, and presence of children at home—offers a more detailed profile of the consumers.

Social Groups are based on urbanization class and affluence. There are four urbanization class categories—Urban, Suburban, Second City, or Town, and Rural. Within each of these urbanity categories, the segments are then sorted into groups based on affluence (i.e., household income).

Retailers, marketers, and retail planners can use the search tool (known as the ZIP Code Look-Up Tool) provided by Claritas on its website (www.mybestsegments.com) to find out suitable segments in the U.S. for their product and services.

Canada's leading consumer segmentation system is *PRIZM5*, offered by Environics Analytics. PRIZM5 is the latest release of the pioneering segmentation system from Environics Analytics that classifies Canada's neighborhoods into 68 unique lifestyle types, to capture current demographics, lifestyles, consumer behaviors, and settlement patterns in Canada. Continuing with methodology that integrates geographic, demographic, and psychographic data, PRIZM5 incorporates the latest authoritative data from nearly a dozen demographic, marketing and media sources to help retailers and commercial service providers to better analyze and understand their customers and markets (Environics Analytics, 2015).

Other available commercial segmentation systems are ESRI's *Tapestry*, MapInfo's *PSYTE*, and Applied Geographic Solutions' *MOSAIC*. They all use a large number of classification variables, from both population census and third-party data.

A CASE STUDY OF MARKET SEGMENTATION USING CLUSTER ANALYSIS[2]

To illustrate how market segments are identified and mapped using a coupling of cluster analysis and GIS, a case study of Dollarama is presented. Dollarama is the largest dollar store chain in Canada. As of January 2017, it operated 1,095 stores across the country. In the retail industry, dollar stores are known as the "extreme value retailer". Unlike convenience stores that are typically small in size, the modern dollar stores are much bigger, carrying a large assortment of merchandise. They aim to meet basic and daily household needs, and focus on frequently used and replenished goods (such as consumables, packaged food/perishables/snacks, health and beauty products), and, to a limited extent, apparel. They also aim to provide a fun, exciting treasure hunt experience. All dollar stores target low- and fixed-income households, including ethnic minorities and new immigrants. Capitalizing on the 2008 recession, the Dollarama stores now also target middle-income consumers. Given their low price points ($1–$4), they are exclusively bricks-and-mortar stores with no online sales and no home delivery (except bulk purchase of party supplies). In this case study, the statistical method of cluster analysis is used to identify the market segments in the Toronto CMA that fit Dollarama's consumer profiles (Ware, 2017; LeBlanc, 2018).

Cluster analysis is a method of data partition and classification, grouping similar cases into a class that is different from other classes. It is also a data reduction method. However, unlike principal component analysis and factor analysis, which group similar variables (i.e., columns in a data set) into factors, cluster analysis groups similar cases (i.e., rows in a data set) into a smaller number of classes, known as clusters. Each resulting cluster is a group of relatively homogeneous cases (or observations) in the data set. On the basis of combination of classification variables, cluster analysis maximizes the similarity of cases within each cluster, while maximizing the dissimilarity between clusters. Cases in each cluster are similar to each other, and are dissimilar to the cases in other clusters.

There are two types of cluster analysis: *hierarchical cluster analysis*, and K-*means cluster analysis*. The former is used when the researcher has no "idea" of how many clusters may exist in the data set. The latter is used when the researcher has a hypothesis about the number of clusters in the data set. In both types of cluster analysis, the method depends on the classification variables being used. It is advised that the data set should contain at least four classification variables, because fewer than four variables result in meaningless clusters. Depending on data sets, the biggest challenge is to identify the optimum number of clusters: too large a number results in many small clusters that do not have much differentiation from each other, while too small a number results in large clusters that may hide important spatial variations due to a high level of generalization. One of the important characteristics of the K-means cluster analysis is its ability to choose the number of clusters desired. Still, the decision is often made with a degree of arbitrariness and after several rounds of experiment, or trial runs, using different values of K. (For a thorough understanding of cluster analysis, students are advised to consult a multivariate statistics textbook.)

The target markets of Dollarama in the Toronto CMA are profiled using the K-means cluster analysis method. Eight classification variables are selected from the 2011 Canadian census at the census tract level of geography. These are:

- median household income (in Canadian dollars)
- number of households with household income under $50,000
- percentage of households living in subsidized housing
- prevalence of low income (i.e., percentage of households living below official poverty line)
- number of unemployed persons
- average dwelling value
- number of home renters
- number of recent immigrants (living in Canada for less than five years at the time of the census)

Median household income and average dwelling values are two most obvious indicators that separate the "less fortunate" neighborhoods from the wealthy neighborhoods. Households that have aggregated income under $50,000 (compared with the median household income of $70,365 for the entire CMA), especially those below the official poverty line, and households that live in subsidized housing are all characteristics of consumers who are likely to buy merchandise from a

Dollarama store. Unemployed persons who have lost their steady income also fit the profile of the Dollarama consumers, though their unemployment status is not necessarily permanent, and many of them re-enter the labor market at some point in time after the census. Recent immigrants are included on the assumption that their income is low and they tend to be price conscious for daily use articles and consumables. It is well documented in the literature that new immigrants are in a period of transition in life and employment, and they struggle to find a job that matches their education credentials and occupation skills in the first five years in Canada. Although some of them are able to purchase a million-dollar house and live in a tony neighborhood, they could be real estate rich but income poor, because the money they had to purchase the house was brought from their home country, not earned in Canada from regular wages or salaries.

The cluster analysis is performed using SPSS (Statistical Package for the Social Sciences). With the eight classification variables, a K-means cluster analysis is trial-run four times, using $K=3$, $K=4$, $K=5$, and $K=6$, respectively. It is found that $K=5$ gives the most distinguishable clusters, with maximum distances between the cluster centroids, which are the means of the cluster scores for the individual census tracts of each cluster.

A new column of Cluster_ID is added to the census dataset, in which a unique ID number is assigned to each of the 1,074 census tracts, linking target market groups to specific areas in the Toronto CMA. Summary and spatial statistics are then calculated including the number of census tracts in each cluster. Demographic, social and economic data for each cluster are also derived. The final cluster centers for each classification variable are presented in Table 3.2. The five clusters, or market segments, are labeled, respectively, as Price Conscious, Middle-Class Thrifty, Middle-Class Well-Off, Rich and Wealthy, and Ultra Rich (LeBlanc, 2018).

Cluster 1, or the Price Conscious segment, which consists of 468 census tracts (out of a total of 1,074 in the entire CMA), should be the primary target market for Dollarama. Clearly, this cluster has:

- the lowest median household income ($64,100)
- the lowest average dwelling value ($345,800)
- the largest number of households with income less than $50,000 (743)
- the highest percentage of persons living below the official poverty line (18 percent)

Table 3.2 Final Cluster Centers for Dollarama Market Segments

Classification variable	1 Price Conscious	2 Middle-Class Thrifty	3 Middle-Class Well-Off	4 Rich and Wealthy	5 Ultra Wealthy
# Census tracts	468	429	126	45	6
Median HH income (1,000$)	64.1 (17.8)	79.5 (22.6)	92.6 (30.1)	114.6 (36.6)	185.1 (34.8)
Average dwelling value (1,000$)	345.8 (69.9)	507.2 (52.4)	735.7 (80.3)	1,092.2 (138.6)	1,789.8 (253.3)
# HH under $50k of income	743 (467.6)	596 (440.5)	511 (378.5)	398 (262.0)	140 (152.4)
Prevalence of low income (%)	18 (9.4)	14 (7.2)	12 (6.9)	10 (5.4)	7 (2.2)
% HH in subsidized housing	14.1 (17.2)	11.1 (16.9)	6.96 (14.2)	3.05 (6.7)	3.88 (9.5)
# Renters	663 (655.7)	530 (644.8)	541 (626.8)	508 (423.0)	177 (129.2)
# Unemployed persons	269 (113.0)	240 (116.3)	195 (88.5)	152 (67.9)	101 (62.8)
# Recent immigrants	436 (372.8)	326 (304.5)	228 (196.2)	182 (156.1)	73 (29.8)

Notes
HH = household.
* Numbers in brackets are standard deviation.

- the highest percentage of households living in subsidized housing (14.1 percent)
- the largest number of home renters (663)
- the largest number of unemployed persons (269)
- the largest number of recent immigrants (436)

The secondary target market for Dollarama should be Cluster 2—the Middle-Class Thrifty segment. This cluster of 429 census tracts has:

- the second lowest median household income ($79,500)
- the second lowest average dwelling value ($507,200)
- the second largest number of households with income less than $50,000 (596)
- the second highest percentage of persons living below official poverty line (14 percent)
- the second highest percentage of households living in subsidized housing (11.1 percent)
- the third largest number of home renters (530; fewer than Cluster 3)
- the second largest number of unemployed persons (240)
- the second largest number of recent immigrants (326)

The other three clusters, which account for 16 percent of all the census tracts in the CMA, contain fewer residents and households that fit Dollarama's consumer profile.

Figure 3.1 maps the spatial distribution of the five clusters, along with the existing 156 Dollarama stores (as of 2016). It is evident that Dollarama has indeed focused heavily on the Cluster 1 "neighborhoods" in store deployment; it has also been extending its market reach to the Cluster 2 neighborhoods, as the retailer stated in its annual reports (Dollarama, 2018). Specifically, 87 (or 56 percent) of the 156 stores are located in (or on the border of) the Cluster 1 census tracts, which are home to 44 percent of the CMA's households; another 46 stores (29 percent) are in (or on the border of) the Cluster 2 census tracts, which contain 41 percent of the CMA's household; only 23 stores are in the census tracts of the other three clusters.

Of the eight classification variables, *median household income* and *average dwelling value* make the most contributions to separating the clusters. *Percentage of households living in subsidized housing* and *number of renters* seem to make the least contribution, because their standard deviations are larger than the cluster means, which suggests that there are wide ranges in the values of these variables within the five clusters.

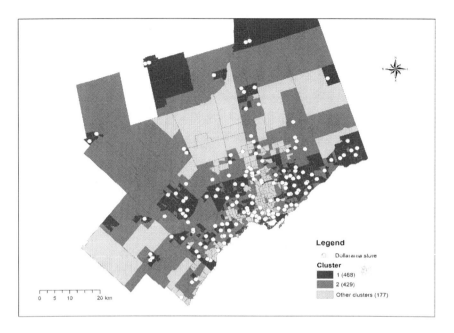

Figure 3.1 Dollarama Market Segments and Store Locations in the Toronto CMA, 2017.

The cluster analysis–based geodemographics is a useful tool for the study of the geography of demand. The same method can be used to identify target markets for other types of retailers and commercial service providers, but with a different set of classification variables. The choice of classification variables depends on the type of business, but also on the knowledge of the market analyst or the retail geographer who performs the market segmentation.

POPULATION PROJECTION

Market condition analysis not only is based on the current population size, but also considers population change within the planning horizon. For this reason, population projection is also an important part of market condition analysis, because retail planners need to estimate not only the current level of demand, but also future demand. This is particularly important for planning of large retail facilities, which are subject to the risk of heavy sunk cost and may require additional land for future expansion.

There are a number of different methods of population projection, including extrapolation methods (both linear and exponential extrapolation); components of growth; and logistic method (Plane & Rogerson, 1994). In this textbook, only the extrapolation methods are described and explained.

Linear Extrapolation Method

The linear extrapolation method projects population on the basis of the past trend of population change, and assumes that the same trend continues in the projection period. The mathematical formula is as the following:

$$P_{(\text{target year})} = P_{(\text{base year})} * (1 + nr)$$

where

- $P_{(\text{target year})}$ is the projected population
- $P_{(\text{base year})}$ is the most recent known population
- n is the number of years between the base year and the target year
- r is the annual population change rate, calculated on the basis of the known populations of two past years, using the formula $r = \{(P_{t2} - P_{t1}) / P_{t1}\} / N$
- N represents the number of years between the two past years P_{t1} and P_{t2}

The operation of this method is illustrated using the Toronto CMA as an example. In this example, we use the 1991 population as P_{t1} and the 2001 population as P_{t2}, to project the 2006 population. Since the real 2006 population is known, the projected population can be compared with the real population for accuracy. According to the Canadian census, the Toronto CMA had a population of 3,892,750 in 1991; the population increased to 4,668,142 in 2001. The 2006 population is projected as the following:

$$r = \frac{(4,668,142 - 3,892,750)}{3,892,750} / 10 = 0.02$$

$population\ 2006 = 4,668,142 * (1 + 5 * 0.02) = 5,134,956$

To assess the accuracy of the projection, the projected population is compared with the real population of the CMA as reported in the 2006 census, which is 5,106,485. The error of projection (i.e., the difference between the real population and the projected population) is only 28,471 persons, or a mere 0.6 percent, indicating a high level of accuracy.

Exponential Extrapolation Method

Unlike the linear extrapolation method, which assumes a constant growth rate in the recent past years, the exponential method assumes that population grows exponentially. Mathematically, the method is expressed as:

$$P_{(target\ year)} = P_{(base\ year)} * e^{nr},$$

where

- $P_{(target\ year)}$ is the projected population
- $P_{(base\ year)}$ is the most recent known population
- e is the base of the natural logarithm, a mathematical constant approximately equal to 2.718.
- n represents the number of years between the base year and the target year
- r is the annual population change rate, calculated on the basis of the known populations of two past years, using the formula of $r = \{\ln (P_{t2} / P_{t1})\} / N$
- N is the number of years between P_{t1} and P_{t2}

The operation of the method is illustrated using the same Toronto CMA example:

$$r = \left\{ \ln\left(\frac{4,668,142}{3,892,750} \right) \right\} / 10 = 0.018$$

Population 2006 = 4,668,142 * $e^{0.018*5}$ = 5,107,761

With the exponential extrapolation method, the error of projection is even smaller:

5,107,761 – 5,106,485 = 1,276 persons, or 0.02 percent.

For retail planning purpose, population projection at smaller geographies is much more useful. The same methods can be used to project the

2006 population at the census tract level, as illustrated in Table 3.3 with a sample set of 20 census tracts in the Toronto CMA. In both linear and exponential methods, the 1991 and 2001 populations from the national census are used as P_{t1} and P_{t2}, respectively, for projecting the 2006 population. The 2001 population is also used as $P_{(\text{base year})}$. The real 2006 population from the Canadian census is also listed to check for projection errors. The same operations can be implemented in a GIS environment, and the projected population can be mapped for visualization and trade area analysis.

From the sample census tracts in Table 3.3, it can be observed that the projections derived from the two methods are similar, with no big difference. However, the projection errors among the 20 census tracts are much larger than the error of projection for the CMA population: ranging from 4.3 to 62.5 percent. As well as that, populations of some census tracts are over-projected (with positive projection errors), while others are under-projected (with negative projection errors). This has happened because the extrapolation methods assumed that the trend of population change in the ten-year period of 1991–2001 would continue in the following five years, 2001–2006. Apparently, this was not always the case in all census tracts. These errors also point to the limitations of population projection in general at small-scale geographies. Small areas of geography, such as census tracts, are sensitive to short-term or one-time population change, possibly resulting from demolition and redevelopment. A short-term change or a one-time change in the recent past, either increase or decrease, could lead to significant errors in a projection, because the projection is based on the assumption that the past trend will continue in the same direction and at the same rate. A significant one-time change (such as an addition of a high-rise condo tower) could also lead to a projection that exceeds the census tract's carrying capacity in a short period of time.

In sum, population projection works better for shorter periods of time and for larger areas of geography. The longer the projection period and the smaller the geographic area, the less accurate the projection is. Population projection also works better for "mature" areas, but is less accurate for areas of new subdivisions, which occur mostly in suburban areas. Relatively speaking, the exponential method tends to produce better results than the linear method when used for a shorter projection period, while the linear method is better for a longer projection period. With both methods, the challenge is to determine the optimum level of geography. In retail planning, larger-than-census-tract geographies, such as trade areas or planning districts, should be

Table 3.3 Examples of Population Projection at Census Tract Level of Geography in the Toronto CMA

Census tract,	Census reported population			Projected 2006 population	
	1991 (P_{t1})	2001 (P_{t2} and $P_{base\ year}$)	2006	Linear method (with error of projection in %)	Exponential method (with error of projection in %)
5,350,001.00	618	626	571	630 (10.3)	630 (10.3)
5,350,002.00	592	658	627	695 (10.8)	694 (10.6)
5,350,004.00	7,050	7,417	6,861	7,610 (10.9)	7,608 (10.9)
5,350,005.00	5,087	5,438	5,089	5,626 (10.5)	5,622 (10.5)
5,350,006.00	280	262	156	254 (62.6)	253 (62.5)
5,350,007.01	3,545	3,786	3,615	3915 (8.3)	3,913 (8.2)
5,350,007.02	5,325	5,941	5,292	6,285 (18.8)	6,275 (18.6)
5,350,008.00	1,336	1,692	3,821	1,917 (−49.8)	1,904 (−50.2)
5,350,009.00	300	226	264	198 (−25.0)	196 (25.7)
5,350,010.00	6,715	9,527	10,742	11,522 (7.3)	11,348 (5.6)
5,350,011.00	836	2,081	4,642	3,631 (−21.8)	3,283 (−29.3)
5,350,012.00	1,955	2,995	8,053	3,792 (−52.9)	3,707 (−54.0)
5,350,013.00	4,573	6,365	6,315	7,612 (20.5)	7,509 (18.9)
5,350,014.00	304	516	548	696 (27.0)	672 (22.7)
5,350,015.00	1,364	2,468	2,742	3,467 (26.4)	3,320 (21.1)
5,350,016.00	1,133	2,532	4,484	4,095 (−8.7)	3,785 (−15.6)
5,350,017.00	4,671	6,427	6,378	7,635 (19.7)	7,539 (18.2)
5,350,018.00	1,822	1,770	1,623	1,745 (7.5)	1,745 (7.5)
5,350,019.00	3,209	3,738	3,284	4,046 (23.2)	4,034 (22.8)
5,350,021.00	5,199	5,235	5,038	5,253 (4.3)	5,253 (4.3)

used for population projection. For a longer projection period, the logistic method is recommended, which caps projection errors by the calculated or prescribed carrying capacity of the geographical area.

KEY POINTS OF THE CHAPTER

- A number of factors in combination influence demand for consumer goods in a geographically confined market. The most fundamental are population size, population composition, and disposable income. Additional factors are family composition, price of goods, inflation rate, consumer expectation of the economic future, and government regulations.
- Because neighborhoods are stratified by social class, economic status, and ethnicity, demand for consumer goods varies across the surface of a city or region. Understanding the geography of demand is the first step in market condition analysis.
- Market analysts often use the household expenditure data to develop profiles of purchasing patterns in different parts of a market. Some marketing firms create such profiles through their own consumer survey. In most countries, relevant government agencies collect and disseminate household expenditure data for various levels of geography. In the United States, consumer expenditure data are collected by the Census Bureau. Similarly, Statistics Canada conducts a national Survey of House Spending annually.
- Market segmentation, which is based on the "science" of geodemographics, is the process of analyzing people by where they live and subdividing a large market into identifiable segments that have similar needs, wants, or demand characteristics. Cluster analysis is the main tool that retail geographers use for market segmentation. Some leading business consulting firms offer off-the-shelf commercial segmentation systems, such as Claritas' *PRIZM Premier*; Environics Analytics' *PRIZM5*; ESRI's *Tapestry*; MapInfo's *PSYTE*; and Applied Geographic Solutions' *MOSAIC*.
- Retail planners need to estimate not only the current level of demand, but also future demand. This is particularly important for planning of large retail facilities. Therefore, population projection is an important part of market condition analysis. There are a number of methods of population projection, including extrapolation, components of growth, and logistic method. In

general, population projection works better for shorter periods of time and for larger areas of geography; the longer the projection period and the smaller the geographic area, the less accurate the projection is. With all methods, the challenge is to determine the optimum level of geography.

NOTES

1 Clusters are selected from both urban and rural areas. In urban areas, the following groups of centers are represented:
   • small population center: 1,000 to 29,999
   • medium population center: 30,000 to 99,999
   • large urban population center: 100,000 and over
2 This case study is based on two graduate research papers authored by Daniel LeBlanc and Sandra Ware, and supervised by the lead author of this book.

REFERENCES

Birkin, M., Clarke, G. & Clarke, M. (2002). *Retail Geography and Intelligent Network Planning*. Chichester, England: John Wiley & Sons, Ltd.

Black, T. (2019). As millennials buy everything online, trucks reap riches. *Toronto Star*, January 12, B3.

Bruce, O. (2017). Social factors affecting retail business. *BizFluent*. https://bizfluent.com/info-8483338-social-factors-affecting-retail-business.html.

Claritas. (2019). Introduction to PRIZM PREMIER. www.claritas.com/prizm-premier.

Condon, G. (2013). Yes, you should pay attention to ethnic grocers. *Canadian Grocer*, April 1. www.canadiangrocer.com/top-stories/yes-you-should-pay-attention-to-ethnic-grocers-8663.

Dollarama. (2018). Annual Information Form Fiscal Year Ended January 28. www.dollarama.com/wpcontent/uploads/2018/04/2018-Annual-Information-Form-English.pdf.

Environics Analytics. (2015). Introduction to PRIZM5. https://environicsanalytics.com/docs/default-source/webinars/prizm5-introduction-20150417.pdf?sfvrsn=57bbf0b1_2.

Jones, K. & Simmons, J. (1993). *Location, Location, Location: Analyzing the Retail Environment* (2nd edition). Toronto, Canada: Nelson Canada.

Karlan, D., Kuhn, M., & Zinman, J. (2009). Does ad content affect consumer demand? *Alliance Magazine*. www.alliancemagazine.org/opinion/does-ad-content-affect-consumer-demand/.

LeBlanc, D. (2018). *Dollarama's Location Strategy: A Retail Estate Perspective.* (Major Research Paper). Toronto, Canada: Ryerson University.

Leventhal, B. (2016). *Geodemographics for Marketers: Using Location Analysis for Marketers*. London, England: Kogan Page Ltd.

Omar, O. E., Hirst, A., & Blankson, C. (2004). Food shopping behavior among ethnic and non-ethnic communities in Britain. *Journal of Food Products Marketing, 10*(4), 39–57.

Plane, D. A. & Rogerson, P. A. (1994). *The Geographical Analysis of Population: with Applications to Planning and Business.* New York, NY: John Wiley & Sons.

Press, J. (2017). The greying of Canada. *Toronto Star,* May 2, A1.

Samuelson, P. & Nordhaus, W. (1983). *Microeconomics.* New York, NY: McGraw-Hill Book Company.

Sleight, P. (2004). Targeting customers: how to use geodemographic and lifestyle data in your business. Henley-on-Thames, England: World Advertising Research Center.

Statistics Canada. (2018). User Guide for the Survey of Household Spending, 2017. Ottawa. www150.statcan.gc.ca/n1/pub/62f0026m/62f0026m2018001-eng.htm.

Tripathi, S. & Sinha, P. K. (2006). *Family and Store Choice—A Conceptual Framework (Working Paper No. 2006–11–03).* Ahmedabad, India: Indian Institute of Management.

Wang, S. & Hernandez, T. (2018). Contemporary ethnic retailing: an expanded framework of study. *Canadian Ethnic Studies, 50*(1): 37–68.

Ware, S. (2017). *The Evolving Location Strategy of Dollarama: a GIS-assisted Analysis* (Major Research Paper). Toronto, Canada: Ryerson University.

4 Retail Structure Analysis

On the supply side, retail structure refers to the mix of different types of retail activity in a given area of geography, or a geographically confined market. The area can be as large as a country, a province, or a metropolitan area; it can also be as small as a retail strip or a shopping center. A good retail structure is one that has a balanced mix of stores that suit the needs of the local consumers; various stores complement each other with minimal internal competition, while facilitating a healthy level of comparative shopping. In contrast, a poor retail structure is one that has too many stores of the same type, with excessive internal competition or over-supply of retail space.

Retail structure analysis often goes hand in hand with demographic analysis and analysis of the geography of demand. It helps business owners to gauge the level of market saturation, the strengths and weaknesses of the competitors, and the market space or gaps left for them (especially new entrants) to fill. It also helps shopping center management to assess if the current store mix suits the local demographics. As an extension of its application, retail structure analysis has been used by social geographers to identify "food deserts" in metropolitan areas. For commercial real estate developers, retail structure analysis is useful for calculating supply density (i.e., per capita retail space) and determining what type(s) of facilities should be built to meet the needs of the growing/changing retail sector. Equally important, municipal planners conduct retail structure analysis to determine if there is an over-supply of certain types of stores, which therefore should be controlled, and if there is an under-supply of other types of businesses, which should be encouraged and promoted, through denying or issuing of new business licenses and building permits. After all, municipal planners need to answer the question of whether the market justifies the additional commercial space that is proposed. Through analysis of changes in the past, future trends can be projected, which is valuable in retail planning for retailers and commercial property developers alike.

Retail structure can be disaggregated in many different ways, such as business structure, format structure, geographical structure, and ownership structure. This chapter explains what factors drive retail structure change, what data are needed for retail structure analysis, and how retail structure analysis can be conducted and interpreted.

DRIVING FACTORS

Retail structure in a market is by no means static; it changes over time. A number of factors, often working in combination, give rise to structural changes.

The fundamental factor for retail structure change has been the restructuring of the larger economy. In most countries, as the primary sector activities continue to shrink, and as the manufacturing sector pumps out more consumer goods due to increasing use of technology and increased productivity, the service economy (or tertiary sector), of which retail is a part, expands accordingly, both in magnitude and variety.

Business consolidation has led to numerous mergers and acquisitions, and has therefore resulted in concentration of retail capital in the hands of a small number of retail corporations. "In the process of increasing concentration, some popular street names have been swallowed up and renamed by their new owners; others continue to operate under the old trading names but are now part of large retail conglomerations" (Gardner & Sheppard, 1989: 26). This has not only resulted in corporate reconfiguration, but also reduced the number of market players. In the 1990s, there was a wave of mergers and acquisitions of drug stores in the U.S. As a result, regional chains and independents were consolidated into a small number of major firms. Store network rationalization after the mergers and acquisitions also resulted in the emergence of super drugstores and the closure of many smaller ones at a rate of approximately 2,000 stores each year (Wrigley & Lowe, 2002).

Retail innovation is another important factor. The emergence and booming of big box retailing and power centers has been supported chiefly by retail innovations. The diffusion of innovation is often coupled with retail internationalization. Most retail innovations originated from a small number of countries (especially the U.S.) that have a strong and innovative retail industry. As the innovative retailers enter foreign markets, they transplant the new formats to the receiving countries, giving rise to changes in local retail structure, including ownership structure. For example, the modern big box format was introduced to Canada by the U.S. retailers in the early 1990s, and most big box stores in Canada are operated by U.S.-based companies, such as Walmart, Costco, Home Depot, Lowes, Staple Business Depot, and Best Buy. More recently, the digital revolution and e-commerce gave rise to virtual stores, leading to the shrinking of "bricks-and-mortar" stores, as the latter are often bypassed by the alternative channels of retailing. In one example, digital photography has led to the disappearance of many film processing stores. Black's Cameras, a Canadian retail chain focusing on photography equipment and film processing since 1939, once had more than 100 stores and was present in almost every regional shopping center in Canada. The entire chain had to close in 2015 due to diminishing demand, and it sold its assets to Montreal-based Les Pros de la Photo, which now operates the brand as an online business only.

Suburbanization of population generates new demands for consumer goods and services in the outskirts of the metropolitan areas, thus expanding the metropolitan market surface into the outer suburbs. Both retailers and commercial property developers have responded to the shift in demand by developing stores, shopping centers, and warehouse retail parks (the European term for power centers) in the suburbs, altering the spatial structure of retailing. This retail decentralization has weakened the relative importance of the downtown and inner-city retail activities. In some metropolitan areas, immigration is the largest source of population growth. The increase in immigrants, who are increasingly ethnic minorities, has led to considerable growth of ethnic retailing in many North American cities (Wang & Hernandez, 2018). In metropolitan Toronto, there are now over 50 Chinese-theme shopping centers, with many more ethnic Chinese supermarkets (Wang et al., 2013).

Finally, national policies and regulations can cause changes in a country's retail structure, in both ownership and format. In 1985, Canada's Foreign Investment Review Agency, which was created in 1973 to scrutinize the entry of foreign firms, was abolished and was replaced by the new agency Investment Canada. One of Investment Canada's objectives is to encourage foreign investment. The North

America Free Trade Agreement, which was signed by the U.S., Canada, and Mexico in 1989, further facilitated investments from the United States. As a result, American retailers entered Canada in large numbers, leading to a continent integration of companies, mostly to the benefit of U.S.-headquartered companies, and to the Canadian consumers (Yeates, 2011). The role of national policy and regulations in retail structure change is more obvious in contemporary China than in any other country in the world, which will be illustrated later in this chapter.

DATA NEED

Retail structure analysis is conducted using databases that ideally should include the following fields:

- name of the retail store
- name of parent company
- street address or postcode (for small-scale geographic analysis)
- name of municipality and province (for large-scale geographical analysis)
- standard industrial classification (SCI) code
- store size (floor area, number of employees, etc.)
- store format
- open year
- close year
- vacancy
- store sales
- ownership (domestic vs. foreign; private vs. public)
- ethnicity

The names of store and parent company inform the researcher of the owner and operator of the business. Street address, postal code, and names of municipality/province provide necessary location information for analysis of spatial structure. SIC code is critical for analyzing business structure. In Canada, SIC is a four-digit code that identifies the type of retail activity. In 1997, the U.S. Federal Statistical Agency, in cooperation with the statistical agencies of Canada and Mexico, developed the *North American Industry Classification System (NAICS)*, with the goal of establishing a North American standard. NAICS is a six-digit code that identifies types of retail activity.

Store size and format are valuable information for examining scales of retail operations. Open year and close year, along with sales (if available) and vacancy rate are indicative, directly or indirectly, of the health of a retail market, in terms of business performance and survival rate. Finally, information on ownership is informative for understanding the economic sovereignty of a country, the level of penetration by foreign retailers, and state involvement in retail business. In metropolitan markets with a large concentration of immigrants and ethnic consumers, ethnic retailing has become an important component of the local retail economy.

A multi-year comprehensive database that includes all of the above fields rarely exists. Often, researchers need to compile their own database with information from different sources. In some jurisdictions, part of the information is published in their statistical yearbooks in aggregate form, but store-level data (such as sales, number of employees, and floor space) are seldom reported. In many cases, researchers need to collect relevant information at small-scale or micro-level geography through fieldwork or from corporate websites. Ryerson University's Centre for the Study of Commercial Activity (CSCA) has been collecting and updating such data for over 20 years. It currently maintains four databases: (1) a Toronto region database of major retail strips; (2) a national database of shopping centers and power centers; (3) a national database of major retail chains; and (4) a national database of food service chains.

Because of the vast variety of retail activity and the large number of SIC codes, aggregation is always necessary to reduce the number of categories in order to reveal meaningful patterns. The challenge for the analyst is to determine how to group them. It is unavoidable that researchers aggregate data differently to suit their own study need. Students are advised to work with 7–8 categories in practicing retail structure analysis. In the rest of this chapter, case studies and examples are presented to demonstrate how retail structure analysis is conducted and results interpreted.

MACRO-LEVEL ANALYSIS

Macro-level retail structure analysis is illustrated with two case studies: one for the Greater Toronto Area in Canada; the other for the City of Beijing and Shanghai in China.

Retail Structure of the Greater Toronto Area

The Greater Toronto Area (GTA) is the most populous metropolitan area in Canada. It consists of the City of Toronto (i.e., the central city or the urbanized core), along with 25 surrounding municipalities organized into four regional municipalities: Durham, Halton, Peel, and York (see Figure 4.1). The total area of the GTA is 7,124 km², with a population of six million (as in the 2016 census). It also has the largest retail economy in the country.

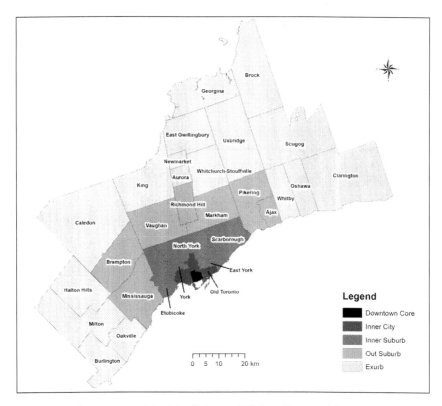

Figure 4.1 Component Municipalities and Urban Zones of the Greater Toronto Area.

Note

The Greater Toronto Area is similar to but slightly larger than the Toronto Census Metropolitan Area. The Downtown Core is bounded by Javis Street on the east, Davenport Road on the north, Spadina Avenue on the west, and Toronto harbor on the south. The Inner City is the area within the old city of Toronto but outside the Core. The Inner Suburb consists of the five former municipalities of York, East York, North York, Scarborough, and Etobicoke. The rest of the GTA forms the vast Outer Suburb and Exurbs.

A study by CSCA (Simmons et al., 1996) showed that *food retailing* was the largest subsector of GTA's retail economy in the mid-1990s, with 9,640 store locations, accounting for one-quarter of all retail outlets in this vast metropolitan region (Table 4.1). The same subsector provided 75,700 jobs (accounting for 33 percent of all retail jobs), and generated 8.78 billion dollars of retail sales (29 percent of total retail sales). Except *auto dealership, clothing* was the next largest retail subsector, with 6,470 stores (17 percent of the total), providing 20,800 jobs (9 percent of the total), and generating 2.41 billion dollars of retail sales (8 percent of the total). *Furniture* was also a thriving subsector due to high demand resulting from a booming housing market at the time. *General merchandise retailing* had fewer locations than clothing and furniture retailing, but this subsector provided more employment (35,000), attributed to many of the stores being department stores that were much larger than the specialty stores.

Table 4.2 shows the broad commercial structure of the GTA by format and geography in 1994. In addition to retailing, this table includes commercial and financial services. Format structure was analyzed with three distinct types of store clusters: retail strips, shopping centers, and new format stores (i.e., big box stores in power centers). Geographical distribution was examined with a four-zone framework: the downtown core, inner city, inner suburbs, and outer suburbs/ exurbs, as depicted in Figure 4.1.

Retail strips are unplanned clusters of businesses, and are pedestrian-scale shopping environments along main streets and public

Table 4.1 Retail Structure of the Greater Toronto Area by Subsector, 1994

Subsector*	Store**		Employment		Sales	
	No.	Share (%)	In 1,000s	Share (%)	In million $	Share (%)
Food	9,640	24.9	75.7	32.8	8,784	29.0
Clothing	6,470	16.7	20.8	9.0	2,413	8.0
Furniture	3,240	8.4	13.4	5.8	2,019	6.7
Auto	6,500	16.8	48.9	21.2	10,059	33.2
General	1,930	5.0	35.0	15.2	3,043	10.1
Miscellaneous	10,970	28.3	37.0	16.0	3,940	13.0
Total	38,750	100.0	230.8	100.0	30,258	100.0

Source: Simmons et al., 1996.

Notes
* by two-digit SIC codes.
** including only those stores that use paid employees, about one-half of all retail outlets in the Greater Toronto Area.

Table 4.2 Commercial Structure of the Greater Toronto Area by Format and Geography, 1994 (Including Commercial and Financial Services)

Zone	Format	Stores			Floor area		
		Number	Share of zone (%)	Share of GTA total (%)	1,000 m²	Share of zone (%)	Share of GTA total (%)
Downtown core	retail strips	2,900	33.0	3.4	520	36.3	2.0
	shopping centers	2,000	22.7	2.4	481	33.6	1.8
	new format	0	0.0	0.0	0	0.0	0.0
	residual*	3,900	44.3	4.6	430	30.0	1.6
	zone total	*8,800*	*100.0*	*10.5*	*1,431*	*100.0*	*5.4*
Inner city	retail strips	8,900	64.5	10.6	1,269	65.0	4.8
	shopping centers	600	4.3	0.7	247	12.7	0.9
	new format	5	0.0	0.0	47	2.4	0.2
	residual*	4,300	31.1	5.1	388	19.9	1.5
	zone total	*13,805*	*100.0*	*16.4*	*1,951*	*100.0*	*7.4*
Inner suburbs	retail strips	3,200	13.5	3.8	524	6.1	2.0
	shopping centers	7,000	29.6	8.3	2,344	27.3	8.9
	new format	17	0.1	0.0	127	1.5	0.5
	residual*	13,400	56.7	15.9	5,600	65.2	21.3
	zone total	*23,617*	*100.0*	*28.1*	*8,595*	*100.0*	*32.6*

Outer suburbs/exurbs	retail strips	4,100	10.8	4.9	1,030	7.2	3.9
	shopping centers	7,500	19.8	8.9	3,412	23.8	13.0
	new format	40	0.1	0.1	357	2.5	1.4
	residual*	26,200	69.2	31.2	9,566	66.6	36.3
	zone total	*37,840*	*100.0*	*45.0*	*14365*	*100.0*	*54.5*
GTA	retail strips	19,100	22.7	22.7	3,344	12.7	12.7
	shopping centers	17,200	20.5	20.5	6,484	24.6	24.6
	new format	71	0.1	0.1	531	2.0	2.0
	residual*	47,700	56.7	56.7	15,984	60.7	60.7
	grand total	*84,100*	*100.0*	*100.0*	*26,342*	*100.0*	*100.0*

Source: Simmons et al., 1996.

Note

* The residual category consists of non-new format retail establishments that are located outside shopping centers and retail strips, including all of the automotive sector.

transit corridors. CSCA collected data only for those retail strips that have a total retail area of 30,000 square feet or more in each of them. Businesses in retail strips typically provide convenience services to local consumers, though some also serve a market generated by the transport corridor. Most stores are owner operated, independent of retail chains. Retail strips are particularly evident within the downtown core and the inner city, where a grid street pattern prevails. In the mid-1990s, 33 percent of all stores in the downtown core, and 65 percent of all stores in the inner city were in retail strips. Retail strips also exist in the inner suburbs and outer suburbs, but in the CSCA study they accounted for less than 14 percent of all the stores there. In suburban areas, especially outer suburbs, residential areas are often subdivided in such a way that houses along arterial roads are reversed to face the inside of the neighborhood, instead of facing the street front, reducing the possibility of retail strip formation. There are two types of retail strips in the suburbs: one is the old main streets; the other is linear-shaped plazas, known as "ribbons". Strip share of the GTA commercial space increased slightly from 23 percent in 1994 to 24 percent in 2010 (Yeates, 2011).

Shopping centers were dominant forms of retail clusters in both the inner suburbs and the outer suburbs, accounting for 30 percent of all retail stores and 27 percent of all retail space in the inner suburbs, and 20 percent of all stores and 24 percent of all retail space in the outer suburbs (see Table 4.2). They also had a considerable share in the downtown core, with 23 percent of the zone's stores and 34 percent of the zone's retail space, mainly because of the presence of the large Eaton Centre (a superregional shopping center) and a number of ancillary malls in the podiums of office towers. The shopping center as a form of retail cluster was much less evident in the inner city, accounting for only 4 percent of the stores and 13 percent of retail space in the zone.

The 1970s was the golden age of mall development in the GTA (Doucet, 2001; Yeates, 2011). A number of superregional malls were built in this period. Within the City of Toronto (as it is today), they were built in the inner suburbs, with the exception of the Eaton Centre. In the outer suburbs and exurbs, they were built as "town centers". Most shopping centers that were built in the 1980s were in outer suburbs. The last superregional shopping center built in the GTA was Vaughan Mills Mall, which opened for business in 2004. Since then, no new large shopping center has been built in the entire region. The subsequent trend has been "mall transformation", with re-tenanting of anchors, adding of big boxes either within shopping centers or on their parking pads, and redevelopment of existing centers in the form of scaled-down lifestyle centers.

The big box format was introduced to the GTA in the early 1990s by American retailers. Development soon gained momentum and accelerated in the late 1990s. In 1994, there were only 71 big box stores in the entire region; they accounted for only 2 percent of the region's total retail space (see Table 4.2). It is no surprise that 69 percent of them were in the outer suburbs and exurbs, and another 24 percent in the inner suburbs, where land for development was more readily available. By 1998, the number of big box stores in the GTA had increased to 325; more than half of them were clustered in power centers, with 20 of the 27 existing power centers in outer suburbs (Yeates, 2000: 53).

The 1990s' studies of the GTA retail structure had at least two important implications for both retailers and commercial property developers. First, retail strips were surviving persistently at a time when big box retailing was radically altering market shares among the GTA retailers, mainly because businesses in retail strips provide goods and services at convenient locations to meet local demand, and are able to adapt to market changes quickly (e.g., no long-term lease, low sunk cost, and relocating easily). Today, they are still viable and affordable locations for small, independent retailers. Second, big box retailing in the GTA was under-developed in the 1990s, relative to its market size and compared with the U.S. metropolitan regions; so there was enormous development potential at the turn of the new millennium. Indeed, big box stores and associated power centers grew explosively and permeated all suburban municipalities in the GTA in the following decade, increasing from 325 in 1998 to 1,500 in 2010 (Yeates, 2011), most of them in outer suburbs.

Retail Structure of Beijing and Shanghai

For nearly 30 years before the economic reform began in 1978, retailing in China was a simple yet rigid distribution system, limited to the distribution of necessities to consumers. Within a planned economy and with a shortage of consumer goods, retailing was a passive activity, and any response by merchants to consumer preference was out of the question. No competition existed, in direct contrast to the competitive nature of a market economy. Private business ownership was banned; the entire retail system was either state-owned or collectively owned.

The department store was the predominant retail format, and retail chains were non-existent. As a result, Chinese cities had a very different retail structure from that of cities in Canada and the United States.

After 1978, the retail sector underwent an enormous transformation with profound changes. Store ownership diversified considerably; foreign retailers were allowed to enter the country; and almost all the new retail formats that were invented in the Western economies were introduced. These included supermarkets, shopping centers, factory outlets, warehouse retail stores, membership clubs, and retail chains. In essence, the sector has moved away completely from a state-planned, towards a market-oriented, retail economy. The retail structure is still different, but it has been converging towards that of the Western economies.

In the Western market economies, retail businesses are typically private-sector activities. Government is rarely involved in owning and operating of retail businesses. Retail structure analysis by ownership is therefore not important, except when examining the depth of market penetration by international retailers. In China, however, ownership structure is still relevant and important, even after 30 years of economic reform.

Table 4.3 shows the legally registered retail enterprises in Beijing and Shanghai by ownership. By the late 1990s, state-owned and collectively owned enterprises were still predominant in the retail sector in both Beijing and Shanghai—the country's two largest metropolitan markets. Together, they accounted for 64 percent of all retail

Table 4.3 Legally Registered Retail Enterprises in Beijing and Shanghai by Ownership

	Beijing (1998)		Shanghai (1999)	
	No.	%	No.	%
State-owned	2,589	22.1	9,480	20.3
Collective	4,882	41.7	13,955	29.9
Co-operatives	133	1.1	357	0.8
Joint-stock	1,818	15.5	593	1.3
Private	2,206	18.8	21,799	46.6
Hong Kong/Taiwan/Macao	32	0.3	160	0.3
Foreign	45	0.4	231	0.5
Others	7	0.1	175	0.4
Total	11,712	100.0	46,750	100.0

Source: Wang & Guo, 2007, with information from Beijing Statistics Bureau, 1999, and Shanghai Office of Commercial Activity Census, 2001.

establishments in Beijing and 50 percent in Shanghai. At the same time, other types of ownership had not only occurred, but expanded rapidly, especially joint-stock and privately owned enterprises. In Beijing, joint-stock ownership accounted for 16 percent of the total retail businesses, and the privately owned businesses accounted for 19 percent. In Shanghai, however, joint-stock ownership was much weaker, accounting for less than 2 percent of the total retail businesses; yet, privately owned retailers reached a whopping 47 percent. Overseas-invested retail establishments include both the foreign operations and those operated by the overseas Chinese from Hong Kong, Taiwan, and Macao, as dictated in state regulations. While they constituted less than 1 percent of the total retail enterprises in both cities, they were expanding steadily, considering that the first foreign-operated stores opened only in 1995. They were much larger in store size and, more importantly, had a much higher employment capacity than most domestic retailers (Wang & Zhang 2005). Table 4.4 shows that the state-owned and the collectively owned large retailers continued to decline in proportion between 2000 and 2003; so did co-operatives (see the columns of percentage change between 2000 and 2003). At the same time, joint-stock, limited liability, and private companies were all on the rise, especially in Shanghai. In fact, they already exceeded the state-owned and collectively owned by large margins.

After more than two decades of economic reform, both the state- and collectively owned stores had lost their absolute monopoly. Modern types of enterprises (including joint-stock, limited liability, private, and foreign-invested) all expanded significantly. They were promoted by both the state and the municipal governments of Beijing and Shanghai in their reformative policies as new means of raising retail capital and creating new consumption spaces (Wang & Guo, 2007).

Where data are available, comparative studies can be conducted across metropolitan markets in different countries. Such an analysis was documented in a study by Wang and Jones (2002). As Table 4.5 shows, Beijing, at the time of the study, had many more stores and a much larger retail workforce than any other city being compared. However, its total retail sales were the smallest with only US$10.5 billion. The total retail floor space in Beijing was estimated at 17,000,000 m²—68 percent of that in metropolitan Toronto—but it generated only half of the sales volume of Toronto's retail economy. Furthermore, the sales performance of the Beijing retailers seemed to be much lower than that in all other cities. In Beijing, sales per

Table 4.4 Large Retailers* in Beijing and Shanghai by Ownership, 2003

Type of ownership	Beijing			Shanghai		
	No. of stores	%	2000–2003 % change	No. of stores	%	2000–2003 % change
Domestic	1,120	97.1	-12.5	9,497	95.3	190.8
State-owned	256	22.2	-17.1	710	7.1	-34.9
Collectively owned	159	13.8	-16.1	140	1.4	-82.8
Co-operatives	20	1.7	-0.6	5	0.1	-54.5
Joint stock	48	4.2	0.6	2,893	29.0	7,132.5
Joint stock/Co-operatives	76	6.6	-0.7	25	0.3	-83.3
Limited liability	280	24.3	10.4	4,701	47.2	309.5
Private	280	24.3	10.9	1,008	10.1	7,100.0
Others	1	0.1	0.1	15	0.2	
HK-MC-TW	16	1.4	0.1	161	1.6	101.3
Foreign	18	1.6	-0.1	304	3.1	-18.7
Total	1,154	100.0	-12.5	9,962	100.0	167.8

Source: Wang & Guo, 2007, with data compiled from China Chamber of Commerce, 2004.

Notes

* Large retailers are defined as those that have annual retail sales of at least RMB5 million ($625,999) and 60 or more employees.

HK-MC-TW = Hong Kong/Macao/Taiwan

Table 4.5 Comparing the Retail Structure of Nine Metropolises by Stores, Employees, Floor Space, and Sales, 1990s

Metropolises	Stores (1000s)	Retail employees (1000s)	Floor area (million m²)	Sales (US$ billion)	Sales/employee (US$1000)	Sales/m² (US$)	% Chain stores	% Chain store sales
Beijing	468.1	1,026	17.2	10.5	10	610	2	15
Toronto	38.8	207	10.2	21.7	105	2,130	12	42
Barcelona	81.2	187	7.9	19.3	103	2,640	10	27
Dallas-Fort Worth	46.0	267	7.6	34.1	128	2,780	30	54
Hong Kong	55.5	214	4.1	24.0	112	5,800	6	62
Melbourne	30.9	172	5.5	11.8	103	3,240	1	38
Mexico City	175.5	425	–	11.4	27	–	<1	29
Munich	12.0	85	3.3	13.6	160	4,153	2	57
Nagoya	100.6	446	8.6	76.7	172	9,000	7	42

Sources: (1) Data (except retail chains) for Beijing are 1998 figures from Beijing Statistics Bureau, 1999, and include individually owned businesses and retail stalls in the urban markets. Data for Beijing's retail chains are from Wu, 1998. Data for all other cities are 1990 figures from Simmons et al., 1998.

employee and per square meter of retail space were US$10,000 and US$610 respectively: the former was only one tenth or less of those in all other cities except Mexico City, and the latter was only 7 to 28 percent of those in the other cities. As well as that, the role of retail chains in Beijing was still insignificant: their sales accounted for merely 15 percent of the city's total. In 2000, the largest chain in Beijing was a supermarket with 45 locations (China Association of Commercial Chains, 2000). This clearly indicates that the retail sector of Beijing as a whole was much less efficient and less competitive than the comparative cities, subjecting it to tough competition from the resourceful multinational retailers.

The retail structure of Beijing and Shanghai at the turn of the new millennium presented many opportunities to international retailers. Shanghai seemed to be more open than Beijing was to new types of retailing including overseas-invested businesses. Although state-owned and collectively owned retail enterprises were still dominating the retail sector in both cities, they were fragmented and were operating in dated formats with low productivity. The particular structure suggested that the time was ripe for international retailers to expand in China with innovative formats and large-scale operations; and they would benefit from the weak competition in the local retail environment. All of these indeed happened in China in the first decade of the new millennium (Wang, 2014).

MICRO-LEVEL ANALYSIS

Micro-level retail structure analysis is illustrated in a case study of two shopping centers in the City of Toronto: Dufferin Mall and Bayview Village Shopping Centre. The former is located in the inner city of Toronto in a high-density area, with 128 stores spanning 52,700 m^2 of floor space. The latter is located in the inner suburb with 113 stores occupying 41,000 m^2 of floor space (See Figure 4.2). Unlike Dufferin Mall, which caters to customers who seek for affordable goods and services, Bayview Village is an upscale mall that caters to affluent consumers and offers a unique and luxurious shopping experience.

Their retail structure is analyzed and compared with an eight-category classification scheme, consisting of *department store, grocer, eatery/restaurant, electronics/communication, fashion/accessories, health/beauty, service,* and *others* (see Table 4.6). The category of *others* consists of stores for which the numbers are too small to form a separate category. Analysis reveals that the two shopping centers have a vastly different store mix not only in proportion of stores by category, but, more importantly, in the quality of stores.

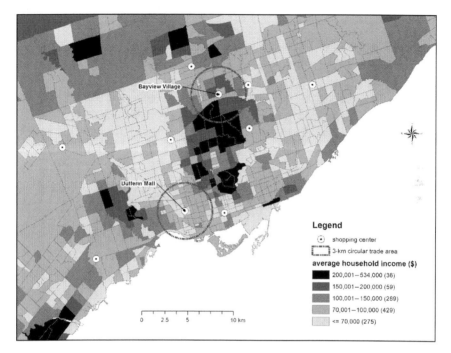

Figure 4.2 Locations of Dufferin Mall and Bayview Village Shopping Centre.

Note
Background shows average household income.

Table 4.6 Store Categories and Percentages in Dufferin Mall and Bayview Village, 2019

Retail category	Dufferin		Bayview	
	# Stores	%	# Stores	%
Department store	3	2.3	0	0.0
Grocer	1	0.8	2	1.8
Eatery/restaurant	27	21.1	16	14.4
Electronics/communication	18	14.1	3	2.7
Fashion/accessories	35	27.3	43	38.7
Health/beauty	20	15.6	15	13.5
Service	12	9.4	21	18.9
Others	12	9.4	11	9.9
Total	128	100.0	111	100.0

Dufferin Mall is anchored by a Walmart department store, a Winners department store, a Marshalls department store, a No Frills supermarket, and a Dollarama store—all discounters selling off-price goods. Bayview Village has no department store at all, but has two high-end supermarkets: a Loblaws and a Pusateri's Fine Food. The former is a premium supermarket, owned by the same company that owns No Frills supermarket. The latter is a family-owned and operated grocery chain specializing in high-quality foods, at prices even higher than in the Loblaws supermarket.

Dufferin Mall has more *eateries* than does Bayview Village: 27 vs. 16. However, most eateries in Dufferin Mall are fast food stalls clustered in a food court. These include KFC, A&W, Thai Express, Pizza Pizza, Manchu Wok, New York Fries, and Subway. The only sit-in restaurant is a Swiss Chalet. In contrast, Bayview Village offers many secluded sit-in restaurants with their own storefront, such as Oliver-Bonacini, Tablule, GOA Kitchen, Elxr Juice Lab, Il Fornello, Aroma, and Pearl. They are more expensive, referred to in the food service industry as "gourmet".

In Dufferin Mall, *electronics and communication* makes up 14 percent of all stores, with 18 outlets in total. In stark contrast, Bayview Village has only three. Yet, the majority of the 18 outlets in Dufferin Mall are quick service kiosks and the subsidiaries of the major brands selling scaled-down mobile phone plans. Those in Bayview Village are all full-service outlets operated by Canada's three largest telecommunication service providers: Bell, Rogers, and Telus; there is no presence of kiosks and discount service providers in Bayview Village.

The highest proportion of retail space in both malls is dedicated to *fashion and accessories*: 27 percent in Dufferin Mall vs. 39 percent in Bayview Village. Again, most fashion stores in Dufferin Mall sell popular, affordable, and dependable apparel and accessories, such as H&M, Forever21, Footlocker, American Eagle, and Garage, though the mall has begun to introduce more expensive stores in recent years, such as Tommy Hilfiger, La Senza, and La Vie en Rose. The fashion options in Bayview Village emphasize high-quality products and reflect the mall's "prestigious, upscale, and unique" image. In a more telling note, none of the fashion stores in Bayview Village is actually present in Dufferin Mall. The high-end fashion boutiques in Bayview Village include Brooks Brothers, Judith&Charles, GEOX, TONI Plus, jacadi Paris, Riani, Talbots, and Stuart Weitzman. Many of them are independent boutiques, featuring high-end fashion designers, which are not available in other malls.

Although Bayview Village has a smaller number of *health and beauty* shops than Dufferin Mall (15 vs. 20), they are all upscale spas, hair and nail salons, and cosmetics stores. While the variety of health and beauty stores in Dufferin Mall is similar, they are not the same quality as those in Bayview Village.

The *service* category includes, but is not limited to, banks, medical clinics, legal offices, and travel agents. Bayview Village has more of them than does Dufferin Mall—21 vs. 12—suggesting that it serves a higher-income clientele in its trade area. One notable difference is that Dufferin Mall has a Catholic Children's Aid Society, which indicates the socioeconomic status of some residents in its trade area.

In sum, Dufferin Mall has a mix of affordable retail stores, responsive to the basic needs of low-to-medium income households, whereas Bayview Village is composed of upscale stores, restaurants, and service outlets that are responsive to the wants of high-income consumers. Since its gentrification and redevelopment in 1998, Bayview Village has frequently overhauled the property to keep up with current trends and stay competitive.

The analysis of the two shopping centers' retail structure would be incomplete without also analyzing and comparing the demographics in their respective trade areas. After all, the choice of a store mix for a shopping center is not a random act on the part of the retail planners; it is a purposeful design to meet the needs of the consumers in its prescribed trade area. For Dufferin Mall and Bayview Village Shopping Centre, this will be presented in Chapter 8 (*Trade Area Delineation and Analysis*) to justify their respective retail structures.

KEY POINTS OF THE CHAPTER

- Retail structure analysis often goes hand in hand with demographic analysis and analysis of the geography of demand. It helps business owners to gauge the level of market saturation, the strengths and weaknesses of the competitors, and the market space or gaps left for them (especially new entrants) to fill. It also helps shopping center management to assess if the current store mix suits the local demographics. Equally important, municipal planners conduct retail structure analysis to determine if there is an over-supply of certain types of stores, which therefore should be controlled, and if there is an under-supply of other types of businesses, which should be encouraged and promoted, through denying or issuing of new business licenses and building permits.

- A good retail structure is one that has a balanced mix of stores that suit the needs of the local consumers; various stores complement each other with minimal internal competition, while facilitating a healthy level of comparative shopping. A poor retail structure is one that has too many stores of the same type, with excessive internal competition or over-supply of retail space.
- Retail structure can be disaggregated in many different ways, such as business structure, format structure, geographical structure, and ownership structure.
- Retail structure in a market is by no means static; it changes over time. A number of factors, often working in combination, drive structural changes. These include business consolidation in the retail industry, retail innovation, suburbanization of population, and national policies and regulations.

REFERENCES

Beijing Statistics Bureau. (1999). *Census of Commercial Activity in Beijing* (Beijing Shi Shehui Shangye Pucha Ziliao Huibian). Beijing: China Commerce Publishing House.

China Association of Commercial Chains. (2000). A list of retail chains with sales over 50 million yuan in 1999. *Commerce Economy and Management, 4* (back cover).

China Chamber of Commerce. (2004). *Almanac of China's Commerce.* Beijing: China Almanac Publishing House.

Doucet, M. (2001). *The Department Store Shuffle: Rationalization and Change to the Greater Toronto Area.* (Research Report 2001–05). Toronto, Canada: Center for the Study of Commercial Activity, Ryerson University.

Gardner, C. and Sheppard, J. (1989). *Consuming Passion: the Rise of Retail Culture.* London, England: Unwin Hyman.

Shanghai Office of Commercial Activity Census. (2001). *The 1999 Census of Commercial Activities in Shanghai, Summary Statistics.* (1999 Shanghai Shi Shangye Fuwuye Pucha Ziliao Huibian). Shanghai: Shanghai Shi Shangye Fuwuye Pucha Bangongshi.

Simmons, J., Biasiotto, M., Montgomery, D., Robinson, M., & Simmons, S. (1996). *Commercial Structure of the Greater Toronto Area.* Toronto, Canada: Center for the Study of Commercial Activity, Ryerson Polytechnic University.

Simmons, J., Jones, K., Kamikihara, S., & Yeates, M. (1998). International comparisons of commercial structure and public policy implications. *Progress in Planning, 50*(4), 291–313.

Wang, S. (2014). *China's New Retail Economy: a Geographical Perspective.* New York, NY: Routledge.

Wang, S. & Guo, C. (2007). A tale of two cities: restructuring of retail capital and production of new consumption space in Beijing and Shanghai (Chapter 13). In Fulong Wu (Ed.), *China's Emerging Cities: The Making of New Urbanism* (pp. 256–282). New York, NY: Routledge.

Wang, S. & Hernandez, T. (2018). Contemporary ethnic retailing: an expanded framework of study. *Canadian Ethnic Studies, 50*(1), 37–68.

Wang, S., Hii, R., Zhong, J., & Du, P. (2013). Recent trends of ethnic Chinese retailing in Metropolitan Toronto. *International Journal of Applied Geospatial Research, 4*(1), 49–66.

Wang, S. & Jones, K. (2002). Retail structure of Beijing. *Environment and Planning A, 34*(10), 1785–1808.

Wang, S. & Zhang, Y. (2005). The new retail economy of Shanghai. *Growth and Change, 36*(1), 41–73.

Wrigley, N. & Lowe, M. (2002). *Reading Retail: A Geographic Perspective on Retailing and Consumption Spaces.* London, England: Arnold.

Wu, X. (1998). Beijing shangye liansuo fazhan zhanluo yanjiu. *Shangchang Xiandaihua, 12,* 17–19. [Strategics for retail chain development in Beijing. *Commerce Modernization, 12,* 17-19].

Yeates, M. (2000). *The GTA@Y2K: The Dynamics of Change in the Commercial Structure of the Greater Toronto Area.* (Research Report 2000–01). Toronto, Canada: Center for the Study of Commercial Activity, Ryerson University.

Yeates, M. (2011). *Charting the GTA: The Dynamics of Change in the Commercial Structure of the Greater Toronto Area.* (Research Report 2011–06). Toronto, Canada: Center for the Study of Commercial Activity, Ryerson University.

5 The External Retail Environment

Role of Regulations and Community Attitude

This chapter discusses the external retail environment, which includes both government regulations and local attitudes toward certain retailers and formats, as illustrated in Box 4 of Figure 1.1. Regulation is a significant force "shaping competition between firms, the governance of investment, the use of labor, and the overall extraction of profit from retailing of goods" (Lowe & Wrigley, 1996: 13). Further, the regulatory environment varies greatly, or is in various stages of development, from country to country, and also within a country among provinces and municipalities. Even in the capitalist free-market economies, where both retail corporations and individual entrepreneurs enjoy a high degree of freedom in business decision making, governments do intervene in the retail industry with regulatory measures, often in the form of public policies, such as foreign investment policies, business tax law, anti-competition law, and land use zoning bylaw (Dawson, 1980). In turn, these policies, which are supposed to reflect a society's values, impose limits on retailers' freedom to deal with competitors and conduct business with suppliers and consumers, thus affecting capital flows, retail operations, and the overall market structure, as explained in Chapter 4. Because the local regulatory and tax environment can have enormous influence on retail development through land use zoning, development density, level of commercial property taxation, and development charges, developers often play one jurisdiction against another to gain special concessions. In this chapter, the four types of public intervention, which are often imposed by different levels of government and implemented at different spatial scales, are expounded with examples.

FOREIGN INVESTMENT POLICIES

For retailers contemplating entering a foreign market, the first thing to examine is perhaps the host country's foreign investment policy. Most countries have policies regulating foreign investment, especially foreign direct investment (FDI), either for national security in general or for economy security in particular to protect their domestic retailers. Usually, the economic superpowers have less restrictive policies than do other countries, because they are much less susceptible to foreign control as a result of receiving FDI. It is usually the smaller economies or the emerging markets that have strict FDI policies.

The United States is the largest FDI receiving country. It receives most foreign investment from its traditional allies, including Canada, Germany, France, Israel, and the United Kingdom. In recent years, countries such as China have also sought to invest in the U.S. Still the world's economic superpower, the United States has virtually no law that prohibits, or subjects to review, foreign investment based on national origin. It does, however, impose some sector-specific limitations and review procedures on foreign investment in a handful of regulated industries, including the airline, telecommunication, and nuclear energy industries (Cooley & Laciak, 2018). Retailing is not one of the regulated sectors. After all, many of the largest sector-specific retailers in the world are U.S. based, and most retail innovations are made in the U.S.; few non-U.S. retailers are able to compete with them anyway. Former President Barack Obama, while addressing the 2015 SelectUSA Investment Summit encouraging foreign investment in the United States, proclaimed that "America is proudly open for business, and we want to make it as simple and attractive for you to set up shops here as is possible" (Cooley & Laciak, 2018). Recently, the Trump administration has been critical of certain foreign investments, particularly those from China, and has threatened to impose greater restrictions on them.

Being very much susceptible to American dominance and control over its economy, Canada has long had protective FDI review policies. Its first Foreign Investment Review Act, which was the culmination of a series of government reports and debates to protect Canadian interests in the age of multinational corporations, was passed by the Canadian Parliament in 1973. The Act resulted in the establishment of the Foreign Investment Review Agency (FIRA) to ensure that the foreign acquisition and establishment of businesses in Canada was beneficial to the country. As outlined in Section 2(2) of the Act, takeovers by foreign investors were assessed based on their contribution to job creation, Canadian participation in management, competition with existing industries, new technology transfer, and compatibility with federal and provincial economic policies.

In 1985, the Foreign Investment Review Act was rescinded and replaced by the Investment Canada Act (ICA). Accordingly, FIRA was renamed Investment Canada, with its mandate drastically reduced. While the Foreign Investment Review Act was emblematic of Canada's protectionist stance towards FDI in the 1970s and early the 1980s, its replacement by the ICA made Canada a friendlier environment for foreign investment (Koch & Olscher, 2018). The purpose of ICA is to provide for the review of significant FDI in Canada in a manner that encourages investment, economic growth, and employment opportunities in Canada, and to provide for the review of FDI in Canada that could be injurious to national security.

Since 1994, Canada, the United States and Mexico have operated as one of the world's largest free trade zones under the North American Free Trade Agreement (NAFTA). The trade and investment rules set in this agreement eliminated both tariff and non-tariff barriers, and opened the Canadian market further to the U.S. retailers.

China did not allow foreign retail operations until 1992, either as sole foreign ownership or in joint ventures. Since then, China has made a series of policy changes to open up its consumer market to international retailers (Wang, 2014). In July 1992, China designated six cities and five Special Economic Zones (SEZ), all located in the eastern coastal region, to open to overseas retail investment for experiment. Overseas retailers were distinguished into two categories: retailers from foreign countries, and those known as overseas Chinese-invested enterprises based in Hong Kong, Taiwan, and Macau. To control the experiment process effectively, the Chinese government cautiously imposed a series of restrictions on the entry and operation of foreign retailers, ranging from geographical limitations to restrictions on capital participation, business format, and sourcing. For example, only the designated cities and SEZs were allowed to participate in the experiment, and each of them was permitted to host only one or two overseas retailers. The entry of foreign retailers had to be approved by the state government; local governments were prohibited from admitting foreign retailers independently. Approved foreign retailers had to operate in joint ventures with at least one Chinese partner; whole foreign ownership was prohibited. In joint ventures, foreign investors' stakes had to be less than 50 percent. With regard to format, joint ventures were strictly limited to single-store operations; retail chains and wholesaling were prohibited. While foreign retailers were allowed to import certain types of merchandise for retailing, total import could not exceed 30 percent of their total sales, meaning that at least 70 percent of the merchandise had to be purchased from domestic manufacturers and suppliers.

In October 1995, the state government took the second step to open its retail sector, but only slightly wider. This time, it authorized Beijing to experiment with expanding joint ventures from single-store operations to retail chains. It also allowed the expansion of foreign participation from retailing to wholesaling, and from general merchandise to food products. As a precautionary measure, the state government still insisted that partnership with Chinese retailers was mandatory, and that the Chinese partners must have a controlling ownership. In addition, the length of the business contract was limited to 30 years or less.

To speed up its negotiations with the World Trade Organization (WTO), the state government in June 1999 made its third major move with further and more significant deregulations. The experiment was expanded geographically to include all provincial capitals and those municipalities that were designated to be independent of their province in economic planning. Sole foreign ownership was still prohibited, but majority foreign ownership was allowed in retail chains that would purchase large quantities of domestically made products and export these products through their own distribution channels, as a relaxation of restrictions on foreign ownership. While all joint ventures were allowed to engage in wholesaling as well as retailing, more stringent criteria were set forth for the selection of foreign retailers and Chinese partners. In correspondence with the country's newly devised national strategy of "Developing the West", preferential treatment was offered to those joint ventures that were willing to set up business operations in Western China. Evidently, the new policies aimed at raising the entry bar and selecting only large international retailers as future entrants. These policies were expected to bring to China its much needed capital, information technology, merchandising techniques, and managerial know-how. At the same time, the new policies were meant to ensure that only the large domestic retailers that had adequate resources and experience would become partners. This would also raise the level of participation by the Chinese retailers in business decision making, so that their role in joint ventures would not be reduced to a liaison or messenger between the foreign retailer and the government.

After 15 years of prolonged negotiation and numerous concessions, China was finally admitted to the WTO in December 2001, and was given a three-year "grace period" to gradually remove all the remaining trade barriers to FDI. In April 2004, as the three-year "grace period" was about to end, the state government announced further policy changes with regard to the participation of FDI in commercial sectors including retailing, marking the end of the 12-year-long experiment. The new policies lifted virtually all remaining restrictions and promised a fully open retail market to international retailers for fair competition. The key points of the new policies are highlighted as the following:

- With the exception of solely foreign-owned enterprise and the foreign-controlled large joint ventures, provincial governments are delegated the autonomy to approve future entrants and opening of new retail outlets in their respective jurisdictions.
- The life span of business contracts for foreign-invested enterprises is limited to 30 years (or 40 years if the business operation is set up in Western China).
- Business plans of foreign-invested enterprises must conform to the local municipal plan and to the commercial activity development plan of the host city. Land for building new business premises must be obtained through public bidding on the land market in a transparent process.
- Foreign-invested enterprises must agree to accept annual inspections with audited financial reports. Those that fail to pass the inspections will not be allowed to open new stores, or may be ordered to close their existing operations.

For the first time, regulatory powers became decentralized and shared with provincial and municipal governments. A vertically integrated and power-sharing regulatory system was in the making. These policies were particularly welcomed by the big international chains, whose operations expanded rapidly through both organic growth (with opening of new stores) and acquisition of existing retailers, posing new challenges to the emerging Chinese regulatory system. With the removal of unconventional barriers, China began to shift to regulating foreign retailers by legal means commonly acceptable to the WTO members, as alluded to in the aforementioned 2004 policies.

India, the world's second largest emerging market, also launched an economic reform, but much later than China did. Until 2010, India's retailing industry was essentially owner-operated small shops; larger format convenience stores and supermarkets accounted for only 4 percent of the industry, and they were present only in large urban centers. Before 2011, the central government of India denied FDI in multi-brand retail, forbidding foreign groups from any ownership in supermarkets, convenience stores, or any retail outlets. Even single-brand retail was limited to 51 percent ownership. Tesco, which had long voiced an interest in India's under-developed retail market, was limited to a joint venture with Tata, one of India's largest multinational corporations, to develop supermarket logistics and warehousing, but not retail stores.

In January 2012, India approved reform for single-brand stores, welcoming international retailers to help innovate India's retail industry with 100 percent ownership, but imposed the requirement that the single-brand retailer source 30 percent of its goods from India. On September 14, 2012, the government of India moved one step further and passed a law to allow multi-brand foreign retailers to take majority stakes in joint ventures (Nelson, 2012). Its cabinet ministers, who made the decision, hoped that foreign retailers would bring not only capital but also expertise in logistics and cold-chain warehousing to modernize its out-of-date retail sector and cut prices. This paved the way for international supermarket chains such as Tesco, Carrefour, and Walmart to set up retail stores in India to help modernize the country's retail industry, but left the approval decisions to individual state governments.

CORPORATE TAX

A retailor planning to enter a new market also wants to know local tax laws and rates. Two types of tax affect the profitability of a retailer: corporate tax and sales tax.

Corporate tax, also called company tax, is a direct tax imposed by a jurisdiction on the income or capital of a corporation. Many countries impose such taxes at the national level, but a similar tax may also be imposed at state, province, or municipal levels. A country's corporate tax may apply to:

- corporations incorporated in that country,
- corporations doing business in that country on income from that country,

- foreign corporations that have a permanent establishment in the country, or
- corporations deemed to be resident for tax purposes in the country.

Countries may tax a corporation on its net profit, and may also tax shareholders when the corporation pays a dividend to them. Where dividends are taxed, a corporation may be required to withhold tax before the dividend is distributed.

Corporate tax rates vary widely by country. For example, corporate tax rates across the Organization for Economic Co-operation and Development (OECD) vary from a low of 12.5 percent in Iceland to a high of 34 percent in France. Some countries have sub-country level jurisdictions (such as provinces and cities) that also impose corporate income tax. In Canada, the provincial corporate tax rates range from 11.5 to 16 percent, in addition to the federal tax rate of 15 percent, resulting in a combined tax rate of 26.5–31 percent (Government of Canada, 2019). Similarly, although the central government tax rate in Switzerland is 8.5 percent, the combined rate including local tax is 21.2 percent (Wikipedia, 2019).

Some countries also impose branch profits tax, which applies to foreign corporations that carry on business in these countries through a "branch" (Osler, 2019). For example, a 25 percent branch profits tax is imposed on the after-tax income that non-resident corporations earn in Canada, if such earnings are not reinvested in the Canadian business (Atlas, 2016). The 25 percent rate may be reduced under a tax treaty between Canada and the country of residence of the foreign corporation. Under the Canada–U.S. tax treaty, the rate of branch profits tax is reduced to 5 percent.

A sales tax is a consumption tax imposed by the government on the sale of goods and services and paid by consumers. A conventional sales tax is levied at the point of sale (POS), collected by the retailer, and passed on to the government. Again, different jurisdictions charge sales taxes at different rates and in different forms, which often overlap when states, counties, and municipalities each levy their own sales taxes.

In Canada, the federal government levies a 5 percent goods and services tax (GST) and the Province of Ontario levies a 7 percent provincial sales tax (PST), resulting in a harmonized sales tax (HST) of 13 percent. (Essential items such as food, medicine, and baby clothes are exempted from HST.) The only province that does not levy a PST is

Alberta, where consumers pay only the 5 percent GST. Municipalities do not have the legislative power to levy sales tax.

In the United States, it is not the federal government that charges sales taxes. Sale taxes are charged by the states and municipalities. In New York City, for example, consumers pay an 8.875 percent sales tax—a combination of the New York State tax (4 percent), the New York City tax (4.5 percent), and a special tax (0.375 percent).

In India, sales tax is levied at multiple rates ranging from 0 to 28 percent, with lower rates for essential items and the highest rates for luxury and de-merits goods. Sales tax rate in India averaged 14 percent from 2006 until 2016. Since then, it has increased to 18 percent (Trading Economics, 2019b). In China, a 13 percent sales tax (2019 rate) is included in the price of goods and services in the form of Value Added Tax (Trading Economics, 2019a). This tax is hidden, not shown in the receipt issued by retailers.

REGULATIONS ON COMPETITION AND ANTITRUST LAWS

Most countries have laws regulating competition for the purpose of maintaining fair and sustainable competition. These regulations may affect the entry of a retailer into a new market, either domestic or foreign, through the path of merger and acquisition.

In the U.S., most states have antitrust laws; so does the federal government. Under the Hart–Scott–Rodino Act (the antitrust law), the Federal Trade Commission (FTC) and the Department of Justice review most of the proposed merger/acquisition transactions that are over a certain size and affect commerce in the United States. Either agency can take legal action to block deals that it believes would "substantially lessen competition". For the most part, current law requires companies to report to the FTC and the Department of Justice any deal that is valued at more than $90 million, so they can be reviewed. After the companies report a proposed deal, the agencies will do a preliminary review to determine whether it raises any antitrust concerns that warrant closer examination. The majority of deals reviewed by the FTC and the Department of Justice are allowed to proceed after the preliminary review. However, if a second request is issued, the companies must provide more information (Federal Trade Commission, 2019).

In Canada, merger control is governed by the federal Competition Act, which includes both notification provisions and substantive merger review provisions (Kilby & Kwinter, 2018). The Competition Act is administered and enforced by the Commissioner of Competition with the support of the Competition Bureau—an independent law enforcement agency. While the Commissioner and the Bureau investigate and evaluate mergers, only the Competition Tribunal—a specialized, quasi-judicial body—can issue a formal remedial order with respect to a merger. Proposed merger transactions that exceed each of the following thresholds generally trigger a pre-merger notification requirement:

- The target business either has assets in Canada of which the book value exceeds CAD92 million, or has annual gross revenues from sales in or from Canada, generated from assets in Canada, that exceed CAD92 million.
- The purchaser and target, together with their respective upstream and downstream affiliates collectively, either have assets in Canada of which the combined book value exceeds CAD400 million or have combined annual gross revenues from sales in, from, or into Canada that exceed CAD400 million.

While only mergers that surpass the thresholds are subject to notification, any merger can be challenged by the Commissioner of Competition and may be subject to the substantive review provisions. During its review of a transaction, the Bureau of Competition will contact market participants, such as consumer groups, labor unions, suppliers of the merging parties, and competitors, to solicit their views on the transaction. Third parties can also proactively contact the Bureau to provide their views on a transaction and raise questions about the merger implications. While third parties do not have the right to challenge a proposed merger, complaints to the Bureau may influence the review and result in closer scrutiny by the Bureau. The proposal is then subject to a substantive test to find out whether the merger/acquisition transaction is likely to substantially prevent or lessen competition in a relevant market. On the other hand, arguments for efficiency gains and customer benefits resulting from the merger or acquisition may be used to counter competition issues.

Similar regulations exist in the UK, which stipulate that clearance from the authorities may be required if a business merger is large enough to impact on competition. Specifically, merger control applies if the total sales of the target in the UK are over £70 million; or if both the acquirer and the target buy (or sell) goods (or services) of a similar kind, and after merger, they would buy (or sell) 25 percent or more of those goods (or services) in the UK or a substantial part of it (Critchley, 2012). Larger mergers, in which involved parties have total sales more than €250 million, or do business in three or more EU member states, may even have a "European dimension", making them subject to EU regulations.

Before 2014, there were two principal competition regulators in the UK—the Office of Fair Trade (OFT) and the Competition Commission. Accordingly, the merger control procedure was divided into two phases: Phase 1 before the OFT, and Phase 2 before the Competition Commission. In 2014, the two regulators were merged into a new single body—the Competition and Markets Authority (the "CMA"), but the two phases of review have been maintained and are handled by different divisions of the new body. In Phase 1, when CMA is notified of a merger, it must decide whether its jurisdiction is triggered under the £70 million or 25 percent test and, if so, whether it thinks the merger may result in a substantial lessening of competition in the affected market. If it thinks so, the review enters Phase 2 for detailed analysis, which starts with fact-finding, including meeting the parties and inquisitorial hearings to stress-test the views of the parties and any third parties who feel they could be affected by the proposed merger. CMA will then decide whether to block the merger, allow it, or allow it but subject to "remedies", such as imposing price caps or obligations to refrain from conduct that may hinder competitors entering the market, compulsory licensing of intellectual property rights (IP) to competitors, and removing non-compete clauses in contracts (Critchley, 2012).

Anti-competition regulations were introduced to China much later than in the Western countries. After China's admission to the WTO, the battle among foreign retailers for a bigger share of the Chinese market had heated up. A number of them were moving toward "independence" (i.e., dropping their Chinese partners) in an effort to consolidate their resources and their decision-making power. To prevent foreign monopoly, the Ministry of Commerce issued *Regulations on Foreign Merger and Acquisition of Enterprises in China* in 2006. While not retail specific, these regulations apply equally to retailing. According to the regulations, the foreign retailer (or investor), if planning to acquire, or merge with, a domestic Chinese enterprise, must in any of the following circumstances apply to both the Ministry of Commerce and the National Bureau of Industry and Commerce Administration for approval (Ministry of Commerce, 2006):

- the foreign retailer's gross sales exceed RMB1.5 billion *yuan* in the year of application;
- the foreign retailer has already merged more than ten domestic retailers (large and small) within one year;
- the foreign retailer's market share in China has reached or exceeded 20 percent;
- the foreign retailer's market share in China will reach or exceed 25 percent after the proposed merger or acquisition.

Similar regulations were announced for acquisition and mergers among foreign retailers themselves that have business operations in China. Specifically, the regulations stipulate that foreign investors (including retailers) must also apply to the Ministry of Commerce and the National Bureau of Industry and Commerce Administration for approval if:

- the acquirer owns capital assets of RMB3 billion *yuan* or more in China;
- the acquirer's gross sales in China exceed RMB1.5 billion *yuan* in the year of application;
- the acquirer's market share in China has already reached or exceeded 20 percent;
- after acquisition or merger, the foreign retailer's market share in China will be 25 percent or higher;
- after acquisition or merger, the foreign retailer and the business entity of which the acquirer is a shareholder will have more than 15 enterprises.

The Ministry of Commerce and the National Bureau of Industry and Commerce Administration will then hold, within 90 days of receiving the application, a public hearing meeting, to be attended by relevant government agencies, affected enterprises, and other interest groups. Depending on the consultation results, the state government can either approve or reject the merger or acquisition application.

To emphasize, it is important to investigate the various regulations when planning for a market entry through the path of merger and acquisition. In most cases, anti-competition regulations do not necessarily prevent store development proposals from being approved. However, regulators may impose remedies on retailers. There are two types of remedies: structural and behavioral (Campbell & Halladay, 2002; Ezrachi, 2005). A typical structural remedy is divestiture of assets and divisions after merger/acquisition. Behavioral remedies are broader in range, including general commitments to behave, or not to behave, in a certain manner. For example, when Canada's two largest bookstore chains—Chapters and Indigo— applied for merger, the Competition Bureau of Canada imposed, in addition to structural remedies, a detailed five-year code of conduct upon Chapters/Indigo as behavioral remedies. The code set out constraints on terms of trade with publishers as well as additional behavioral restraints upon Chapters and Indigo in the downstream sector. The code protected publishers by limiting Chapters/Indigo's ability to demand discounts from them, setting minimum payment deadlines, and governing the timing and volume of Chapters/Indigo's book returns to publishers. In the downstream business, Chapters/ Indigo was prohibited from acquiring/opening any new stores for two years or enforcing restrictive covenants against the opening of other bookstores in any of its shopping center leases. It was also required to seek Bureau approval before re-entering the wholesale book business (Campbell & Halladay, 2002).

Most authorities favor structural over behavioral remedies. Behavioral remedies are usually directed or imposed when the absence of a suitable buyer makes divestiture impossible, or a structural remedy may generate costs, risks, or inefficiencies, which would render it inappropriate (Ezrachi, 2005). If a proposal is denied, the applicant has the right to appeal.

ZONING BYLAW

Most municipalities have an official plan that sets out the city's general policies for future land use. Many municipalities also have a comprehensive zoning bylaw that divides the municipality into different land use zones, with detailed maps. The bylaw specifies the permitted uses (e.g., commercial, residential, industrial, institutional, and transportation) and the required standards (e.g., building size and location) in each zone, which are legally enforceable (Province of Ontario, 2019). Construction or new development that does not comply with the zoning bylaw is not allowed, and the municipality will refuse to issue a building permit. Zoning bylaws are needed as a legal means to implement the objectives and policies of a municipality's official plan, manage land use and future development, and protect citizens and stakeholders from conflicting land uses.

In general, retail stores can only be developed on land zoned for commercial use. However, zoning bylaws are not carved in stone, and a parcel of land can be rezoned if an application for amendment is submitted by a retailer or commercial property developer, and is approved by the municipal council. Before filing an application, the retailer or commercial property developer is advised to talk to the municipal planning staff to determine if an application can be made and what information needs to be included in the application.

In Canada, if the local council refuses a rezoning application, the applicant may be able to appeal to the Local Planning Appeal Tribunal (LPAT). The LPAT is an independent administrative tribunal that is responsible for hearing appeals. The appeal must be accompanied by written reasons, usually economic benefit for the city, such as job creation and municipal tax contributions. In cases of appeal, the LPAT will hold a mandatory case management conference to discuss opportunities for settlement, such as mediation, and may hold a hearing. If a hearing is required, appellants and others permitted by the LPAT may be given the chance to provide a summary of their cases. Appealing a local decision to the LPAT is a serious matter. It can take time, effort, and, in some cases, money, for everyone involved.

If the matter is returned to the municipality by the LPAT, the council is obligated to address any shortcomings, while continuing to have the opportunity to address local matters in making a new decision. When reconsidering a matter returned by the LPAT, the municipality will need to re-assess the matter, hold a public meeting, and issue a new decision. In the Province of Ontario, the second decision will be final unless it is appealed. If this happens, the LPAT will hear the matter and make a determination on whether the municipality's new decision aligns with provincial and municipal policies. If it does align, the municipal decision will be final. If the municipal decision again does not align with local or provincial policies, the Tribunal will make a final decision on the matter (Province of Ontario, 2019).

Increasingly, large retail facilities such as big box stores and power centers are developed on green fields (idle farmland in suburbs) or on brown fields (old industrial land and railway yards in built-up areas). It is important for retailers and developers to find out how easy it is to have a rezoning application accepted and approved by city council in the market they plan to enter, and if there exists an appeal mechanism. In the Province of Ontario, no application for a rezoning will be approved if the municipality passed a new comprehensive zoning bylaw within the past two years.

COMMUNITY ATTITUDE

A good market, or even a favorable location, does not necessarily mean stores can be developed there to capture the demand. Community opposition may prevent a business plan from being materialized. Community opposition takes place mainly in democratic societies; it rarely happens in non-democratic countries though.

Walmart Stores Inc. reported, at the end of its fiscal year in January 2014, that it had operated 3,288 supercenters, 508 discount stores, and 407 small-format stores in all 50 states of the U.S. Yet, it did not have stores in five of the country's largest cities—New York City, San Francisco, Detroit, Seattle, and Boston (Goldstein, 2018). Reasons for Walmart's absence in these cities vary, but local businesses often fight Walmart's entry into their market and many consumers join forces with the opposition. City officials elected by local residents listen carefully to these objections (Ausick, 2014).

Walmart had long planned to enter New York City. In 2007, it proposed opening stores in the Queens and Staten Island boroughs of the city, but was met with opposition, and had to abandon the hope of opening a store in New York City (Hughes, 2012). In 2010, 2011, and part of 2012, Walmart mounted a vigorous public relations campaign to open a supercenter in Brooklyn, New York City. According to Kantar Media, during the first nine months of 2012, Walmart spent $1.8 million on ads (television, radio, outdoor, internet, and magazine or newspaper) in the New York market. Targeted charitable donations were also made to win community support (Greenhouse & Clifford, 2013). For example, after Hurricane Sandy, Walmart made donations and sent truckloads of goods to victims. It also donated to groups like City Meals on Wheels and the Eagle Academy. It even hired five lobbyist-consultants to help it win approval from the city for that project. Although a poll conducted by the *New York Times* in August 2011 showed that 62 percent of the city residents thought that Walmart should be permitted to open in the city, its entry plan met strong opposition from the local business community and labor unions, who influenced municipal politicians. There even existed a citizen group named "Walmart Free NYC". Mayor Bill De Blasio, the United Food & Commercial Workers (the union covering grocery workers), and some local residents continued to oppose having a Walmart in their community.

The Walmart plan to enter New York City was a case of opposition targeting a particular retailer, not necessarily the big box format itself; other retailers, such as Target and Costco, do have big box style stores at multiple locations in New York City (Lodge, 2017). There are both social and political reasons for the opposition. Walmart is criticized for being anti-union and for paying its employees low wages and giving poor benefits, which could put the unionized supermarkets in New York City out of business. The New York City Council speaker (and a candidate for mayor at the time), Christine Quinn, said, "As long as Walmart's behavior remains the same, they're not welcome in New York City"; she added, "New York isn't changing. Walmart has to change" (Greenhouse & Clifford, 2013). Due to strong opposition, Walmart announced in September 2013 that it was giving up its plan to open a store in Brooklyn.

Community opposition does not always target a particular retailer. It can be a fight against a particular format, especially large format. In 2014, Walmart Canada planned to open a supermarket in downtown Toronto on Bathurst Street near Kensington Market. The building was to be developed by RioCan—Canada's largest REIT, which focuses exclusively on retail real estate, with its core strategy being to own and manage community-oriented neighborhood shopping centers anchored by supermarkets. The proposed building was to be a three-story structure, with a Walmart supermarket on the second and the third floors.

The city planning regulations require that a public hearing be held, and the local community have the right to express their concerns at the public hearing meeting. Many residents in the neighborhood and the retailers in Kensington Market opposed the development (Ballingall, 2013; Davidson, 2013). Kensington Market is a distinctive multicultural neighborhood in Downtown Toronto. In November 2006, it was designated a National Historic Site of Canada. Most shops in Kensington are family run, and the vendors there make their living selling fresh food. Concerned residents and vendors argued that it is a predatory move to set up a large format supermarket in an area that is already well served by local food retailers. More than 50,000 people signed an online petition opposing the Walmart development (CBC News, 2013). Local interest groups also lobbied elected politicians to block the proposal. The city councilor, Adam Vaughan, who represented that riding, took the community concern to the city council. Council passed an interim bylaw, temporarily banning new retail development in the area for a period of one year. The ban would give the Planning Department more time to study the area and recommend development limits.

To give balance, planning regulations also give developers the right to appeal a local government decision. Taking advantage of the right, RioCan filed an appeal to Ontario Municipal Board (OMB)—an unelected board in the Province of Ontario which is delegated the power to hear applications and appeals related to municipal planning and to make arbitrations. The CEO of RioCan said, "We just did not think it was an appropriate thing for council to pass. If they were right, then the OMB will say so" (Dempsey, 2013). Adam Vaughan counter-argued that "We are seeking to have Torontonians build Toronto, and not the OMB or Walmart". Due to community opposition, the RioCan plan had to be modified. According to the new plan, only half of the building space would be used for retailing; the other half would be used for offices. As a result, Walmart gave up its plan of opening a store at the Kensington location (Armstrong, 2014). RioCan went ahead with building the community shopping center, which is now anchored by a much smaller FreshCo banner supermarket owned by Sobeys.

Not all community opposition is successful. In 2013, Loblaw, Canada's largest grocery chain, announced a plan to open a new "urban format" supermarket, also near Kensington Market, as part of a mixed-use development. The building would be a 15-story condo complex, and the store would be located on the second floor of the building (CBC News, 2014). By "urban format", the company meant a store that is much smaller than its regular stores: around 20,000 square feet, compared with its regular stores which can be as large as 85,000 square feet. A group of citizens, known as the "Friends of Kensington Market", said that the grocery store would do more harm than good for the neighborhood. They took actions to oppose the plan for the same reasons as they did against the Walmart plan. In an email statement to CBC News, Steven Deveaux, the Vice President of Land Development at Tribute Communities, the company behind the condo development where the Loblaws supermarket would be hosted, said that

> the forthcoming grocery store will not be out of place in Kensington Market.... While we understand the concern of some of those in the community, Tribute believes that the introduction of a first-class grocery store to the second floor will be complimentary to the surrounding neighborhood.
>
> (CBC News, 2014)

This time, the local councilor Adam Vaughan conceded that while he was concerned about the Loblaws store competing with the dwindling number of small food merchants in Kensington Market, there was no way for the city to fight the store's arrival because the commercial use conformed to existing zoning for that location. So, the Loblaws store opened for business as planned, despite the community opposition.

KEY POINTS OF THE CHAPTER

- Regulation is a significant force shaping competition between firms, the governance of investment, the use of labor, and the overall extraction of profit from retailing of goods.
- There are four types of regulations or public policies that govern the retail industry: foreign investment policies, business tax law, anti-competition law, and land use zoning bylaw.
- The regulatory environment varies greatly, or is in various stages of development, from country to country, and even within a country among provinces and municipalities. Regulations are often imposed by different levels of government and implemented at different spatial scales.
- It is important to investigate the various regulations when planning for a market entry through merger and acquisition. In most cases, anti-competition regulations do not necessarily prevent store development proposals from being approved, but regulators may impose remedies on retailers.
- In general, retail stores can only be developed on land zoned for commercial use. However, zoning bylaws are not carved in stone, and a parcel of land can be rezoned if an application for amendment is submitted by a retailer or commercial property developer, and is approved by the municipal council. Before filing an application, the retailer or commercial property developer is advised to talk to the municipal planning staff to determine if an application can be made and what information needs to be included in the application.
- Community opposition may derail a well-conceived business plan. It takes place mainly in democratic societies, but rarely happens in non-democratic countries. Therefore, "local temper" should be explored in the planning stage as well.

REFERENCES

Armstrong, J. (2014). Developer backs away from Walmart in Kensington Market. *Global News*, February 14. https://globalnews.ca/news/1151521/developer-backs-away-from-walmart-in-kensington-market/.
Atlas, M. (2016). Canada's "branch" tax on foreign corporations—an overview. https://wolterskluwer.ca/blog/canadas-branch-tax-on-foreign-corporations-an-overview/.

Ausick, P. (2014). Eight largest cities without Walmart. https://247wallst. com/retail/2014/06/16/eight-largest-cities-without-walmart/.

Ballingall, A. (2013). Proposed Walmart near Kensington Market has residents fuming. *Toronto Star*, May 28. www.thestar.com/news/ gta/2013/05/28/proposed_walmart_near_kensington_market_has_ residents_fuming.html.

Campbell, A. N. & Halladay, C. W. (2002). The use of behavioural remedies in Canadian merger law (paper presented at Canadian Bar Association 2002 Annual Fall Conference on Competition Law). McMillan Binch LLP. www.mcmillan.ca/Files/The%20Use%20of%20Behavioural_ Campbell_1002.pdf.

CBC News. (2013). 50,000 sign petition against proposed Wal-Mart in Kensington. June 5. www.cbc.ca/news/canada/toronto/50-000-sign-petition-against-proposed-wal-mart-in-kensington-1.1342714.

CBC News. (2014). Loblaws coming to Toronto's Kensington Market. January 28. www.cbc.ca/news/canada/toronto/loblaws-coming-to-torontos-kensington market-1.2513661.

Cooley, S. & Laciak, C. (2018). The foreign investment review (edition 6)—United States. *Lawreviews*. https://thelawreviews.co.uk/edition/the-foreign-investment-regulation-review-edition-6/1174923/united-states.

Critchley, S. (2012). Competition law: regulation of mergers and acquisitions. UK: Collyer Bristow LLP. www.lexology.com/library/detail. aspx?g=74f87ca6-6cca-4a29-a446-a8199c81fba0.

Davidson, J. (2013). At a packed meeting, Kensington Market Says "no" to Walmart. *Torontonist*, June 7. https://torontoist.com/2013/06/at-a-packed-meeting-kensington-market-says-no-to-walmart/.

Dawson, J. (1980). Retail activity and public policy. In J. A. Dawson (Ed.), *Retail Geography* (pp. 193–235). London, England: Croom Helm.

Dempsey, A. (2013). Bylaw that blocked Kensington-area Walmart to be appealed to OMB. *Toronto Star*, September 17. www.thestar.com/news/ gta/2013/09/17/bylaw_that_blocked_kensingtonarea_walmart_to_be_ appealed_to_omb.html.

Ezrachi, A. (2005). *Under (and Over) Prescribing of Behavioural Remedies* (working paper). Centre for Competition Law and Policy, The University of Oxford. www.law.ox.ac.uk/sites/files/oxlaw/cclp_l_13-05.pdf.

Federal Trade Commission. (2019). Merger review: how mergers are reviewed. www.ftc.gov/news-events/media-resources/mergers-and-competition/merger-review.

Goldstein, M. (2018). Why is there not a single Walmart store in New York City? www.quora.com/Why-is-there-not-a-single-Walmart-store-in-New-York-City.

Government of Canada. (2019). Corporate tax rates. www.canada.ca/en/ revenue-agency/services/tax/businesses/topics/corporations/ corporation-tax-rates.html.

Greenhouse, S. & Clifford, S. (2013). A respite in efforts by Walmart in New York. *New York Times*, March 7. www.nytimes.com/2013/03/07/ business/a-respite-in-efforts-by-wal-mart-in-new-york.html.

Hughes, M. (2012). Walmart fails to crack New York City. *Telegraph.* www.telegraph.co.uk/news/worldnews/northamerica/usa/9546569/Walmart-fails-to-crack-New-York-City.html.

Kilby, M. & Kwinter, G. (2018). Merger control in Canada: overview. Toronto, Canada: Stikeman Elliott LLP. https://ca.practicallaw.thomsonreuters.com/6-500-7423?transitionType=Default&contextData=(sc.Default)&firstPage=true&bhcp=1.

Koch, M. & Olscher, R. (2018). The foreign investment review (edition 6)—Canada. *Lawreviews.* https://thelawreviews.co.uk/edition/the-foreign-investment-regulation-review-edition-6/1174863/canada.

Lodge, M. (2017). Walmart is still being banned from one of the world's biggest cities, but oddly Target isn't. *TheStreet.* www.thestreet.com/story/14051569/1/walmart-is-still-being-shut-out-of-one-of-the-world-s-biggest-cities-but-oddly-target-isn-t.html.

Lowe, M. & Wrigley, N. (1996). Towards the new retail geography. In N. Wrigley and M. Lowe (Eds.), *Retailing, Consumption and Capital: towards the New Retail Geography* (pp. 3–30). Essex, England: Longman Group Ltd.

Ministry of Commerce. (2006). Regulations on foreign merger and acquisition of enterprises in China. Beijing.

Nelson, D. (2012). Tesco and Walmart get green light to move into India. *Telegraph,* September 14. www.telegraph.co.uk/finance/newsbysector/retailandconsumer/9544107/Tesco-and-Walmart-get-green-light-to-move-into-India.html.

Osler. (2019). Branch profits tax. www.osler.com/en/resources/business-in-canada/browse-topics/additional/branch-profits-tax.

Province of Ontario. (2019). *Citizen's Guide to Land Use Planning: Zoning Bylaws* www.ontario.ca/document/citizens-guide-land-use-planning/zoning-bylaws.

Trading Economics. (2019a). China sales tax rate—VAT. https://tradingeconomics.com/china/sales-tax-rate.

Trading Economics. (2019b). India sales tax rate—GST. https://tradingeconomics.com/india/sales-tax-rate.

Wang. S. (2014). *China's New Retail Economy: a Geographic Perspective.* New York, NY: Routledge.

Wikipedia. (2019). Corporate tax. https://en.wikipedia.org/wiki/Corporate_tax.

6 Spatial Growth Strategies

There are two types of corporate strategies to achieve business growth: *non-spatial growth strategies* and *spatial growth strategies*. The former include increasing store size, expanding merchandise offerings, and altering merchandise mix, in order to increase sales and market shares. The latter refer to store network expansion either by adding more outlets at more locations in an existing market, or by opening stores in a new market. Once a new market is chosen on the basis of favorable market conditions and friendly external retail environment, the retailer considers a suitable spatial growth strategy. (See Box 6 in Figure 1.1). Alternative spatial growth strategies include organic growth, merger, acquisition, joint ventures, and franchising. Each strategy has its own merits and limitations (Birkin et al., 2002, Alexander & Doherty, 2009). This chapter compares the different spatial strategies, with a particular emphasis on their geographical implications. The comparisons are supported with stories of success and failures.

ORGANIC GROWTH

In retail geography, organic growth, also known as internal expansion, refers to the opening of new stores in a market using the firm's own resources. This does not include growth attributable to acquisitions or mergers. From a real estate point of view, this can be achieved through either construction of new store shells on the retailer's own land, or lease of space from other property owners. Organic growth has the advantage of giving the retailer control over the pace of store development and operation, according to its available resources and its assessment of the retail environment, while keeping the retailer's identity (i.e., the brand) in the process. It also prevents a company from taking on substantial debt through loans or borrowed resources as in the case of acquisition, therefore subjecting the retailer to a low level of investment risk. On the flip side, spatial growth can be slow because of the lengthy process of store location selection, the trouble of acquiring land for new store development, or the difficulty of negotiating leases for suitable properties. This is particularly true in a foreign market because of unfamiliarity and uncertainties in the overseas retail environment. The retailer adopting this strategy may be pre-empted by its competitors and therefore lose future growth opportunities. There can also be high investment risks due to "sunk cost" associated with building new store shells, which may not be easily recovered if the store has to be closed prematurely, Organic growth is usually the preferred growth strategy for a company in the initial stages of the business. When this strategy is chosen, detailed location analysis and site selection are required.

Birkin et al. (2002) distinguish two types of organic growth with regard to the sequence of expansion: *hierarchical diffusion*, and *contagious diffusion*. In hierarchical diffusion, the retailer opens new stores in the largest cities first, and then working systematically down to medium-sized and smaller urban centers. In contagious diffusion, the retailer establishes its presence from a single location, usually the city of its headquarters, and then spreads to the adjacent markets. With the second strategy, the retailer first builds high regional/local market shares, rather than national market shares. The early development of Walmart from the State of Arkansas in the U.S. was an example.

MERGER, ACQUISITION, AND TAKEOVER

Merger, acquisition, and takeover are all means of inorganic, or external, growth, but they have different legal definitions (Birkin et al., 2002).

A merger occurs when two separate business entities combine forces to create a new, joint organization. Mergers require no cash to complete but dilute each company's individual power. In a legal merger, the merging companies no longer exist. Instead, they are subsumed in a new corporation with a new ownership and management structure (see Figure 6.1A). There are four different types of merger. In a *horizontal merger*, two companies that are in direct competition and

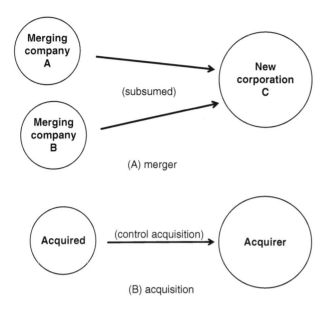

Figure 6.1 Illustration of Corporate Merger and Acquisition.

share the same product lines and the same markets are subsumed. In a *vertical merger*, a retail company and a supplier are merged. When two companies that sell the same products in different markets come together, it is defined as a *market-extension merger*. When two companies selling different but related products in the same market are merged, it is defined as a *product-extension merger* (Hayes, 2019).

An acquisition takes place when one (usually a bigger) company purchases another (usually a smaller) company, but a new company does not emerge. It is defined as the purchase of more than 50 percent of the ownership by an acquiring retailer (known as the *buyer* or the *acquirer*) from another company (known as the *target* or *acquired firm*). This leads to a change of control in the acquired firm. The merging companies still exist, though the acquired firm often becomes a subsidiary of the acquirer (see Figure 6.1B). Depending on marketing need, the acquirer may change the banner of the acquired, or choose to retain the banner and operate the business with dual or multiple banners.

Takeover is similar to a control acquisition, but carries a negative connotation—an "unfriendly" acquisition. It implies that the acquirer is in a much stronger market position than is the acquired, and the former takes over the entire control of the latter. In some cases, a smaller firm acquires management control of a larger and/or longer-established company and retains the name of the latter, known as a "reverse takeover". A hostile takeover takes place when the target firm's board of directors shows resistance to being bought, but a tender offer is made directly to the shareholders, bypassing the board of directors.

In common, merger, acquisition, and takeover all lead to business expansion through "external" growth, as opposed to internal growth. In practice, friendly mergers of equals do not take place very often, and it is uncommon that two companies would benefit equally from combining forces and two different CEOs agree to give up some authority to realize the benefits (Majaski, 2019). Since mergers are uncommon and takeovers carry a negative connotation, contemporary corporate restructuring is often referred to as "merger&acquisition" transactions (M&A), rather than simply a merger or an acquisition. Also due to the negative connotation, many acquiring companies refer to an acquisition as a merger.

M&A have many advantages over organic growth. First of all, they lead to rapid store network growth and swift geographic expansion, and help retailers to penetrate a market where they have previously been un- or under-represented, thus improving market reach and firm visibility. Second, M&A help retailers to acquire a larger customer base and new channels of distribution, and provide better cash flow and sales growth. They also help retailers to obtain a stronger line of credit, because of the combined value of the two businesses, and to achieve economies of scale. Third, retailers benefit from the added expertise from personnel of two different firms, while also reducing duplication of services. In addition, this can be an effective way of eliminating or pre-empting competition in the market. Furthermore, it can be used as a means to realize "corporate tax inversion" for tax benefit: that is, the acquirer buys a foreign company and assumes its tax nationality to cut overall tax costs. In 2014, Burger King (a Florida-based quick service restaurant chain) purchased Tim Hortons (a Canadian coffee-and-doughnuts chain), and contemplated putting the headquarters of the combined company in Canada for the lower corporate tax rate. It was estimated that the move could save Burger King $275 million in taxes each year. Such use of acquisition and takeover has been blasted in the U.S. as tax dodging, and President Barack Obama has criticized a "herd mentality" by companies seeking deals to escape U.S. taxes (Drawbaugh, 2015). Finally, M&A offer the potential opportunity for subsequent organic growth once an operational infrastructure is established (Alexander & Doherty, 2009).

There are also challenges and risks associated with M&A. Acquiring an existing chain, especially a large chain, requires a large investment, and the upfront cost can be very high. If calculations about increased income are inaccurate, the company may be strapped with a debt it has difficulty repaying. When joining forces with another business, there is often a need to expand management capabilities. However, achieving organizational and cultural fit in the stage of M&A implementation and corporate integration can not only be a challenge but also be very costly (Birkin et al., 2002). "Synergy opportunities" may exist only in the minds of the corporate leaders and the deal makers. Where there is no value to be created, the CEO and investment bankers—who have much to gain from a M&A deal—will try to create an image of enhanced value. M&A may also lead to "growth" in unanticipated directions, exposing the company to heavy losses or even failure.

JOINT VENTURE

Joint venture is a business arrangement in which two or more companies agree to pool their resources for the purpose of creating a new business venture. The new entity, which can be a corporation, limited liability company, or partnership, is separate and apart from the participants' other business interests. The participating companies share the profits, but they are also responsible for the losses and costs associated with the new business venture (Hargrave, 2019). Businesses form joint ventures for four main reasons: to combine resources; to combine expertise; to save money (Murray, 2019); or when required by the host country, as was the case in China. This growth strategy is often used when an international retailer enters a foreign country, where the retailer forms a new business entity with a local partner. Local partners allow foreign retailers to connect with the host government and compatible organizations to gain strategic advantages in activities such as obtaining business licenses and development permits, as well as sourcing and logistics. Local partners can also be relied upon for their expertise in exploring the domestic market and managing the local workforce. The participating businesses can work together on a particular business endeavor, while still maintaining the rest of their business apart from each other.

There are two general types of joint ventures. The first type is *equity joint venture,* in which partners share profits, losses, and risk in equal proportion to their respective contributions to the venture's registered capital. Depending on the proportion of contributions, this type of joint venture can be differentiated as majority ownership, minority ownership, and equal ownership. The second type is *cooperative joint venture*, in which the foreign retailer provides the majority of funds and technology, and the local partner provides land, buildings, equipment, etc. Once the joint venture has reached its goal, it can be liquidated like any other business. It often also leads to takeover or buy-out of the weaker local partners by the more resourceful international retailers.

A challenge to the success of a joint venture is the integration of human resources and knowledge sharing. Since joint ventures are built upon trust and convergent goals, risks may occur when partners from different cultures do not trust operating a certain way or have divergent goals, and therefore lack the willingness to reciprocate (Allen, 2019). Joint venturing in less developed economies may entail a higher level of risk due to a lack of knowledge of the local legal system, communication problems, and divergence on agreed-upon objectives.

FRANCHISING

Franchising is another form of spatial growth strategy. In a franchising arrangement, a franchisor grants the franchisee the right to use its trademark or trade-name as well as certain business systems and processes, such as a tested product, standard building design and decor, detailed techniques in running and promoting the business, and training of employees (Quinn, 1998). The franchisee usually pays a one-time franchise fee plus a percentage of sales revenue as royalty, but receives the benefit of gaining immediate name recognition. The franchisee also agrees to comply with certain obligations as set out in a franchise agreement. The franchisor–franchisee relationship continues until the end of the agreement. Among the largest franchised retail chains in the U.S. are Subway, McDonald's, 7-Eleven, Pizza Hut, Walmart, and Starbucks.

Franchising as a business model is used under the following circumstances: (1) the market is adjudged not big enough to justify the cost of operating corporate-owned stores; (2) the retailer wants to test a new market first; (3) a local partner's knowledge of the market is critical for selling the products; and (4) the host country's regulations require local partnership.

There are two main forms of franchising: *direct franchising agreement*, and *master franchising agreement*. Direct franchising links the franchisor and the franchisee directly. In a master franchise agreement, the franchisor grants the master franchisee the right to sub-franchise to other franchisees within an exclusive market, therefore developing a three-way relationship. The master franchise has been a popular way to spread American businesses to international territories, which allows a master franchisor to find many franchisees in an overseas market. The master franchisor is responsible for training and providing support to the new franchisees within a large area, which can include an entire country. A typical example of master franchising is 7-Eleven in China, with three master franchisees, which are believed to have the native knowledge of Chinese customers in different regions. The Hong Kong Dairy Farm International Ltd. was granted permission by 7-Eleven to master franchise in south China's Guangdong Province. The Taiwan-based President Chain Store Corporation was authorized to franchise in Shanghai. The Beijing 7-Eleven Co. Ltd., which is a joint venture of Japan-based Ito Yokado, Beijing Shoulian Group, and China National Sugar & Alcohol Group Corporation, recruits and supports the regional franchisees in Beijing (Pan et al., n.d.).

The biggest advantage of franchising is that it enables a retailer to expand its store network fast with minimal capital investment, because investment is born by the franchisees. This greatly reduces the financial risks for the franchisor. Studies have shown that failure rates are much lower for franchise businesses than for independent business start-ups. In a foreign country, the franchisor may be able to take advantage of favorable government regulations. For example, in many countries, the franchisor does not have to submit to the same types of regulations that govern direct foreign investment in retailing. On the other hand, the level of profit for the franchisor is much lower. Because a great deal of standardization (in logo, store design, products, and service) is required, there can also be weak quality control by the franchisor over the operation of the franchisee stores (Zwisler & Krakus, 2015).

STORIES OF SUCCESS AND FAILURE

Most retailers have used organic growth at some stage of their store network development. In many cases, a retailer uses more than one strategy in combination to achieve its goal of business growth and spatial expansion. There are also plenty of stories of success and setbacks associated with the various strategies. Retailers adjust their growth strategy when the market conditions and the retail environment change. Inability to adjust often leads to devastating results, as told in the subsequent Canadian and Chinese stories.

U.S. Retailers in Canada

With a population of only 37 million, Canada is a relatively small market. However, due to its short physical and cultural distance from the U.S., Canada has been the first foreign market that many U.S. retailers seek to enter as part of their internationalization strategy. American retailers started operating in Canada around the turn of the twentieth century, but the much intensified process of retail internationalization in the 1990s ushered in many new American retail chains. They arrived in new formats not seen in Canada before, and offered many products outside the normal range of merchandise found in a typical domestic store (Arnold & Luthra, 2000).

Walmart entered Canada in 1994 through the acquisition of Woolco—a department store chain. At the same locations, Walmart opened 122 discount department stores on the same day across the country—a case of rapid geographical expansion and swift market penetration. With the initial infrastructure established, its post-entry expansion switched to organic growth. In 2003, it began to open Sam's Club—its membership retail warehouse branch—following the contagious diffusion approach: from the largest urban center of metropolitan Toronto outward to medium-sized cities in southern Ontario. In the next six years, it opened six Sam's Clubs, an average of one store per year—a much slower growth rate. Unable to compete with Costco, which had already established a firm presence in southern Ontario and other Canadian metropolitan areas, Sam's Club did not linger for long and closed all of the six Canadian locations in 2009.

Beginning in 2006, Walmart shifted its growth focus to opening supercenters, also through organic growth, due to the lack of a suitable acquisition target. The large format supercenter combines two "stores" under one roof: a supermarket, and a general merchandise division. Its inventory includes such non-food items as pharmacies, books, hardware, clothes, and kitchenware. Most also have a garden center. To simplify the site selection process, Walmart Canada turned to work closely with a Canadian shopping center/power center developer: SmartCentres. At the time of writing, SmartCentres is the landlord of over 100 Walmart supercenters. Walmart also acquired leaseholds from Target (as described in Chapter 2): 52 in total. What

Walmart acquired were merely store leases, not Target per se. By 2019, Walmart has expanded to operate 410 stores in Canada.

Target, also a U.S. discount retailer, ventured into Canada in 2011 by acquiring leaseholds of the former Zellers stores from the parent company The Hudson's Bay. Zellers ceased to exist, but its employees were not retained by Target and had to re-apply for their position to continue working in their same locations. At the time of its bankruptcy, Zellers had a store network of 279 locations spread over 175 cities and municipalities. However, Target purchased only 189 of the leaseholds. Normally, a retailer entering a new market through acquisition does not need to conduct detailed location analysis and trade area analysis, because retail sites and real estates are already in place. Since Target did not intend to open stores at all the 279 Zellers locations, it must have conducted comprehensive market and location research to decide which ones were desirable locations and therefore should be acquired. In a short period of three years, Target opened 133 stores at the former Zellers locations in most provinces and in all major urban centers. Everyone thought Target would open more stores on the remaining leaseholds it had acquired, but in 2015, it suddenly closed its entire Canadian operation and withdrew from Canada completely due to its inability to break even. It was reported that in the three-year period, Target lost $2.1 billion. While acquisition of the leaseholds was not the only factor in the failure of Target in Canada, it was the main cause of the retailer's heavy losses, making Target's high-profile entry a high-profile failure.

Another example of an American retailer using a combination of organic growth and acquisition (but in reverse order) to enter and expand in Canada is Lowe's. In the same business sector as is Home Depot, Lowe's specializes in do-it-yourself home improvement. It entered Canada in 2007, 13 years after Home Depot did. Initially, Lowe's adopted the organic growth strategy and expanded slowly: by 2016, it still had only 44 stores in Canada (Shaw, 2016), compared with 180 stores operated by its rival Home Depot. In 2016, Lowe's entered into an agreement with the Canadian home improvement retailer Rona Inc. for Lowes to acquire Rona's entire network of 496 corporate and franchise stores, plus nine distribution centers (Lowe's Canada, 2016). The acquisition represented a key step in accelerating Lowe's growth and created one of the largest home improvement retailers in Canada, with 539 store locations and pro forma revenues of approximately CAN$6 billion from its Canadian operations.

Before the acquisition, Lowe's had no presence in the Province of Québec, which accounts for 25 percent of Canada's home improvement market (Shaw, 2016), but the majority of the Rona stores were in that province; so the acquisition brought a significant market gain for Lowe's in Canada. The current plan is to maintain Rona's retail banner, its management team, and its employees, known in the retail industry as a "dual-brand" strategy (or multi-brand strategy, because Rona itself operates stores under different banners), but the effectiveness of this strategy remains to be seen and the synergy opportunities to be tested. In fact, Lowe's Canada has begun to convert some Rona stores to the Lowe's banner (Marowits, 2016).

The case of Best Buy in Canada deserves a longer account here. The largest retailer of consumer electronics in the U.S., Best Buy entered Canada in 2001 through the acquisition of Future Shop—a domestic market leader in consumer electronics, which at the time already had a well-established network with 88 store locations across the country (Strauss, 2000; 2001). Originally, Best Buy planned to enter the Canadian market through organic growth by opening Best Buy brand stores (Hess & Kazanjian, 2006). For that purpose, Best Buy negotiated and signed eight property leases for new store development: seven in the Province of Ontario and one in the Province of British Columbia. In 2001, it saw an acquisition opportunity.

Future Shop was started in 1983 as a family-owned business with a single store in the City of Vancouver. It followed an organic growth strategy and took the contagious diffusion approach to store development. With that approach, Future Shop first diffused to the surrounding municipalities of Richmond, Coquitlam, Surrey, and Burnaby in the Greater Vancouver Region. Beginning in 1986, it expanded eastward into the provinces of Alberta, Manitoba, and Ontario. In 1993, the company went public on the Toronto Stock Exchange, raising fresh capital of $30 million for further expansion. Throughout the 1990s, Future Shop progressively expanded into the remaining provinces in Canada. Encouraged by its success, Future Shop ventured into the United States to become an international retailer. Unfortunately, its U.S. entry was short lived and proved a disaster. Unable to replicate its business model south of the border in the face of fierce competition from both Best Buy and Circuit City, Future Shop had to retreat to Canada in 1999.

After intense negotiations in August 2001, Future Shop conceded to the bid and sold its ownership to Best Buy at a value of CAN$580 million. The original arrangement was for Future Shop to take on the name of Best Buy to form a single-brand business entity, but the then president of Future Shop, Kevin Layden, pushed for a proposal to retain the Future Shop banner and implement a dual-brand strategy in Canada (Hucker, 2008; Strauss, 2008). In explaining the rationale of the strategy, John Noble, Senior Vice President of Best Buy International, offered four considerations (Chandrasekhar, 2006). First, the Canadian consumer electronics market was fragmented. Even the market leader Future Shop had only 16 percent of the market share; so, the national market had room for a new brand. Second, Best Buy had already signed eight real estate leases in Canada as part of its original plan; cancelling these leases would be costly. Third, conversion of the Future Shop stores into Best Buy outlets would take a considerable amount of time and money, in both store redesign and staff transition. Lastly, and most importantly, Future Shop was a well-established brand, with 95 percent of unaided brand awareness among the Canadians. The dual-brand strategy could make Canadian consumers "believe" that the U.S.-based Best Buy would not monopolize Canada's consumer electronics industry.

In the following decade, Best Buy expanded both brands in Canada, through organic growth, to own nearly 200 stores. The Best Buy outlets are typically big box stores, ranging from 30,000 to 36,000 square feet in floor space. Many are located in power centers, but some are free-standing; a few were opened in regional and superregional shopping centers to replace defunct department stores. The Future Shop stores varied in size, with the earlier stores being smaller than the newer ones, primarily because they were developed before the big box format was introduced to Canada. After the acquisition, Best Buy also developed large format Future Shop stores in power centers.

While operating two brands in the same foreign market may have merits, its successful implementation requires carefully defined differentiation between them (Thrall, 2002). If not sufficiently differentiated, the two brands will unavoidably cannibalize one another, resulting in wasting of corporate resources, higher overhead costs, and loss of revenue. In the case of Best Buy, both chains had their stores concentrated in the large urban centers; they thus shared the same metropolitan markets. Geographical proximity had also been employed in store deployment within the large metropolitan areas. At many locations, a Best Buy store and a Future Shop store co-tenanted the same power center (Valencia Saravia & Wang, 2016). Besides, the stores were hardly differentiated enough in product mix, operation format, and price structure. With such spatial proximity and store similarity, cannibalization was almost unavoidable.

In fact, there was evidence all the way that Best Buy's dual-brand strategy was not working well. Only a few years after the retailer's entry into Canada, the Vice-Chairman and CEO of Best Buy, Brad Anderson, acknowledged that "Clearly, we [have] over-invested [in Canada]" (Flavelle, 2005). Best Buy's head of retail for North America, Brian Duun, was also disappointed by the company's performance in Canada. On January 31, 2013, Best Buy announced it would close 15 outlets (seven Best Buy stores and eight Future Shop stores) and lay off 900 workers (Shaw, 2013), in order to "reduce unnecessary costs, eliminate redundant operating systems, and ... optimize its real estate strategy to reflect ... a changing retail landscape" (Best Buy Canada News Release, quoted in the *Canadian Press*, 2013). Two years later on March 28, 2015, Best Buy announced it was to close all the remaining 131 Future Shop stores and re-open 65 of them under the Best Buy banner, ending its dual-brand operation in Canada. Best Buy's Canadian experience may offer a useful lesson for Lowe's.

International Retailers in China

After the economic reform began in the early 1980s, China became a market sought after by international retailers. In the early years of opening up, approved foreign retailers had to operate in joint ventures with at least one Chinese partner; wholly owned subsidiaries were prohibited (as described in detail in Chapter 5). In joint ventures, foreign investors' stakes had to be less than 50 percent. In such a rigid retail environment, the early entrants as international retailers in China invariably took the path of joint ventures, and the local business partners were all state-owned enterprises, matched to them by the Chinese government. While joint venture does offer opportunities for foreign retailers to learn the market conditions and the retail environment in general, few of them were content with being reduced to minority ownership, because it curbed their ability in business decision making, such as the freedom to impose their own operating methods with minimal friction. In a more restrictive manner, the Chinese government required that foreign retailers have a local partner in each city where they were approved to operate.

Walmart entered China in 1996 in the form of joint ventures. It obviously had to take the organic growth strategy in store development because the Walmart stores were completely new formats in China. It also followed the hierarchical diffusion approach to geographical expansion: starting from the first-tier cities of Shenzhen (one of the four

SEZs), Beijing, and Shanghai, and gradually diffusing to the provincial capitals, most of which are second-tier cities. This allowed Walmart to focus on the "islands of prosperity", or plum markets with affluent consumers, to ground its first retail capital in the country. In the city of Shenzhen, Walmart opened both a supercenter and a Sam's Club in the same year. However, as dictated by the Chinese regulations of the time, Walmart had to have two different local partners: Shenzhen International Trust and Investment Corporation for its supercenter, and Shenzhen SEZ Development Corporation for its Sam's Club. Not surprisingly, the store development process was slow, also because of the difficulty in obtaining suitable real estate for its large format stores. In eight years, by the end of 2004, Walmart opened only 42 outlets in the vast country of 1.3 billion consumers, compared with 241 stores in Canada and 671 in Mexico in the same year (Wang & Zhang, 2006).

The French Carrefour also entered China by forming a joint venture with a Chinese company named Zhongguan Commerce. While the joint venture was registered under the name of Zhongguan Commerce exclusively, it was actually operated by Carrefour. In 1995, Carrefour opened its first hypermarket (the Carrefour version of supercenter) in Beijing. Shortly after, it negotiated and obtained approval from other local governments to open stores in Shanghai, Shenzhen, and a number of other cities. In 1999, Carrefour settled its China headquarters office in Shanghai and entered a new partnership with the Shanghai-based Lianhua Group, the largest domestic supermarket chain in China at the time. Carrefour expanded much more aggressively than did Walmart. It not only opened stores without state government approval but also quietly maintained controlling stakes in all its joint ventures. Its aggressiveness and disregard for the Chinese regulations irritated the state government so much that it admonished Carrefour in 2001 by suspending any further expansion; the suspension brought Carrefour's CEO to Beijing to apologize in person (Wang & Zhang, 2006). Similarly, the German Metro AG entered China in 1996 through a joint venture with the Shanghai-based Jinjiang Group. Until 1999, Metro limited its operation to Shanghai and the neighboring provinces of Jiangsu and Zhejiang. It was not until 2006 that Metro opened its first store in Beijing.

After China's admission to the WTO, and with progressive deregulations, international retailers shifted to entering and penetrating the China market through acquisition. These included the earlier entrants, who accelerated their spatial growth by a combination of greenfield development (another term for organic growth) and M&A. In 2004, the British Tesco entered China by purchasing 50 percent ownership of Hymart-Hymall—a Taiwanese retail chain with 25 hypermarkets in China. Two years later, Tesco augmented its ownership to 90 percent and changed the Hymart-Hymall brand to the Tesco-Legou banner. In 2007, Walmart acquired 35 percent of the total shares of Trust Mart—another Taiwanese supermarket chain with 100 stores in China. By the same agreement, Walmart had the option to acquire the remaining shares by 2010. According to Alexander (1997), international retailers sometimes acquire a minor interest in a retail operation, in order to monitor the performance of that company. If things proceed as expected, minority interest may lead to outright acquisition. Shortly after China was admitted to the WTO, major international retailers were moving towards "independence" in an effort to consolidate their business decision-making powers. In 2005, Carrefour formed a wholly owned subsidiary in Haikou of Hainan Province, and also bought out its Chinese partners in several cities. In the same year, Metro increased its ownership in the joint venture from 60 to 90 percent (Wang, 2014).

The American Best Buy and Home Depot were among a small number of international retailers that entered the China market through acquisition but were unsuccessful. Best Buy first entered China in 2006 through the acquisition of China's then fourth largest consumer electronic retailer Jiangsu Five Star Electronics. As with its operation in Canada, Best Buy adopted a dual-brand strategy in China, retaining the Five Star brand whilst opening Best Buy–branded stores as a second corporate entity. Between 2006 and 2009, Best Buy opened a total of six large format stores, all of which were in the City of Shanghai. It was not until 2010 that Best Buy began to expand beyond Shanghai to test the neighboring markets by opening one store in each of Suzhou and Hangzhou. Despite its international reputation, organizational strength, and rich resources, Best Buy was unable to turn its China operation into a profitable international division. On February 22, 2011, it announced it was to close all of the Best Buy banner stores in China and focus on expanding the domestic Five Star store network, a totally different ending from its Canadian operation (Wang, 2012). Home Depot arrived in China in the same year as did Best Buy through the acquisition of domestic retailer Homeway. Adopting a single-brand strategy, it acquired 14 Homeway stores and turned 12 of them into Home Depot brand stores. Also unable to make a profit, it had to downsize its business by closing five of the 12 Home Depot stores between 2009 and 2012, reducing its presence from six to three urban markets and abandoning the Beijing market completely. In 2012,

Home Depot closed all seven remaining stores, joining a growing list of international retailers that failed to grasp the local consumer culture (Wang, 2014).

KEY POINTS OF THE CHAPTER

- There are two types of corporate strategies to achieve business growth: *non-spatial growth strategies* and *spatial growth strategies*. The former include increasing store size, expanding merchandise offerings, and altering merchandise mix, in order to increase sales and market shares. The latter refer to store network expansion either by adding more outlets at more locations in an existing market, or by opening stores in a new market.
- Alternative spatial growth strategies include organic growth, merger, acquisition, joint ventures, and franchising. Each strategy has its own merits and limitations.
- Organic growth has the advantage of giving the retailer control over the pace of store development and operation, while keeping the retailer's identity in the process. On the flip side, spatial growth can be slow because of the lengthy process of store location selection, the trouble of acquiring land for new store development, or the difficulty of negotiating leases for suitable properties. This is particularly true in a foreign market.
- Merger&acquisition can lead to rapid store network growth and swift geographic expansion, and help retailers to penetrate a market where they have previously been un- or under-represented. M&A can also help retailers to acquire a larger customer base and new channels of distribution, and to eliminate or pre-empt competition. There are also challenges and risks associated with M&A, because they require a large upfront investment.
- Joint venture is a business arrangement often used when an international retailer enters a foreign country, where the retailer forms a new business entity with a local partner. Risks may occur when partners from different cultures do not trust operating a certain way or have divergent goals, and therefore lack the willingness to reciprocate.
- The biggest advantage of franchising is that it enables a retailer to expand its store network fast with minimal capital investment, because investment is born by the franchisees. This greatly reduces the financial risks for the franchisor. On the other hand, the level

of profit for the franchisor is much lower, and there can be weak quality control by the franchisor over the operation of the franchisee stores.

• Most corporate retailers have used organic growth at some stage of their store network development. In many cases, a retailer uses more than one strategy in combination to achieve its goal of business growth and spatial expansion.

REFERENCES

Alexander, N. (1997). *International Retailing*. Oxford, England: Blackwell Publishing Ltd.

Alexander, N. & Doherty, A. M. (2009). *International Retailing*. Oxford. England: Oxford University Press.

Allen, S. (2019). Joint venture 101: grow your business with a joint venture. *The Balance Small Business*. www.thebalancesmb.com/joint-venturing-101-1200766.

Arnold, S. J. & Luthra, M. N. (2000). Market entry effects of large format retailers: a stakeholder analysis. *International Journal of Retail & Distribution Management*, 28(4/5), 139–154.

Birkin, M., Clarke, G., & Clarke, M. (2002). *Retail Geography and Intelligent Network Planning*. Chichester, England: John Wiley & Sons, Ltd.

Canadian Press. (2013). Eight Future Shop and seven Best Buy big box stores closing across Canada. January 31. www2.macleans.ca/2013/01/31/reports-of-best-buy-closures-across-canada/.

Chandrasekhar, R. (2006). *Best Buy Inc—Dual Branding in China (Research Report)*. London, ON: Richard Ivey School of Business, The University of Western Ontario.

Drawbaugh, K. (2015). Burger King's move to Canada could save it $275 million in taxes. *Reuters*, Business, February 10. www.huffpost.com/entry/burger-king-inversion-deal-millions_n_6306206.

Flavelle, D. (2005). Rivals, costs hit Best Buy. *Toronto Star*, December 14, E4.

Hargrave, M. (2019). Joint venture. *Investopedia*. www.investopedia.com/terms/j/jointventure.asp.

Hayes, A. (2019). Mergers and acquisitions. *Investopedia*. www.investopedia.com/terms/m/mergersandacquisitions.asp.

Hess, E. D. & Kazanjian, R. K. (2006). *The Search for Organic Growth*. Cambridge, England: Cambridge University Press.

Hucker, W. (2008). Kevin Layden to resign at Best Buy International. *Marketnews*, July 2. www.marketnews.ca/content/index/page?pid=3855.

Lowe's Canada. (2016). Lowe's completes acquisition of Rona. www.lowescanada.ca/en/news/lowes-completes-acquisition-of-rona.

Majaski, C. (2019). What is the difference between mergers and acquisitions? *Investopedia*. www.investopedia.com/ask/answers/021815/what-difference-between-merger-and-acquisition.asp.

Marowits, R. (2016). Lowe's Canada to convert 40 Rona big-box stores starting in early 2017. *Canadian Press*, December 12. www.theglobeandmail.com/report-on-business/lowes-canada-to-convert-40-rona-big-box-stores-starting-in-early-2017/article33298243/.

Murray, J. (2019). What is a joint venture and how does it work? *The Balance Small Business*, www.thebalancesmb.com/what-is-a-joint-venture-and-how-does-it-work-397540.

Pan, Y., Oh, H., & Weitz, B. (n.d.) Entering Shanghai: 7-Eleven's choice of master franchisee. (Presentation prepared for the International Retailing Education and Training Program). The University of Florida: David F. Miller Center for Retailing Education and Research.

Quinn, B. (1998). Towards a framework for the study of franchising as an operating mode for international retail companies. *The International Review of Retail, Distribution and Consumer Research, 8*(4), 445–467.

Shaw, H. (2013). Best Buy to close 15 stores in Canada; lay off 900 workers. *Financial Post*, January 31 http://business.financialpost.com/2013/01/31/best-buy-to-close-15-stores-in-canada-lay-off-900-workers/.

Shaw, H. (2016). Lowe's Cos to buy Canada's Rona for $3.2 billion in cash to create home improvement giant. *Financial Post*, February 3. file:///C:/Users/Shuguang%20Wang/OneDrive/Lowe's%20buys%20Rona/Lowe's%20Cos%20to%20buy%20Canada's%20Rona%20for%20$3.2%20billion%20in%20cash%20to%20create%20home%20improvement%20giant%20_%20Financial%20Post.html.

Strauss, M. (2000). Best Buy confirms expansion into Canada. *Globe and Mail*, December 8, B6.

Strauss, M. (2001). Electronics retailers gearing for big box battle. *Globe and Mail*, March 21, B1.

Strauss, M. (2008). Kevin Layden: can a dual-brand strategy travel? *Globe and Mail*, June 30. www.theglobeandmail.com/report on business/kevin-layden-can-a-dual-brand-strategy-travel/article692432/.

Thrall, G. I. (2002). *Business Geography and New Real Estate Market Analysis*. New York, NY: Oxford University Press.

Valencia Saravia, J. & Wang, S. (2016). Why Best Buy's dual-brand strategy failed in Canada. *Professional Geographer, 68*(4), 650–662.

Wang, S. (2012). The setback of Best Buy in China. *The Retail Digest*, Summer Issue, 20–25.

Wang, S. (2014). *China's New Retail Economy: a Geographic Perspective*. New York, NY: Routledge.

Wang, S. & Zhang, Y. (2006). Penetrating the Great Wall and conquering the Middle Kingdom: Walmart in China. In S. D. Brunn (Ed.), *Walmart World* (pp. 293–314). New York, NY: Routledge.

Zwisler, C. E. & Krakus, B. (2015). *Avoiding Common Mistakes in International Franchising*. Chicago, IL: International Franchise Association. https://higherlogicdownload.s3.amazonaws.com/FRANCHISE/33a13346-4a02-4ab3-81b8-eb69580a680c/UploadedImages/Top%205%20Mistakes%20Made%20by%20Franchisors%20Expanding%20Internationally%20Paper.pdf.

7 Market Screening, Retail Location Analysis, and Site Evaluation

In economic geography, location analysis is concerned with the search for a location that has comparative territorial advantages, namely favorable physical, socioeconomic, and political conditions, for a specific type of economic activity to achieve high efficiency and generate maximum profit. In any type of economic activity, location is considered the most important factor in keeping operating cost low and accessibility to customers high. In a simple territorial context, this means that the area and location with better conditions will receive the first consideration for the type of economic activity (Boyce, 1978; Healey & Ilbery, 1990).

Location theories are rooted not only in geography but also in the disciplines of engineering, mathematics, and economics. There are three fundamental laws in location theories (Church & Murray, 2009: 8–10):

> LL1: some locations are better than others for a given purpose (that is, some locations afford more efficiency than other locations, and therefore are optimal);

> LL2: spatial context (i.e., social, economic and political conditions) can alter site efficiencies;

> LL3: sites of an optimal multi-site pattern must be selected simultaneously, rather than independently one at a time.

As explained in Chapter 1, the success of a retail store depends on two general factors: the location of the business, and the management of the business. Although both factors contribute to the success of a retail venture, location is undeniably a dominant consideration. A good location allows ready access to the site, attracts large numbers of customers, and increases potential sales of retail outlets (Ghosh & McLafferty, 1987). Conversely, a poor location can economically punish the retailer and doom a store to failure. For corporate retailers that operate large retail facilities, detailed location analysis is necessary before committing a lease, investing in site acquisition and improvements, or actually building a new facility (Church & Murray, 2009), because the disadvantages of a poor location are difficult to overcome. In importance for retailers, store location research is viewed as an "insurance policy" (Thompson, 1986).

Retail location analysis is conducted in two stages and at two spatial scales: *macro-scale* area-based selection, and *micro-scale* point-based selection. In the first stage and at macro scale, the analyst focuses on market condition analysis (or market appraisal) and identifies areas with a concentration of target consumers. This is known as market screening. It is done based on demographic and socioeconomic conditions, and is often conducted using census data, along with consumer data if such data are readily available (Hoffman, 2006). In the second stage and at micro scale, site selection is conducted to investigate the following location factors (Jones & Simmons, 1993):

- availability, suitability, and affordability of real estates
- visibility and accessibility of the potential sites
- types of location (such as retail strip, shopping center, power center, or freestanding)
- presence of competition and complimentary co-tenants
- zoning regulations

Retail outlets of different formats have different location and space requirements. For example, fashion stores, on average, are much smaller than supermarkets, and are usually located in regional or superregional shopping centers. Big box stores are much larger than conventional supermarkets and require more selling space. Suitable property needs to be not only available but also affordable in order for a business to maintain a healthy level of profit. This is especially important for the low-margin retailers such as discount supermarkets. Site visibility and accessibility play an important role in self-advertising and facilitating customers to travel to the location. Ideally, stores should be located where they are visible to passing traffic. Accessibility refers to how easy it is for a customer to get to the store, which depends on nearby road patterns, number and position of ingress and egress, road conditions, and barriers. Type of location may enhance or reduce visibility and accessibility, but also affect rent. For example, store rent in a regional or superregional shopping center is typically higher than on a retail strip; however, many regional and superregional shopping centers are located at or near public transit hubs or at highway inter-changes, and provide free parking. In general, being close to competi-tors should be avoided because competitors dilute the demand and reduce market shares in the trade area. However, there could be benefit if the presence of competitors helps to generate a larger trade area due to agglomeration effects. Organic growth is often accompanied by greenfield development on land that is not readily zoned for commercial use. This is a common occurrence in outer suburbs where big box stores and power centers are built on idle farm-land. In such cases, application for rezoning is necessary.

In accordance with Box 7 in Figure 1.1, this chapter covers selected methods of location analysis and site evaluation. These methods make location analysis and site selection less subjective and more systematic through the eyes of retailers.

METHOD OF MACRO-SCALE LOCATION ANALYSIS FOR MARKET SCREENING

A useful method of market screening is cluster analysis. An application of cluster analysis has already been shown in Chapter 3 in the case study of Dollarama. In this section, two more case studies are pre-sented to further illustrate how this method is used in market screening.

Case Study 1: Tiering China's Urban Markets

Since the economic reform began in the early 1980s, China has made significant progress in economic development, and become the second largest economy in the world. Its level of urbanization has also increased substantially, and it now has 52 percent of the population living in urban areas (compared with 70–80 percent in the Western developed economies). A disproportionate amount of retail sales is generated in cities, where the increasing concentration of population and the growing accumulation of wealth empower the urban dwellers with high purchasing power.

Due to the vast variations in population size, economic structure, settlement patterns, and wealth accumulation among the Chinese cities, levels of demand and market size differ significantly within the nation's urban system. When international retailers plan to penetrate the Chinese market and execute their spatial growth strategies, they invariably enter the large urban markets first and then diffuse to smaller cities. They often use such names as first-, second-, and third-tier cities to describe and label the Chinese urban markets of various sizes. While a hierarchy of urban markets can be a useful agent for retail diffusion, no systematic classification of Chinese cities had ever been proposed and applied for the study of retail geography. As one blogger put it squarely,

> We often hear of China's first-, or second-, or third-tier cities; yet, what actually makes a city tier? The terms are so often used, yet there is actually no official formula for determining what tier a city falls in. Instead, everyone makes up their own rules.
>
> (Barry, 2011)

To fill the void, Wang (2014) proposed and experimented with a multivariate classification of the Chinese cities, specifically for macro-scale market screening. Such a classification scheme is useful in a number of ways. Methodologically, it puts forward a clear formula as a systematic way of differentiating urban markets, so that comparative studies by different researchers can be facilitated. Practically, such an objectively constructed hierarchy can be used by retailers as a reference in search of urban markets according to their geospatial strategies and growth priority.

Nine variables are selected for the construction of the classification scheme, as listed in Table 7.1. The first five are indicators of demand, purchasing power, and size of the retail economy. Ideally, disposable income should be used instead of wage, because wage is not the only, though it is the major, source of disposal income. According to the 2010 National Survey of Household Spending conducted by the National Bureau of Statistics of China, wage accounts for only 65 percent of the total income; the other 35 percent is derived from business income, investment income (interest and stock gain), income from properties (rent), and public transfers (pension, employment insurance, etc.) (National Bureau of Statistics of China, 2011a). However, total income or disposable income is never a part of the Chinese census. Total wage is

Table 7.1 Classification Variables for Cluster Analysis

Variable	Pearson correlation coefficient r (with retail sales)
Total population	0.867**
GDP	0.979**
Retail sales	1.00**
Total wage	0.938**
Average wage	0.627**
Internet subscriptions	0.864**
Smartphone users	0.934**
Number of buses	0.900**
Population density	0.216**

Note
**Correlation is significant at the 0.01 level (two-tailed).

therefore used as an alternative to reflect relative purchasing powers in different cities. Average wage is also used in the classification scheme to signify the level of affluence at individual level in various cities. GDP indicates not only a city's ability to develop and provide retail-related infrastructures, but also institutional and corporate purchasing powers, which account for a significant portion of retail sales in China.

The four remaining variables are facilitating factors. For example, more and more urban consumers use the internet and smartphone to not only search for product features, availability, and price, but also make purchases and have the merchandise delivered to their home. Retailers typically favor cities with high population density, as high density means compact trade areas with high sales potentials. Private automobile ownership is an important indicator of consumer mobility. Unfortunately, this information is not available at the city level in official statistics. In the absence of automobile ownership data, the number of buses is used to differentiate cities with regard to levels of mobility. A number of cities have also built extensive subway and light rail transit (LRT) lines, but no systematic information was available on those either (at the time of research).

Given the large number of urban centers in China, only the provincial-, sub-provincial-, and prefecture-level cities (a total of 287) are included in this multivariate classification exercise. The smaller cities are excluded. As the correlation coefficients in Table 7.1 show, retail sales in the 287 cities are highly correlated with all the selected classification variables, except population density. This suggests that the choice of the variables is appropriate and reasonable for classifying the Chinese cities for the purpose of screening the urban retail markets.

K-means cluster analysis is used to classify the Chinese cities. This is because references in literature are often made to three to five tiers of cities in China, meaning that the number of tiers is definite. Original, instead of standardized, variables are used in the cluster analysis. $K = 3$ is used to begin with, which results in two small clusters and one extremely large cluster that contains 89 percent of all the 287 cities. Different values of K are then experimented with progressively. At $K = 8$, the largest cluster (Cluster 7) still contains 224 cities, or 78 percent of the 287 cities (see Table 7.2). At this point, it is decided to break up this large group of cities with a separate run of cluster analysis: this time, with $K = 2$ (see Table 7.3). The two runs result in nine distinctive clusters. Analysis of variance (ANOVA) tests (F-tests) show that all nine clusters are statistically significant.

Of the nine resultant groups of cities, three are still single-case clusters (Beijing, Shanghai and Tianjin) and one cluster comprises only two cites (Guangzhou and Shenzhen). On the basis of the cluster centers (i.e., the cluster centroids in the multi-dimensional space) and the distances between them, it is decided to combine the nine clusters into five tiers of cities for the purpose of the study (see Table 7.4). The five tiers are labeled as

- mega urban markets, comprising five cities in four natural clusters (Clusters 1, 2, 3, and 4)
- Tier 1, consisting of 18 cities in Clusters 5 and 8
- Tier 2, 30 cities in Cluster 6
- Tier 3, 56 cities in Cluster 7.1
- Tier 4, 168 cities in Cluster 7.2

As Table 7.5 shows, the market size and conditions vary significantly among the cities of different tiers, suggesting conspicuous regional variations. In general, the market size and the size of the retail economy decrease progressively from the mega urban markets and Tier 1 cities down to the lower-tier cities. However, within each tier, some market attributes exhibit wide ranges. These within-group variations have resulted from the classification exercise using multiple variables.

The five mega urban markets have the largest populations, with an average of 8.4 million people living in their city proper. Both Beijing and Shanghai have more than ten million residents. These five mega cities also command the highest levels of GDP and retail sales, particularly Beijing and Shanghai. Although Shenzhen has a population of

Table 7.2 Final Cluster Centers from the First Run (with $K=8$)

Variable	Cluster								ANOVA	
	1 (1 city)	2 (1 city)	3 (2 cities)	4 (1 city)	5 (8 cities)	6 (30 cities)	7 (224 cities)	8 (5 cities)	F	Sig.
Total population (10,000)	1,175	803	450	1,332	279	204	86	437	192.0	0.000
Population density (person/km²)	964	1,085	1,469	2,583	1,592	1,333	884	1,872	3.0	0.004
GDP (billion yuan)	1,197.2	703.0	830.6	1,487.6	261.3	130.4	26.0	369.3	1997.3	0.000
Retail sales (billion yuan)	521.2	227.9	299.9	513.4	101.3	52.2	9.8	150.5	1081.3	0.000
Total wage (billion yuan)	318.3	78.7	103.1	200.4	25.8	14.2	3.2	39.9	1655.1	0.000
Average wage (1,000 yuan)	58.8	45.2	48.7	63.5	39.4	35.2	27.7	41.5	30.6	0.000
Cell phone subscription (million)	17.8	9.9	19.1	21.1	4.5	2.8	0.7	8.7	587.9	0.000
Internet subscription (million)	4.9	5.3	2.6	12.5	1.0	0.5	0.1	1.3	1066.9	0.000
Number of buses (1,000)	21,7	7.9	17.1	16.3	3.8	2.1	0.5	5.6	234.9	0.000

Source: Wang, 2014.

Note
Fifteen cities could not be classified due to missing data.

Table 7.3 Final Cluster Centers from the Second Run (with $K=2$, to Break Up Cluster 7 in Table 7.2)

	Cluster		ANOVA	
	7.1 (168 cities)	7.2 (56 cities)	F	Sig.
Total population (10,000)	75.2	119.5	45.9	0.000
Population density (person/km^2)	814.9	1092.5	4.7	0.031
GDP (billion yuan)	17.9	50.6	519.7	0.000
Retail sales (billion yuan)	7.2	17.8	166.9	0.000
Total wage (billion yuan)	2.3	5.8	176.0	0.000
Average wage (1,000 yuan)	26.5	31.4	38.2	0.000
Cell phone subscription (million)	0.5	1.1	96.9	0.000
Internet subscription (million)	0.08	0.18	92.8	0.000
Number of buses (1,000)	0.4	0.8	77.7	0.000

Source: Wang, 2014.

Table 7.4 Natural Clusters and City Tiers

Tier	Natural cluster*	Member cities
Mega urban market (5)	1, 2, 3, & 4	Beijing[1]; Shanghai[1]; Tianjin[1]; Guangzhou[2,3]; Shenzhen[3,4]
Tier 1 (18)	8	Shenyang[2,3]; Nanjing[2,3]; Hangzhou[2,3]; Dongguan; Chengdu[2,3]; Wuhan[2,3]*; Foshan*; Chongqing[1]*
	5	Dalian[2]; Ningbo[3]; Changchun[2,3]; Wuxi; Suzhou; Jinan[2,3]; Qingdao[3]; Changsha[2]; Harbin[2,3]*; Xian[2,3]*
Tier 2 (30)	6	Shijiazhuang[2]; Tangshan; Taiyuan[2]; Hohot[2]; Baotou; Anshan; Jilin; Daqing; Xuzhou; Changzhou; Nantong; Yangzhou; Wenzhou; Hefei[2]; Fuzhou[2]; Xiamen[3,4]; Nanchang[2]; Zibo; Dongying; Yantai; Linyi; Zhengzhou[2]; Zhuhai[4]; Shantou[4]; Huizhou; Zhongshan; Nanning[2]; Kunming[2]; Lanzhou[2]; Urumqi[2]
Tier 3 (56)	7.1	Haikou[2]; Guiyang[2]; Yinchuan[2] (See Wang, 2014 for others)
Tier 4 (168)	7.2	Lhasa[2]; Sanya; Guilin; Lijiang; Zhangjiajie (See Wang, 2014 for others)

Notes
1. provincial-level city; 2. provincial capital; 3. sub-provincial city; 4. Special Economic Zone.
* Fifteen cities could not be classified due to missing data in at least one of the nine classification variables. They are assigned to the closest cluster by visually inspecting three key attributes, for which data are available: population size, GDP, and total retail sales.

Table 7.5 Market Conditions of Different Tiered Cities*

Attributes	Cluster mean and ranges				
	Mega	Tier 1	Tier 2	Tier 3	Tier 4
Total population (million)	**8.42** 2.46–13.32	**4.38** 1.79–15.43	**2.02** 0.83–5.03	**1.18** 0.25–2.75	**0.74** 0.15–2.04
Population density (person/km²)	**1,514** 964–2,583	**1,543** 592–3,606	**1,315** 243–5,324	**1,090** <100–3,405	**805** <100–4,554
GDP (billion yuan)	**1,010.0** 703.0–1,487.6	**319.8** 205.3–489.2	**128.7** 76.8–192.9	**50.3** 12.2–74.1	**17.7** 2.7–35.0
Retail sales (billion yuan)	**327.5** 227.9–521.2	**130.0** 76.2–196.9	**51.3** 20.7–97.1	**17.8** 1.7–36.6	**7.1** 0.5–28.7
Total wage (billion yuan)	**160.7** 78.7–318.3	**31.5** 9.5–66.6	**13.9** 5.1–27.2	**5.8** 2.0–15.5	**2.3** 0.4–9.9
Average wage (1,000 yuan)	**53.0** 45.2–63.5	**39.6** 31.5–45.1	**35.2** 25.5–44.3	**31.3** 20.9–47.0	**26.7** 12.7–43.2
Cell phone subscription (million)	**17.4** 9.9–21.1	**7.0** 3.5–14.1	**2.8** 0.3–5.2	**1.1** 0.1–3.1	**0.5** 0.1–1.2
Internet subscription (million)	**5.6** 2.5–12.5	**1.1** 0.6–2.0	**0.53** <0.1–1.9	**0.2** <0.1–4.5	**0.1** <0.1–3.5
Number of buses (1,000)	**16.0** 7.9–25.3	**4.9** 1.4–8.1	**2.1** 0.6–5.3	**0.8** 0.1–2.5	**0.4** <0.1–1.8

Source: National Bureau of Statistics of China, 2011b, and Wang, 2014.

Note

* Numbers in bold are cluster averages; numbers in italics are cluster ranges.

only 2.5 million, the smallest of the five, both its GDP and retail sales are larger than those of Tianjin, making it a member of this elite group of cities. No cities of other tiers (including Tier 1) have achieved retail sales higher than the minimum in the mega urban markets. The very high retail sales in the mega markets are certainly attributed to the high levels of wages and the various facilitating factors. Both total wage and average wage in the five mega urban markets are much higher than in any other cities. On average, there are twice as many cell phone users in these five cities as those in the Tier 1 cities, and there are five times the number of internet subscribers. In addition to the large number of buses, these cities are known for high automobile ownership. All five cities also have extensive subway/LRT networks: by the end of 2010, Beijing had 330 km in operation; Shanghai, 410 km; Guangzhou, 220 km; Tianjin, 72 km; and Shenzhen 60 km.

The Tier 1 cities consist of the members of two natural clusters: Clusters 5 and 8. Eleven of them are provincial capitals. Twelve of them, including nine provincial capitals, have been granted sub-provincial status with a high level of autonomy in economic planning, a status higher than ordinary provincial capitals. These cities also have very favorable market conditions. The average population size is five million, with Chongqing having 15 million residents living in its city proper. Both total wage and average wage are much higher than those in the lower-tier cities, with average wage close to 40,000 RMB yuan. Similarly, the numbers of cell phone and internet subscribers are much higher in the Tier 1 cities than in cities of the lower tiers. In addition to the relatively large number of buses, two of these cities, Chengdu and Shenyang, already have subway lines in operation, and another 13 have subway lines under construction. Although Chongqing's population is larger than that of Beijing and Shanghai, it is placed in Tier 1, because its GDP, retail sales, and number of internet subscribers and city buses are all smaller than the minimum for the five mega urban markets. Dongguan in Guangdong Province is the smallest city in this group, with a population of only 1.8 million. However, it is pushed into Tier 1 mainly because of its high GDP value and high volume of retail sales. The average wage in Dongguan, which stands at 42,600 yuan, ranks the fifth among the 18 Tier 1 cities, and is much higher than the cluster average (see Table 7.5). Similarly, Guangdong's Foshan City has a much higher GDP value and much higher retail sales than the group averages, making it a Tier 1 city as well. It should be noted that the Tier 1 cities are not limited to the eastern coastal provinces; five of them are in central China and two in northeast China (see top map in Figure 7.1).

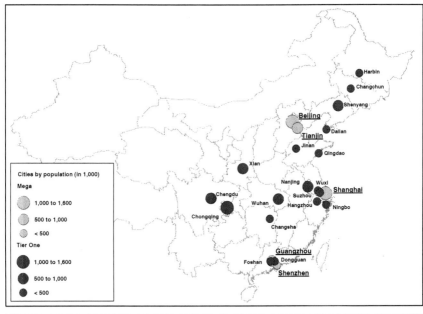

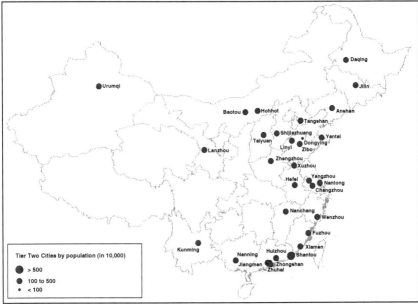

Figure 7.1 Geographical Distribution of Mega Urban Markets and Tier 1 and Tier 2 Cities

Note
Top map shows the mega urban markets and Tier 1 cities; bottom map shows the Tier 2 cities.

Thirty cities are classified as Tier 2 urban markets. This group includes 11 provincial capitals and three SEZs (Xiamen, Shantou, and Zhuhai). Most other Tier 2 cities are regional urban centers with relatively high levels of economic development. Excepting the interior provincial capitals, a large number of cities in this group are situated in three coastal provinces, with four in each of Shandong, Zhejiang, and Guangdong, reflecting high levels of economic development in these provinces and the coastal region in general (see the bottom map in Figure 7.1). The market conditions of the Tier 2 cities are not as favorable as those of the Tier 1 cities. Their average population size and retail sales, two million and 50 billion yuan respectively, are both half of those of Tier 1 cities, indicating much weaker total purchasing power. Largely due to their smaller populations, these cities also have much smaller numbers of cell phone and internet subscribers. Of the 30 cities in this group, none has subway trains in operation, and only six of them (Fuzhou, Xiamen, Changzhou, Zhengzhou, Nanchang, and Nanning) have subway lines under construction. Still, their market conditions are distinctly superior to those of the Tier 3 and Tier 4 cities: their average population size, GDP, and retail sales are all twice as large as those of the Tier 3 and Tier 4 cities (see Table 7.5).

The Tier 3 and Tier 4 cities are mostly smaller municipalities of regional importance, with only three provincial capitals (Guiyang and Haikou in Tier 3 and Lhasa in Tier 4). Accordingly, they have much smaller population size and much lower GDP values and retail sales. None of them have subways in operation or even under construction. Of the 56 Tier 3 cities, only 36 have populations of one million or more. It should be noted that the Tier 4 cities include several popular tourist destinations, such as Sanya, Guilin, Lijiang, and Zhangjiajie. These cities may bring in considerable numbers of tourists, who contribute to local retail sales.

International retailers are invariably interested in the large and affluent urban markets, especially in the early stages of their entry and market expansion. Therefore, city tiers are particularly relevant to the foreign retail giants. In the sequence of store development and for scale economies, it makes business sense for the large retailers to set up multiple stores in a few large urban centers with high population density, so that these stores can be effectively supported by a small number of regional distribution centers. Once a solid market leader position is established, they diffuse to cities of lower tiers. It is not clear if international retailers have developed and used similar classification schemes to screen the Chinese urban markets, but an examination of the presence and market penetration of the major international retailers in China seems to prove that the classification scheme in Table 7.4 coincides with the sequence of their store development and distribution (Wang, 2014). As a final note, individual cities are not necessarily locked into the same tier for a long time; their status may change over time, so the classification scheme should be updated regularly with more recent data.

Case Study 2: T&T Supermarket

T&T Supermarket is a food retailer in Canada targeting ethnic Chinese consumers. Since its creation in 1993 in Metropolitan Vancouver, the company has expanded to operate 27 stores in six metropolitan areas and has become Canada's largest Asian supermarket chain. Unlike the other ethnic Chinese food retailers, T&T focuses on the affluent Chinese consumers with high household income, and adopted characteristics of a mainstream Canadian supermarket in terms of store size, spaciousness, and configuration (Wang et al., 2013). In 2009, it was acquired by the mainstream food retailer Loblaw—Canada's largest grocery retail chain. At present, T&T operates eight stores in metropolitan Toronto. Assuming that it plans to grow the store network in metropolitan Toronto by opening another 1–2 stores, where should the new stores be developed? Among other things, the main location criterion for T&T is a spatial concentration of affluent ethnic Chinese in the surrounding trade area of the potential sites.

K-means cluster analysis is used to screen the metropolitan market and identify target areas where suitable real estate will be investigated and evaluated. For simplicity and easy interpretation, only four census variables are selected as classification variables—the minimum required for cluster analysis. These are:

- Chinese Canadians (including both Chinese immigrants and Canadian born Chinese)
- established Chinese immigrants (who have been in Canada for at least five years from time of the most recent census and are more likely to have a stable income-earning job than are the recent immigrants)
- average household income
- percentage of households who are not low income (i.e., above Statistics Canada defined Low Income Measure)

Chinese Canadians with these characteristics are believed to be relatively affluent and are likely to have the financial resources to purchase foodstuff from a T&T supermarket. Two of the four classification variables need to be calculated from the original census variables (called "derived variables"):

- "established Chinese immigrants" = "total Chinese immigrants"–"recent Chinese immigrants"
- "percentage of households who are not low income" = 1–"prevalence of low income based on after-tax low-income measure"

Using statistical software SPSS, experiments are made with $K=3$, $K=4$, $K=5$, and $K=6$, to find the most suitable classification at the census tract level of geography. The optimal classification is found to consist of five clusters produced by $K=5$. The two large clusters, Clusters 4 and 5, have 499 and 448 census tracts, respectively (see Table 7.6). The two small clusters, Clusters 2 and 3, have 17 and 3 census tracts only. The other cluster, Cluster 1, has 106 census tracts. Fifteen census tracts cannot be classified due to missing data in one or more of the four classification variables.

Both Cluster 4 and Cluster 5 have the largest, and similar, numbers of residents of Chinese ethnicity and established Chinese immigrants; however, Cluster 5 has a much higher average household income than Cluster 4 ($105,200 vs. $68,100). The percentage of households not in poverty is also higher in Cluster 5 census tracts than in Cluster 4 census tracts (89 percent vs. 79 percent). As such, Cluster 5 is considered to

Table 7.6 Final Cluster Centers for T&T Market Screening*

Classification variable	Cluster				
	1	2	3	4	5
Chinese Canadians	424	245	193	513	491
Established Chinese immigrants	383	221	165	424	436
Chinese not in poverty (%)	91.8	93.7	92.3	79.2	89.4
Average household income ($)	168,100	303,800	493,900	68,100	105,200
Number census tracts	106	17	3	499	448

Note
* Fifteen census tracts cannot be classified due to missing data in one or more of the four classification variables.

represent the ideal spatial segments that the new T&T stores should target. Cluster 1 contains smaller numbers of ethnic Chinese and established Chinese immigrants than do Clusters 4 and 5, but it has much higher household income at $168,100; so it constitutes anther target market for T&T. Both Clusters 2 and 3 consist of the wealthiest census tracts, but they also contain the smallest number of Chinese and established Chinese immigrants, and are the smallest spatial clusters as well. There is not enough demand in these areas to support a T&T supermarket.

After joining the SPSS data file (with cluster ID added to it) and the census boundary file, the five clusters are mapped for visualization (see Figure 7.2). The eight existing T&T stores are also added to the map. Four areas in the metropolitan region are identified as having potential demand to support a new T&T store, but do not currently have a T&T supermarket nearby. Three of these areas have a constellation of Cluster 5 census tracts in outer suburbs; the fourth one has a cluster of Cluster 1 census tracts in the central city. Further investigation can be conducted within these four areas to search for suitable real estate.

Figure 7.2 Potential Areas That Warrant Further Investigation of Suitable Real Estates for New T&T Stores.

METHODS OF MICRO-SCALE LOCATION ANALYSIS—SITE EVALUATION

A spectrum of methods and techniques have been used by academics and practitioners for retail site selection and evaluation. These range from simple and subjective methods that are suitable for small and independent retailers, to more complex and systematic modeling methods that are used by corporate retailers and retail chains. Examples of simple methods include *rules of thumb, analogue method,* and *parasitic approach.* Examples of systematic modeling are *ranking, regression,* and *location-allocation.*

With *rules of thumb,* the store developer uses a single key factor to select a site for a new store, which is regarded as directly related to sales performance (Jones & Simmons, 1993). It is called "rules of thumb" because the decision is made largely based on the past experience of the store operator and his/her empirical observations. While this method leads to a fast decision and costs very little money in the process, the decision is often subjective and over-simplified. It is appropriate only for stores that are relatively insensitive to relocation and are flexible to modify their operations, because it does not cost much for the store to relocate after it has been set up.

The *analogue method* is also based on generalizations of a practitioner's experience, not on theories. In 1932, William Applebaum, while working for the Kroger Company, developed a sales forecasting technique that later came to be known as the analogue method (Thompson, 1986). With this method, the analyst uses a successful (i.e., a profitable) store as a model to identify its store attributes and trade area characteristics (Birkin et al., 2002). The analyst then uses the same attributes to search for a new location or site that matches the characteristics of the successful store. The success of this method depends on whether or not similar sites can be found elsewhere, but also on the experience of the location analyst. This method is often used by retail chains, but is not suitable for evaluating greenfield sites, where the trade area and the surrounding transport network are still evolving.

A similar approach to the analogue method is the *parasitic approach* (Birkin et al., 2002). This approach is used typically by smaller retailers, which do not have the resources (both money and data) and expertise to conduct detailed and thorough location analysis. They simply follow the large retailers in selecting store locations, assuming that the large retailers have done the "homework" and the locations that the large retailers have chosen are good locations. It makes business sense that the "parasitic" retailers are supplementary to the larger retailers that they follow, but do not compete with the large retailers.

In the rest of this section, more detailed discussions are devoted to the *ranking method* and the *regression method*. *Location-allocation* will be treated separately in Chapter 9.

The Ranking Method

The *ranking method* is alternatively known as the *rating method, checklist method,* or *multi criteria ranking method*. With this method, the location analyst pre-selects a number of location factors as criteria; he/she then compares and ranks several sites using the same set of criteria, and chooses the "best" available site while recognizing the various constraints (Jones & Simmons, 1993). Since the relative importance of the selection criteria often differs, weighted ranking with varying weights assigned to different criteria is recommended.

Let us assume that T&T Supermarket is searching for a site to develop a new store in one of the four areas identified in the previously described market screening research. The ranking method is used to compare and rank three alternative sites with four pre-selected criteria: visibility, accessibility, parking space, and property cost. Visibility, which is difficult to quantify, is expressed as distance from the nearby arterial roads or whether the site is blocked by other buildings. Accessibility is evaluated by the number of arterial roads and the number of ingress and egress routes that provide access to the site. Parking is measured by the number of parking spaces on the site. Property cost (land cost or rent) is measured in dollars.

Each site is given a score of 1 to 10, with a score of 1 indicating the least favorable for that criterion, and a score of 10 indicating the most favorable. That is, a score of 10 means the best visibility and accessibility, the most parking space, and the lowest cost for acquiring the site and retaining the property. Treating all four criteria as of equal importance, the rankings of the three alternative sites based on their total scores are summarized in Table 7.7a. Site B has a total score of 35, and is therefore ranked the first and the best of the three for the new supermarket. Sites A and C have total scores of 34 and 21, respectively, and are ranked the second and the third.

Table 7.7 Ranking of Three Alternative Sites for Development of a T&T Supermarket

(a) Un-weighted Ranking

Criteria	Site A	Site B	Site C
Visibility	10	8	6
Accessibility	8	10	5
Parking	6	10	4
Cost	10	7	6
Total score	34	35	21
Ranking	2nd	1st	3rd

(b) Weighted Ranking

Criteria	Site A	Site B	Site C
Visibility	$10 \times 0.1 = 1$	$8 \times 0.1 = 0.8$	$6 \times 0.1 = 0.6$
Accessibility	$8 \times 0.1 = 0.8$	$10 \times 0.1 = 1$	$5 \times 0.1 = 0.5$
Parking	$6 \times 0.3 = 1.8$	$10 \times 0.3 = 3$	$4 \times 0.3 = 1.2$
Cost	$10 \times 0.5 = 5$	$7 \times 0.5 = 3.5$	$6 \times 0.5 = 3$
Total score	8.6	8.3	5.3
Ranking	1st	2nd	3rd

In reality, some factors or criteria are bound to be more important than others for a particular retailer. Let us assume that of the above four factors, cost is more important than the other three, because property rent or mortgage affects store profitability over an extended period of time. Free parking is the second most important: without free parking, customers may not want to come to this particular store for grocery shopping. Accessibility and visibility are less important than the other two factors, because if the store has a good reputation with regard to product offerings, price, and the shopping environment in general, regular customers are less bothered by accessibility and visibility: they know where the store is and how to find it. Based on the assumed relative importance, different weights are distributed among the four factors: 0.5 for cost, 0.3 for parking, and 0.1 for each of accessibility and visibility, with the total weights equal to 1. With the application of the respective weights, Site A is found to be the best, instead of Site B (see Table 7.7b.)

While Site B is rated qualitatively better than the other two sites, there is no indication of "by how much". This is one of the limitations of the ranking method. A more elaborate example of the ranking method is presented and illustrated in Chapter 10, where location analysis and site selection of distribution centers is discussed.

Multivariate Regression

Regression modeling is a standard statistical method for retail site evaluation. A much more precise and rigorous procedure than some other methods (such as the ranking method), regression modeling is widely used by large retail chains that own a wealth of corporate data (especially "big data"). There are different forms of regression modeling, including univariate, multivariate, linear, non-linear, and logistic regression. While the models are based on rules of science, they all also build on the philosophy of the analogue procedure (Roger & Green, 1979). In this section, only linear multivariate regression is described and illustrated.

Multivariate regression works by defining a dependent variable and correlating this dependent variable with a set of independent variables. Mathematically, a linear multivariate regression model is expressed as the following:

$$Y = a + b_1 X_1 + b_2 X_2 + b_3 X_3 + \ldots + b_n X_n$$

where

- Y is the dependent variable
- a is the Y intercept, which is a constant
- $X_1 \ldots X_n$ are independent variables
- $b_1 \ldots b_n$ are regression coefficients for the corresponding independent variables

In retail location analysis, the dependent variable is customarily represented by sales potential at that location or site being considered. Either total sales or per-unit-area sales can be used. The independent variables, also described as sales predictors, are represented by both analogue store attributes and catchment area characteristics (Breheny, 1988). The former include store size and amount of parking; the latter include demographic and socioeconomic characteristics, as well as competition, that are believed to directly influence demand and the level of sales. The regression coefficients are calculated from the existing data collected at the other stores in the same retail chain, which reflect the relative contributions to sales potential to be made by the various independent variables. In statistical terms, these coefficients reflect the relative importance of the selected independent variables in explaining the variations in the dependent variable, sales potential.

In order to build a robust and reliable regression model, Birkin et al. (2002) emphasize the importance of the following three conditions: (1) select a set of independent variables that directly influence merchandise demand and sales volume; (2) choose a set of independent variables that are as uncorrelated with each other as possible to avoid the problem of multicollinearity; and (3) find a set of sample stores that have similar trade area characteristics. There are two ways in which researchers choose independent variables. In the first, independent variables are selected based on theoretical reasoning that they have a cause–effect relationship with the dependent variable. In the second, they are selected from a long list of variables through the stepwise regression procedure. The first way should be preferred because the selection process is guided by relevant theories. With the second way, some variables may be selected but have no cause–effect relation with the dependent variable. Collinearity can be checked by examining the simple correlation coefficients among the selected independent variables.

Students are reminded that in the use of regression analysis, a minimum sample size of 30 is required in order for the constant and the regression coefficients to be statistically significant. The resultant model should be assessed against two other statistical indicators: the R-squared (R^2), and the significance level. R^2 is the percentage of the dependent variable variation that is explained by the regression model. It ranges between 0 and 1, with 0 indicating that the model explains none of the variability of the sales data around its mean, while 1 indicates that the model explains all the variability of the sales data around its mean. In general, the higher the R^2, the better the model fits the data. The minimum acceptable R^2 value varies for different subjects of research. In the study of retailing, it is suggested that 0.6 be the minimum, as consumer behaviors, which often form part of the independent variables, are less predictable than in science. As for significance level, $\alpha = 0.05$ (in correspondence with a 95 percent confidence level) is commonly used as a minimum. If the R^2 value is too low or the α value is too high, a different set of independent variables should be tried to calibrate the regression model. Another way of calibrating a regression model is to split the dataset into two portions and run regression analysis twice using one-half of the data a time (Ghosh & McLafferty, 1987). Similar coefficients and R^2 values should indicate model consistency and reliability. Finally, both data and models should be updated regularly to reflect currency in market conditions and to maintain accuracy.

Operation of the regression method is illustrated in Birkin et al. (2002) with a small set of sample data ($n=7$, which is smaller than the required minimal sample size of 30; see Table 7.8). Assume that a supermarket chain already operates a store in each of the seven cities in the UK. Store performance data in terms of (monthly) sales and store size are known for the seven existing stores. Information about market conditions, such as number of competitors within their trade areas, population size, and household income is also known. The supermarket chain wants to develop a regression model and use the model to evaluate whether opening a new store in the City of Canterbury, where a suitable real estate with 8,000 square feet of space has been identified, would be profitable.

With sales as the dependent variable, and store size, number of competitors, population size, and percentage of household with income over £50,000 as independent variables, a regression model is built from the statistical outputs (derived in SPSS; see Table 7.9):

Sales = 193,158 + 134.7(store size) − 448,614(competitors)
+ 19.9(population) + 26,332(percentage of households with
income over £50,000)

Note: the coefficient for number of competitors within trade area is negative because this variable negatively influences store sales. The other three factors positively contribute to store sales, so their regression coefficients are all positive. The coefficients also quantify the contributions of the respective independent variables to store sales. For example, an increase in store size by one square foot would lead to an increase in sales by £134; but each additional competitor within the trade area would reduce stores sale by £448,614, nearly half a million pounds. With the known information for the prospective store location in Canterbury, sales potential is calculated as:

Sales potential = 193,158 + 134.7(8,000) − 448,614(5)
+ 19.9(100,000) + 26,332(40) = £2,070,968 (or £2.07 million)

Further calculation shows that per-unit-area sales for the Canterbury store are predicted to be £265 per square foot, which is higher than that of the seven existing stores in the other cities, suggesting that the Canterbury location would be a viable choice.

When the regression model is evaluated against the R^2 and significance level, it is found that the R^2 value is very high—at 0.9—and the

Table 7.8 Sample Stores for Regression Modeling

City of location	Store size (sq. ft.)	Number of competitors in trade area	Population in trade area	% of households with income over £50k	Monthly sales (£)	Sales per sq. ft. (£)	Predicted sales (£)	Error of prediction (%)
Leeds	10,000	7	140,000	25	1,833,000	183	1,844,160	0.61
Manchester	12,000	8	200,000	20	2,747,250	229	2,727,286	-0.73
Derby	8,000	4	80,000	20	1,598,400	200	1,594,942	-0.22
Sheffield	11,000	5	100,000	15	1,800,750	164	1,816,768	0.89
Croydon	12,000	6	110,000	30	2,108,425	176	2,096,834	-0.55
Cambridge	9,000	4	80,000	30	2,025,400	225	1,992,962	-1.60
Guildford	10,000	5	120,000	35	2,580,000	258	2,606,708	1.04
Canterbury	8,000	5	100,000	40			2,070,968	

Source: adapted from Birkin et al., 2002: 128.

Table 7.9 Regression Coefficients for the Sample Stores in Table 7.8*

Model	Unstandardized coefficients		Standardized coefficients	t	Sig.
	B	Std. error	Beta		
(Constant)	193,157.9	122,517.8		1.58	0.256
Store size	134.7	14.7	0.478	9.19	0.012
Competitors	−448,614.3	31,979.7	−1.608	−14.03	0.005
Population	19.9	1.0	1.974	19.16	0.003
% over £50k	26,331.9	2,136.0	0.441	12.33	0.007

Note
* Dependent variable is sales.

coefficients for the four predictors are all statistically significant, with α less than 0.05. The "robustness" of this model is supported by the very small errors of prediction, which are calculated as:

- (model predicted sales for an existing store – the actual sales from the same store)/the actual sales from the same stores * 100 percent

As shown in Table 7.8, the errors of predictions are very small, all less than 2 percent. The significance level for the constant is much greater than 0.05, at 0.256, meaning that the constant can be accepted only at the 74 percent confidence level, which is much lower than the usual minimum of 95 percent. The reliability of the model should be improved by increasing the sample size to at least 30 stores.

KEY POINTS OF THE CHAPTER

- Retail location analysis is conducted in two stages and at two spatial scales: macro-scale area-based selection, and micro-scale point-based selection. In the first stage, the analyst focuses on market condition analysis and identifies areas with a concentration of target consumers, known as market screening. In the second stage, site selection is conducted by examining specific location factors.
- K-means cluster analysis is a useful method of market screening. However, it does not always produce a straightforward and clear-cut classification of submarkets. Often, several trial runs are needed for experiment, and "human intervention" is sometime necessary, as illustrated in the China case study.

- Market screening based on cluster analysis forms the first step in identifying potential locations for new store development, and some form of visualization on the cluster map (along with existing stores) is needed to narrow down the location search, as shown in the T&T case study.
- The ranking method works with a number of pre-selected location factors to choose the "best" available site while recognizing the various constraints. Since the relative importance of the selected criteria often differs, weighted ranking with varying weights assigned to different criteria is recommended.
- Three conditions are important in building a robust and reliable regression model: (1) select a set of independent variables that directly influence merchandise demand and sales volume; (2) choose a set of independent variables that are as uncorrelated with each other as possible to avoid the problem of multicollinearity; and (3) find a set of sample stores that have similar trade area characteristics. Equally important, the input data should meet the minimum sample requirement ($n \geq 30$), and the resultant model should be assessed against two other statistical indicators: the R-squared (R^2), and the significance level (α).

REFERENCES

Barry. (2011). What makes a city tier in China? *The China Sourcing Blog*, July 28. www.chinasourcingblog.org/2011/07/what-makes-a-city-tier-in-chin.html.

Birkin, M., Clarke, G., & Clarke, M. (2002). *Retail Geography and Intelligent Network Planning*. Chichester, England: John Wiley & Sons, Ltd.

Boyce, R. R. (1978). *The Bases of Economic Geography* (2nd edition). New York, NY: Holt, Rinehart & Winston.

Breheny, M. (1988). Practical methods of retail location analysis: a review. In N. Wrigley (Ed.), *Store Choice, Store Location and Market Analysis* (pp. 39–86). London, England: Routledge.

Church, R. L. & Murray, A. T. (2009). *Business Site Selection, Location Analysis and GIS*. Hoboken, NJ: John Wiley & Sons, Inc.

Ghosh, A. & McLafferty, S. L. (1987). *Location Strategies for Retail and Service Firms*. Lexington, MA: Lexington Books.

Healey, M. J. & Ilbery, B. W. (1990). *Location and Change: Perspectives on Economic Geography*. Oxford, England: Oxford University Press.

Hoffman, C. (2006). Retail keeps rolling. *Real Estate Forum*, 61(5), 58–70.

Jones, K. & Simmons, J. (1993). *Location, Location, Location: Analyzing the Retail Environment*. Toronto, Canada: Nelson Canada.

National Bureau of Statistics of China. (2011a). *China Statistical Yearbook.* Beijing: China Statistical Publishing House.

National Bureau of Statistics of China. (2011b). *China City Statistical Yearbook.* Beijing: China Statistical Publishing House.

Roger, D. S. & Green, H. L. (1979). A new perspective on forecasting store sales: applying statistical models and techniques in the analogue approach. *Geographical Review, 69*(4), 449–458.

Thompson, J. S. (1986). *Site Selection.* New York, NY: Lebhar-Friedman Books.

Wang, S. (2014). *China's New Retail Economy: a Geographic Perspective.* New York, NY: Routledge.

Wang, S., Hii, R., Zhong, J., & Du, P. (2013). Recent trends of ethnic Chinese retailing in metropolitan Toronto. *International Journal of Applied Geospatial Research, 4*(1), 49–66.

8 Trade Area Delineation and Analysis

Trade area delineation and analysis (Box 7 in Figure 1.1) often goes hand in hand with business location analysis and site selection, as they are complementary procedures.

> Choosing a retail site in the absence of sound trade area analysis is a lot like flying an airplane with blinders: it forces a business to commit itself to a course in the absence of vital information such as store patronage, local market opportunities, competing businesses, and barriers that would dissuade consumers from visiting the site.
>
> (Segal, 1998)

However, because site selection and trade area analysis use different sets of techniques, they are treated in two separate chapters. Two groups of techniques are reviewed and elaborated in this chapter. The first group deals with the techniques used to define the trade area of a single store or a single shopping facility, such as the *circular* and *driving distance/time* methods. The second group consists of techniques used to delineate trade areas of a set of stores, including *Thiessen Polygon, Reilly's Law,* and the *Huff Model.* Applications of these methods are demonstrated with examples using different statistical and GIS software. Methods of sales potential estimation are also explained, because for retailers, knowing sales potential is the ultimate purpose of trade area analysis.

TRADE AREA CONCEPTUALIZATION

In retail geography, *trade area* refers to the spatial extent of the distribution of customers around an individual store: it can be viewed as a contiguous area (or a polygon) around a store that contains the majority of the customers or potential customers (Hernandez et al., 2004). It is also known as a *market area* or *customer catchment area*. Within a trade area, a high level of interactions between the retail store and the customers that patronize the store is expected. Interactions are measured in different ways: (1) the number of customers who patronize the store; (2) the number of transactions made by the patronizing customers; and (3) the dollar amount of transactions.

The foundations of contemporary approaches to trade area delineation were laid by William Applebaum based on shopper survey patterns, called customer spotting (Applebaum, 1968; Davis, 1976). Conceptually, a trade area has a spatial dimension and geographical boundaries, though the boundaries are not clear cut and are often fuzzy. Trade areas also vary in size and shape. Factors that affect trade area size and shape include store size, settlement patterns (i.e., residential density), transportation network and barriers to movement, and presence of competitors (Jones & Simmons, 1993). Commonly, larger stores have a larger trade area than do the smaller stores, because they carry a larger assortment of merchandise and tend to attract customers from a wider area. Customers are willing to travel a longer distance for multipurpose shopping. In high-density areas, the spatial dimension of a store's trade area tends to be compact, because a smaller area can contain enough customers and sufficient demand to support the business of the store. The existence of an efficient transportation network (both public transit and road network, including bridges over rivers) facilitates shopping trips by reducing travel friction and overcoming the effects of barriers to movement, thus helping extend the trade area. The presence of competitors negatively affects the size of a trade area because competitors provide alternative choices and intervening opportunities. It should also be noted that trade areas are not static, but are "fluid": they can be modified, temporarily, by price reductions and special promotions, which retailers do from time to time to manipulate customer flows (Ghosh & McLafferty, 1987).

Church & Murray (2009) distinguish two types of trade area: descriptive and prescriptive. Descriptive trade areas are defined based on data about existing customers. With available customer data (usually collected at POS in a retail store) and combined with customer spotting and dot-density maps of customers, the retailer knows who its customers are, where they live, what they buy, and how much they spend. Prescriptive trade areas are delineated using mathematically and statistically based modeling (such as the Huff Model and location-allocation modeling), and are based on assumptions or inference of shopping habits and consumption patterns of potential customers. In the past, when cash was the main means of exchange, use of descriptive trade area was limited because of the difficulty of collecting location-based customer data. As such, most methods of trade area delineation were developed based on mathematical and statistical modeling, which became the mainstay of orthodox retail geography. With the wide use of debit cards and credit cards as alternative methods of payment, and with the use of geotechnologies, corporate retailers have been accumulating a wealth of geo-referenced customer databases. In the modern era of "big data", the importance of descriptive trade area is expected to resurface and grow.

In a parallel theorization, Jones & Simmons (1993) generalize three approaches to trade area delimitation, each of which is represented by different methods and techniques. These are *spatial monopoly, market penetration*, and *dispersed market.*

The *spatial monopoly* (also known as the deterministic) approach makes a clear-cut assumption about the spatial dimension of the trade area. Trade areas defined using this approach are typically non-overlapping polygons with definite boundaries. This approach also assumes that all customers patronizing the store come from within this area and there is no spending leakage; those who live outside are excluded from consideration (Hernandez et al., 2004). This approach is represented by such methods as *circular, travel distance/time, Thiessen Polygon, Reilly's Law,* and *location-allocation* (See Table 8.1).

The *market penetration* approach, also known as the probabilistic approach, makes no clear-cut assumption about the spatial dimension of the traded areas. Trade areas defined using this approach are not polygons but are probability surfaces. Such trade areas overlap with one another and have no definite boundaries. Customers are assigned to each store partially, with the assumption that people do not always go to the closest store. In other words, there is always a probability that a consumer chooses to go to a more distant store to reduce the total

Table 8.1 Three Approaches to Trade Area Delineation

Approach	*Methods*
Spatial monopoly (deterministic)	*Circular; travel distance/time; Thiessen Polygon; Reilly's Law; location-allocation*
Market penetration (probabilistic)	*Huff Model*
Dispersed market	*Customer profiling; geodemographics*

shopping cost. The probabilistic approach is represented by the *Huff Model*. The level of market penetration is usually the highest near the store and declines irregularly with distance depending on the pattern of the local road network (Jones & Simmons, 1993).

The *dispersed market* approach is taken to define trade areas for retailers that carry highly specialized, or a narrow selection of, goods. There is often no obvious spatial concentration of customers for such retailers, and customers are widely dispersed in a city or metropolitan area, where the distance decay relationship is weak. A common method that follows this approach is customer profiling or customer prospecting through geodemographic analysis by age, income, ethnicity, and lifestyle. Through cluster analysis and mapping, the analyst identifies the subareas that have a relative concentration of persons with the desired characteristics of potential consumers. This method has already been described and illustrated in Chapter 3 (*Geography of Demand, Expenditure Patterns, and Market Segmentation*). Highly specialized retailers also use the lifestyle information contained in PRIZM and other market segmentation systems to identify target trade areas in a broader urban market.

Two types of data are used in trade area analysis: primary data and secondary data. Primary data are usually compiled by retailers themselves, at POS or through online orders, either by sales associates asking postal codes and phone numbers, or based on credit card transactions. Through customer data analysis, retailers develop a customer profile consisting of demographic, social, and economic attributes. The commonly used secondary data are from the census. Census data are less expensive, and require less effort, to acquire than much other data. They are useful to identify potential customers, though many of the potential customers in a trade area do not necessarily patronize the store.

METHODS OF TRADE AREA DELINEATION FOR SINGLE STORES

Circular Trade Area (or Simple Ring)

This is the easiest, quickest, and least expensive method of trade area delineation, offering radial or ring-based analysis. With this method, trade area is defined as a circle around a store with a pre-defined radius. This method assumes that the transport surface is uniform, and the store is equally accessible from all directions. Competition is not a major factor, and adjacent trade areas of other stores may overlap or not overlap, depending on the distances between the adjacent stores and the pre-defined radius. Demographic and socioeconomic data for the trade area can be extracted from the circle for further analysis. The operation of this method is illustrated using the same twin-mall case study presented in Chapter 4 (*Retail Structure Analysis*).

To reiterate, Dufferin Mall is located in the inner city of Toronto in a high-density area, with 128 stores spanning across $52,700\,\text{m}^2$ of floor space. Bayview Village Shopping Centre is located in the inner suburb, with 113 stores occupying $41,000\,\text{m}^2$ of floor space (see Figure 4.2). The two shopping centers have a very different tenant mix or retail structure, with Dufferin Mall catering to customers who seek for affordable goods and services, and Bayview Village targeting affluent consumers and offering a luxurious shopping experience. The choice of a particular store mix for a shopping center is not a random act on the part of the mall management and the retail planners; it is a purposeful design to meet the needs of the consumers in its prescribed trade area. A trade area analysis and comparison of the two shopping centers serves to explain the rationale of their respective retail tenant mix.

A circular trade area with a 3-km radius is created around each mall, which is then overlaid on top of the census layer (see Figure 4.2). Because the trade area circle (known as a buffer in GIS) intersects the boundaries of some census tracts, these census tracts are split using the circular buffer. After splitting, only the portions that are inside the buffer, along with the census tracts that are entirely within the buffer, are included in the trade area. Eight census variables are selected for trade analysis and comparison, as they are believed to best represent the market conditions (both demand and purchasing power) for the two shopping centers. These variables are:

- population size
- number of households
- average household income
- prevalence of low income (based on after-tax low-income measure, as a percentage)
- unemployment rate
- average value of dwellings
- percentage of population aged 25–64 years, with a Bachelor or above-Bachelor level of education.
- percentage of recent immigrants

Only the "count" variables (such as population size and number of households) are split, using the method of "*area proportion*". The average/rate/percentage variables are not split because they are not affected by polygon splitting. When the average/rate/percentage variables are aggregated for the entire trade area, their totals are calculated first, and then averaged for the trade area. This is to avoid "calculating average from averages". For example, when average household income for the entire trade area is calculated, the sum of household income for each census tract (CT) (Σ income) is calculated by multiplying that CT's average household income by the number of households in that same CT. The total household income for the entire trade area ($\Sigma\Sigma$ income) is then calculated by aggregating the household income of all the CTs in the trade area. The trade area average is calculated by dividing the total household income ($\Sigma\Sigma$ income) by the total number of households. Similarly, when unemployment rate is calculated for the trade area, the total number of unemployed persons is first calculated for the entire trade area; this is then divided by the total number of persons between 15 and 65 years of age and is multiplied by 100. The market conditions of the two trade areas are summarized in Table 8.2.

The physical size of the two trade areas is the same: $28\,\text{km}^2$ (area$=\pi*3^2$). However, the Dufferin Mall trade area consists of 66 census tracts, whereas the Bayview Village trade area is composed of only 39 census tracts. Accordingly, the Dufferin Mall trade area contains a population of 234,423 persons and 108,255 households, twice as

Table 8.2 Trade Area Comparison for Dufferin Mall and Bayview Village Shopping Centre

Trade area characteristics*	Dufferin Mall	Bayview Village
Number of census tracts	66	39
Population size	234,423	125,563
Number of households	108,255	52,128
Average household income ($)	76,800	103,900
Prevalence of low income (based on after-tax low-income measure, in %)	19.1	21.8
Unemployment rate (%)	5.0	4.5
Average value of dwellings ($)	566,800	614,000
Percentage of population aged 25–64 years, with a Bachelor or above-Bachelor level of education (%)	45.3	61.1
Percentage of recent immigrants	6.1	11.0
Sales potential (in million $)	1,662.8	1,083.2

Note
* based on 2011 Canadian census.

many as in the Bayview Village trade area. This shows clearly that the Dufferin Mall trade area has a much higher population density with a much larger consumer market than does Bayview Village. When average household income is compared, however, the Bayview Village trade area appears to be much more affluent: $103,900 vs. $76,800, or 35 percent higher than the Dufferin Mall trade area. The relative affluence of the Bayview Village trade area is also reflected by its average dwelling value: $614,000 vs. $566,800 (or 8.3 percent higher). The higher household income in the Bayview Village trade area should be closely related to its higher percentage of population with a Bachelor or above-Bachelor level of education—61.1 percent vs. 45.3 percent—as these people tend to hold higher-earning jobs. This part of the population also has a tendency to purchase more expensive and luxury consumer goods. Unexpectedly, the Bayview Village trade area has higher prevalence of low income (based on after-tax low-income measure), at 22 percent, compared with 19 percent for the Dufferin Mall trade area. Also, the proportion of recent immigrants in the Bayview Village trade area, who often have precarious employment and therefore low income (or no income), is higher than in the Dufferin Mall trade area. This may contribute to the high prevalence of low income. It is reasonable to infer (and is also frequently reported in local newspapers) that many recent immigrants who settle in the affluent Bayview Village neighborhood are property rich but income poor, meaning that they purchased expensive homes with cash brought from their home countries, not with money they earned in Canada.

In sum, it is by no coincidence that Bayview Village Shopping Centre hosts expensive and high-end retail stores, because the residents in the trade area tend to be highly educated consumers with higher income. The different tenant mix in Dufferin Mall makes sense because the stores suit the consumer profile of the mall's trade area. The same retailers as those in Bayview Village would not attract enough sales to make a profit if they were located in Dufferin Mall. Such a trade analysis is useful not only for the shopping center as a whole, but also for the individual mall tenants. As the demographic profile evolves and changes over time, the shopping center management can use the analytical results for recruiting new tenants, when existing leases end or are up for renewal.

The two shopping centers can also be compared by the sales potentials (or potential consumer expenditure) in their trade areas. In general, sales potentials are estimated through multiplication of the total number of households by average household expenditure on the types of merchandise carried by the store type under consideration (Richards, 1984). Specifically, sales potential for the two shopping centers can be calculated as the following:

> Sales potential = number of households * average household income * percentage of household income spent on consumer goods and services typically sold in shopping centers * probability of consumers purchasing these goods and services from the shopping center

Based on the Survey of Household Spending data, it is estimated that on average, consumers in metropolitan Toronto spend about 20 percent of their household income on goods and services typically sold in shopping centers. Since the circular method follows the spatial monopoly approach in defining trade area, the probability of the consumers who live in the trade area patronizing the respective shopping center is assumed to be 1. Using the above formula, sales potential in each census tract is calculated first; the figures are then aggregated for the entire trade area. By this estimate, the sales potential in Dufferin Mall's trade area is $1,662.8 million, and that in the Bayview Village's trade area is $1,083.2 million (see Table 8.2). It should be pointed out that the sales potentials are calculated based on census data from estimated expenditures generated by the "night population"; expenditures from the "daytime population" are not captured.

A cautionary note: the circular method may result in an incorrect delineation of the trade area because it does not account for transportation barriers such as rivers or railroad tracks that may cross through a trade area and restrict access to a retail site.

Travel Distance/Time

This method uses travel distance or time to define the trade area. Depending on the type of retail destination, pre-selected travel distance can be 2 km or 5 km; pre-selected travel time can be five minutes or ten minutes. Distance and travel time are influenced by the characteristics of the road network (such as speed limit, one-way street, number of lanes, road capacity, etc.) The trade area defined using this method is irregular in shape, often elongated along major transportation routes (see Figure 8.1). Once an irregular-shaped trade area is delineated, it can be overlaid on top of the census layer in the GIS environment in the same way as is done with the circular method, to extract demographic and socio-

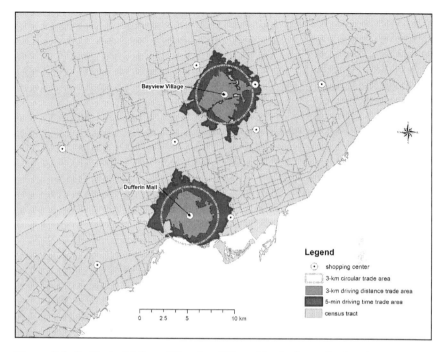

Figure 8.1 Dufferin Mall and Bayview Village Trade Areas Defined Using 3 km Driving Distance and 5-minute Driving Time.

Note
A driving speed of 60 km/h is assumed.

economic data for further analysis. This method has the ability to produce more accurate trade areas than the circular method, because it takes into consideration transportation friction.

Customer Spotting

Customer spotting is an empirically based methodology for trade area delineation. It includes several methods by which retailers can "spot" customer origins on a map. These include license plate survey, customer survey, customer records, and customer activities. Since most corporate retailers keep extensive transaction records linked to residential addresses, the method of customer records is more commonly used than the other methods. Figure 8.2 shows the residential locations (by six-digit postal codes) of a Food Basics supermarket in the City of Toronto. There is obviously a distance decay in the distribution of customers from the location of the supermarket. A buffer can be

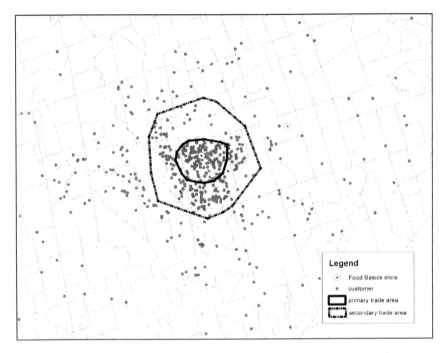

Figure 8.2 Trade Area of a Food Basics Supermarket Defined Using the Method of Customer Spotting.

Note
The primary trade area contains 60% of the reported customers; the secondary trade area—the second ring—contains the next 20% of the reported customers.

drawn that includes 60 or 80 percent of the recorded shoppers, or of the total sales, and be defined as the trade area of the store. ESRI's *Business Analyst* provides the option of drawing circular shaped buffers or convex-shaped trade areas. The buffer can then be used to extract demographic and socioeconomic data for further analysis of the trade area and estimate of sales potentials.

METHODS OF DELINEATING TRADE AREAS FOR A SET OF STORES

Thiessen Polygon

Thiessen Polygon is a geometric procedure for delimiting theoretical trade areas for a network of stores. This method assumes that the retail stores for which trade areas are being delineated are similar in size and sell similar products at similar prices; and that consumers purchase goods from the closest store to minimize travel distance/time. It is most suitable for delimiting trade areas of chain stores.

Thiessen Polygons are constructed following a three-step procedure:

1   Draw lines to join each store with its close neighbors (but no line should cross other lines).
2   Find the mid-point of each line segment.
3   At the mid-point of each line segment, draw a boundary line at a 90° angle with the first set of lines.

The second set of lines form a series of polygons, which represent the theoretical trade areas of the stores. The theoretical trade areas defined with this method never overlap with each other, because each store is the monopoly in its own trade area. This method is rooted on, but a variant of, the central place theory. If the set of stores are evenly distributed, each polygon would be a standard hexagon, as is depicted in the central place theory. In the real urban retail landscape, however, stores are seldom evenly distributed; the trade areas are hence distorted to irregular Thiessen Polygons.

The Thiessen Polygon method has been computerized in all known GIS software, in which it is known as the *equal competition* method. In general, it works well for chain stores that sell the same products at the same prices, but is not recommended for use to delineate trade area for stores that are different in size or sell different products, because it does not take into consideration store attractiveness. This method also works well in areas with minimal physical barriers to movement and transportation, as it does not recognize the existence of barriers and ignores their effects.

In addition to delineating trade areas, the Thiessen Polygon method can be used to assist with store site selection. For example, it is reported that a fast food restaurant chain used it to add new outlets along the edges, or at the vertices, of the Thiessen Polygon-shaped trade areas of the existing stores (Jones & Simmons, 1993). Such locations have the property of maximizing distances from the sister stores and therefore minimizing internal competition.

Reilly's Law of Retail Gravitation

Reilly's Law of Retail Gravitation was one of the first attempts at developing a formal method for demarcating retail trade areas (Reilly, 1929;

1931). It was later formalized by Converse (1949) as the *breaking point formula*. Derived from the gravity model, this method states that if two retail facilities (A and B) share retail trade from the same surrounding area, the market boundary between them can be calculated using the following formula:

$$breaking\ point\ (A-B) = \frac{distance\ (A-B)}{1 + \sqrt{\dfrac{attractiveness(B)}{attractiveness(A)}}}$$

Attractiveness can be expressed as the floor area of a retail store, or as the number of stores in a shopping center, or as parking space. The underlying assumption is that the larger the store, or the more stores a shopping center has, the more varieties of merchandise are carried, and, therefore, the more attractive the retail facility is. *Distance* can be expressed as physical distance, time distance (travel time), or cost distance (travel cost).

Reilly's Law also follows a three-step procedure in delineating trade areas:

1   Draw straight lines to connect each store/center with its close neighbors.
2   Calculate breaking points between each pair of adjacent stores using the formula.
3   Draw boundary lines through the breaking points at 90° angles with the first set of lines.

The first and the third steps are the same as in the Thiessen Polygon method. Only the second step is different: that is, the breaking points are determined by calculation using the gravity model, instead of being pinpointed at the middle of the first set of line segments.

Unlike Thiessen Polygon, Reilly's Law is suitable for delineating trade areas of stores or shopping centers of different sizes. For example, say we wish to determine the market boundary between Eaton Centre and Scarborough Town Centre—two superregional shopping centers in the City of Toronto. Eaton Centre has 326 stores; Scarborough Town Centre has 221 stores; the distance between them is 16.7 km:

$$BP(Eaton - Scarborough) = \frac{16.7}{1 + \sqrt{\dfrac{221}{326}}} = 9.16\ (km)$$

When trade area boundaries are drawn, the distance is measured from Facility A (in this example Eaton Centre) to the breaking point. Logically, the breaking point is always closer to the smaller facility but further away from the large facility. This gives the larger facility a bigger trade area.

Although conceptually sound and a better method than Thiessen Polygon, Reilly's Law has never been computerized in any of the known GIS software. In practice, the probability-based Huff Model (discussed next) is more commonly used, because it produces more realistic trade areas while incorporating all the principles of Reilly's Law. In other words, the Huff Model is a superior method and eliminates the need for Reilly's Law.

The Huff Model

The Huff Model is a spatial interaction model developed by David Huff in 1963 (Huff, 1963), and has since endured the test of time and become an established theory in spatial analysis of commercial activity. The model is based on the principle that the probability of a given consumer visiting, and purchasing goods, at a given store is a function of the distance to that store, the store's attractiveness, and the distance and attractiveness of the competing stores. Specifically, it calculates gravity-based probabilities of consumers at each origin location patronizing each store in the study area. The probability values at each origin location can be used to generate probability surfaces and delineate trade areas for each store in the study area. With the probabilities, sales potential can also be calculated for each origin location, based on disposable income, population, and expenditure.

The original Huff Model was expressed in the form of the following formula:

$$P_{ij} = \frac{\dfrac{(A_j)}{(D_{ij})^\lambda}}{\displaystyle\sum_{j=1}^{n} \dfrac{(A_j)}{(D_{ij})^\lambda}}$$

(the original Huff Model)

where

- P_{ij} = probability of customer living in origin i shopping at store j
- A_j = attractiveness of store j

- D_{ij} = distance between the origin of customer i and the location of store j
- λ = exponent for distance
- n = total number of shopping alternatives in the study area including store j itself

Huff later extended the model to allow inclusion of more than one attractiveness variable and a weight (α) for the attractiveness variables, to reflect their relative importance and contributions to the probability (see Huff, 2003). The extended Huff Model is expressed in the following formula:

$$P_{ij} = \frac{\dfrac{(A_j)^{\alpha}}{(D_{ij})^{\lambda}}}{\displaystyle\sum_{i=1}^{n} \dfrac{(A_j)^{\alpha}}{(D_{ii})^{\lambda}}}$$

(the extended Huff Model)

As a gravity model, the Huff Model depends heavily on the calculation of distance. The underpinning assumption in the Huff Model is also that individual consumers are more likely to shop at the location closest to them. As the distance between the shopping destination and the location of a customer increases, the probability of going to that location decreases. Two conceptualizations of distance can be used: traditional Euclidean (straight-line) distance, and travel time along a road network. The attractiveness of a store can be measured by square footage of floor space, number of parking spaces, or number of stores in a shopping center. Attractiveness can also be expressed as a single number that combines all the factors that make a store/shopping center attractive. This single number is usually referred to as an index of composite attractiveness. The distance exponent is a parameter that models the rate of distance decay in the drawing power of the store, as potential customers are located further away from the store. Increasing the exponent would decrease the relative influence of a store on more distant customers. It is usually estimated empirically, based on survey of shopping preferences of individuals in the study area. Understandably, the task of obtaining actual shopping preferences for different products can be time-consuming and expensive. When survey data are not available, it is suggested that the distance exponent should take a value between 1 and 3: 1 is used for high-order goods that are purchased with low frequency (i.e., durables and specialty goods); 3 is used for low-order goods that are purchased with high frequency (i.e., convenience goods such as groceries); 2 is used for other types of goods (such as apparel and accessories, etc.).

The Huff Model is useful for generating customer volume estimates for either existing stores or proposed new stores. It helps to answer such strategic questions as: (1) what would happen to my trade area if my store expanded by 50 percent? (2) what would happen to my trade area if an existing competitor were to leave the market? (3) what would happen to my trade area if a competitor introduced a new store in the market? (Hernandez et al., 2004)

Operation of the Huff Model requires the use of three sets of data:

- a list of stores (or shopping centers) with their locations and attributes for attractiveness
- a list of building block areas (census tracts or dissemination areas) with associated demographic and socioeconomic data (for market size and purchasing power calculation)
- a matrix of distance (or travel time) between the centroid of each building block and each store

Usually, three critical probabilities are used as markers of trade areas: census tracts or dissemination areas with 0.6 or higher probability form the *primary trade area* of a store; those with a probability of 0.4–0.59 form the *secondary trade area*, and those with probability of less than 0.4 form the *tertiary trade area*. Tertiary trade areas are given much lower priority by retailers in their marketing and promotion efforts.

The Huff Model has been built into a number of GIS software packages, including ESRI's *Business Analyst*. In the GIS platform, not only is calculation of probabilities made faster, but the output can be communicated and visualized easily in understandable forms such as tables and maps. However, these fuzzy trade areas need to be viewed on a store-by-store basis, and, unlike trade areas defined using the deterministic approach, it is impossible to depict carto-graphically the trade areas of an entire store network (Hernandez et al., 2004). Despite the general applicability of the model, it has not always been used correctly; the biggest challenge is to estimate the parameters (Huff, 2003). There are two ways to estimate the parameters. One way is to make an "educated guess". This is used when sample data are not available. It depends on the experience of the analyst and his/her knowledge of the local market. Often, several guesses are made for experiment to find out which parameters generate the best results. The second way is to statistically estimate or calibrate the model. This requires the use of a set of sample data to calibrate the parameters and the weights. Several parameters are experimented with, and a measure of goodness of fit is produced. Calculations are undertaken to estimate the direction and amount that each of the parameters should change to improve the fit. Each change is then entered into the model, and the model is re-run until the best values that give rise to the best fit to the sample data are found (Goodchild, 2005).

In the rest of the chapter, two examples are presented to illustrate the operation and application of the Huff Model. In the first example, the original Huff Model with a single attractiveness variable is used for simplicity. In the second example, the extended Huff Model is used with a composite attractiveness index, for a comprehensive under-standing of the method.

Example 1[1]

Figure 8.3 shows a hypothetical market consisting of ten census tracts (CT), which is served by three supermarkets. For clarity, the three sets of data typically required for the use of the Huff Model are presented in Table 8.3. Since groceries are low-order goods purchased with high frequency, consumers are usually sensitive to travel distance; so $\lambda = 3$ is used in calculating probabilities. It is also assumed that, on average, 12 percent of household income is spent on groceries purchased from supermarkets.

First, $\dfrac{(A_j)}{(D_{ij})^3}$, which represents the perceived utility of store j by a con-sumer at location i, is calculated for each CT and for each supermarket:

- for CT1 and Supermarket 1, this is calculated as: $\dfrac{(12000)}{3^3} = 444.44;$

- for CT1 and Supermarket 2, this is calculated as: $\dfrac{(6000)}{8^3} = 11.72;$

- for CT1 and Supermarket 3, this is calculated as: $\dfrac{(15000)}{6^3} = 69.44;$

- $\sum \dfrac{(A_j)}{(D_{ij})\lambda}$ is therefore 525.61 (see Table 8.4).

The probabilities that residents living in each CT purchase groceries from each of the three competing markets are then calculated:

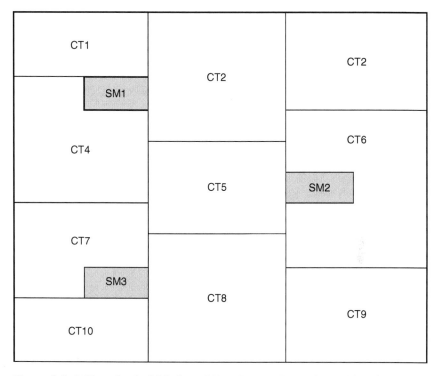

Figure 8.3 A Hypothetical Market of Ten Census Tracts Served by Three Supermarkets.

Note

CT = census tract; SM = supermarket.

$$\text{probability}_{(CT1\text{-}SM1)} = \frac{444.44}{525.61} = 0.846$$

$$\text{probability}_{(CT1\text{-}SM2)} = \frac{11.72}{525.61} = 0.022$$

$$\text{probability}_{(CT1\text{-}SM3)} = \frac{69.44}{525.61} = 0.132$$

Using the calculated probability, sales potentials are estimated for each competing store. For example,

Sales potential for SM1 from
CT1 = 400 * 60,000 * 0.12 * 0.846 = $2.44 million

Table 8.3 Demographic and Socioeconomic Conditions of the Hypothetical Study Area, with Store Size and Distance Matrix

Census tract (CT) no.	No. of households	Average household income ($)	Total household income ($ million)	Total demand for groceries (12% of household income, in $ million)	Distance to supermarket (km)		
					Supermarket 1 (12,000 sq.ft)	Supermarket 2 (6,000 sq.ft)	Supermarket 3 (15,000 sq.ft)
1	400	60,000	24.00	2.88	3	8	6
2	900	45,000	40.50	4.86	4	6	6
3	600	50,000	30.00	3.60	7	5	7
4	850	75,000	63.75	7.65	2	2	4
5	550	70,000	38.50	4.62	6	3	4
6	950	63,000	59.85	7.18	8	2	6.5
7	650	48,000	31.20	3.74	6	8	2
8	1,000	52,000	52.00	6.24	8	4	3.5
9	350	80,000	28.00	3.36	10	5	7
10	550	85,000	46.75	5.61	8	9	1.5
Total	6,800	60,963	414.55	49.75			

Sales potential for SM2 from
CT1 = 400 * 60,000 * 0.12 * 0.022 = $0.06 million

Sales potential for SM 3 from
CT1 = 400 * 60,000 * 0.12 * 0.132 = $0.38 million

The total sales potential for all three supermarkets from CT1 is $2.88 million, which equals the total demand for groceries by residents living in CT1 (see Table 8.4). Also using the calculated probabilities, sales potentials for each of the three supermarkets from all ten census tracts are calculated as $12.79 million, $15.56 million, and $21.39 million, the sum of which equals the total demand for groceries in the entire market (see Table 8.4).

It is important to note that the total probability that residents in each census tract purchase groceries from the three competing supermarkets always equals 1. This is an important property of the Huff Model, which means that every time an existing store is closed, or a new store is added to the market, the probabilities change, and the total demand and the total sales potential are redistributed among the competing stores.

Example 2

Vaughan Mills Mall, an enclosed regional shopping center located in the suburb of metropolitan Toronto, opened for business in 2004. The mall has almost 1.4 million square feet (110,000 m²) of retail space with over 200 retail stores, restaurants, and entertainment outlets. It is also the only superregional shopping center built in the metropolitan region in the new millennium. In January 2013, plans were announced to add 150,000 square feet and 50 new stores to the mall, which was completed in late 2014. On March 17, 2016, Saks Fifth Avenue Off 5th opened a 32,000-square-foot (3,000 m²) store in the mall; on September 28, 2018, the Japanese retailer Uniqlo opened a fashion store there. The mall also introduced the first Legoland Discovery Centre in Canada.

The addition of Vaughan Mills Mall would obviously have had impacts on the adjacent regional shopping centers, as it competes for business with them, particularly Promenade Mall and Yorkdale Shopping Centre (see Figure 8.4). The impacts can be examined through a trade area analysis using the Huff Model. Impacts are described with reference to changes in number of census tracts in their primary ($p \geq 0.6$) and secondary ($0.6 > p \geq 0.4$) trade areas, as well as to changes in sales potential in the trade areas.

Table 8.4 Calculation of Probability and Sales Potential for the Three Hypothetical Supermarkets

CT	A_j/D_{ij}^3				Probability				Sales potential ($ million)			
	for SM1	for SM2	for SM3	Sum	for SM1	for SM2	for SM3	Total	for SM1	for SM2	for SM3	Total
1	444.44	11.72	69.44	525.61	0.846	0.022	0.132	1	2.44	0.06	0.38	2.88
2	187.50	27.78	69.44	284.72	0.659	0.098	0.244	1	3.20	0.47	1.19	4.86
3	34.99	48.00	43.73	126.72	0.276	0.379	0.345	1	0.99	1.36	1.24	3.60
4	1,500.00	750.00	234.38	2,484.38	0.604	0.302	0.094	1	4.62	2.31	0.72	7.65
5	55.56	222.22	234.38	512.15	0.108	0.434	0.458	1	0.50	2.00	2.11	4.62
6	23.44	750.00	54.62	828.06	0.028	0.906	0.066	1	0.20	6.50	0.47	7.18
7	55.56	11.72	1,875.00	1,942.27	0.029	0.006	0.965	1	0.11	0.02	3.61	3.74
8	23.44	93.75	349.85	467.04	0.050	0.201	0.749	1	0.31	1.25	4.67	6.24
9	12.00	48.00	43.73	103.73	0.116	0.463	0.422	1	0.39	1.55	1.42	3.36
10	23.44	8.23	4,444.44	4,476.11	0.005	0.002	0.993	1	0.03	0.01	5.57	5.61
Total	–	–	–	–	–	–	–	–	12.79	15.56	21.39	49.75

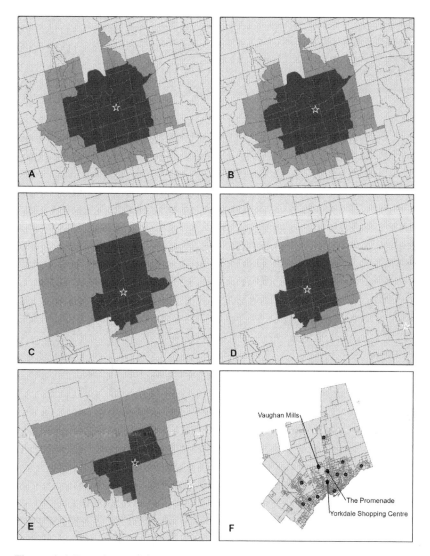

Figure 8.4 Locations of the 13 Regional Shopping Centers and the Primary and Secondary Trade Areas of Yorkdale Shopping Centre, Promenade Shopping Centre, and Vaughan Mills Mall.

Notes
- A (top left) = Yorkdale trade areas without Vaughan Mills
- B (top right) = Yorkdale trade areas with Vaughan Mills
- C (middle left) = Promenade trade areas without Vaughan Mills
- D (middle right) = Promenade trade areas with Vaughan Mills
- E (bottom left) = Vaughan Mills Mall trade areas
- F (bottom right) = the 13 regional shopping centers

Primary trade areas are shown in darker grey, secondary trade areas in lighter grey.

An automated Huff Model posted on www.arcgis.com ("Huff Model", 2012) is used for this case study. This version of the Huff Model is less versatile than the one in ESRI's *Business Analyst*, though both use *ArcGIS* as the platform. It resembles the original Huff Model and allows for use of only one attractiveness variable. However, it is open source and more accessible to instructors and students (as it is free of cost). To mitigate its limitation in handling multiple attractiveness variables, the model is modified by Ryerson University researchers, and a calculator app is added to it for computing a composite attractiveness index.[2]

Two sets of data are used: a list of regional shopping centers with center attributes (see Table 8.5); and the CT-level census for the Toronto CMA. Distances between (the centroid of) each CT and each shopping center are calculated by the automated Huff Model. The model is run twice. In the first run, Vaughan Mill Mall is excluded, and the probabilities that residents in each census tract patronize each of the 12 regional shopping centers are calculated. On the basis of these probabilities, the primary and secondary trade areas of Promenade and Yorkdale shopping centers are delineated and mapped. In the second run, Vaughan Mill Mall is included, and the probabilities that residents in each census tract patronize each of the 13 regional shopping centers are calculated, on the basis of which, the primary and secondary trade areas of Promenade and Yorkdale shopping centers are re-defined and mapped.

There are three important considerations in the use of the Huff Model: (1) selection of appropriate attractiveness indicators—either a single indicator or a composite index; (2) standardizing of the indicators if their ranges of values are vastly different; and (3) weighting of indicators if their relative importance varies. Before running the Huff Model for the shopping center case study, a composite "attractiveness" variable is created using four shopping center attributes: floor space, number of stores, number of fashion stores, and number of department stores. Each attribute variable is re-scaled (or standardized) using the *minimum score* formula, which compares each value of a variable to the minimum value in that variable (see Malczewski and Rinner, 2015; Matadeen, 2019):

$$Standardized\ Variable = \frac{Var\ X}{Min}$$

Taking "floor space" as an example, the standardized "floor space" value for Bramalea City Center becomes: $1{,}052{,}430 / 743{,}900 = 1.41$;

Table 8.5 Thirteen Regional Shopping Centers in the Toronto CMA

Shopping center	Original value				Standardized and weighted value				Composite attractiveness index
	Floor space (sq.ft)	No. of store	No. of department stores*	No. of fashion stores	Floor space	No. of stores	No. of department stores*	No. of fashion stores	
Bramalea City Centre	1,052,430	269	3	65	2.83	4.36	3	2.95	11.64
Eaton Centre	1,723,220	288	2	87	4.63	4.67	2	3.95	14.25
Erin Mills Town Centre	743,900	193	3	55	2.00	3.13	3	2.50	9.13
Fairview Mall	894,400	266	2	82	2.40	4.31	2	3.73	11.44
Markville Shopping Centre	967,780	213	3	59	2.60	3.45	3	2.68	10.23
Pickering Town Centre	800,875	238	3	64	2.15	3.86	3	2.91	10.42
Scarborough Town Centre	1,085,750	226	3	65	2.92	3.66	3	2.95	11.03
Sherway Gardens	1,035,220	217	2	69	2.78	3.52	2	3.14	10.44
Square One	1,376,000	322	4	112	3.70	5.22	4	5.09	16.01
The Promenade	901,925	185	2	61	2.42	3.00	2	2.77	9.19
Upper Canada Mall	1,015,880	240	3	68	2.73	3.89	3	3.09	11.21
Yorkdale Shopping Centre	1,597,450	217	3	72	4.29	3.52	3	3.27	12.58
Vaughan Mills*	1,400,000	224	1	95	3.76	3.63	1	4.32	12.71

Note
* Vaughan Mills Mall does not have any conventional department store; a value of "1" (the smallest value possible) is assigned to number of stores in Vaughan Mills as a value of "0" results in zero probability. The number of department stores in the other shopping centers includes Sears and Zellers, which were recently closed.

the standardized "floor space" for Eaton Centre becomes: 1,723,220 / 743,900 = 2.32; and so on. With this method, all the standardized values are greater than or equal to 1 (see Table 8.5). The standardized variables are then used to compute the composite attractiveness index:

Attractiveness index = (floor space * weight) + (number of stores * weight) + (number of fashion stores * weight) + (number of department stores * weight)

Researchers use different weighting methods to assign weights. Some methods make the total weights for all the participating variables equal to 1; others assign weights from 1 to 10 (see Church & Murray, 2009: 111). Selection of weights depends heavily on a researcher's knowledge and experience. In this shopping center case study, weights between 1 and 3 are assigned to the four attractiveness variables to reflect their relative importance (as perceived by the authors of this book):

2 for floor space
3 for number of stores
2.5 for number of fashion stores
1 for department stores

Larger weights are given to total number of stores and number of fashion stores because they are nowadays the main reasons for shoppers to visit a large shopping center. A low weight is assigned to department store to reflect its declining influence in attracting shoppers to a regional or superregional shopping center. As hard goods (such as home appliances and furniture) have moved out of department stores in shopping centers, more spaces are occupied by soft goods retailers, especially fashion retailers. Calculation of the attractiveness index using the calculator app is illustrated in Figure 8.5. Probabilities are then calculated using the composite attractiveness index (because the automated Huff Model has "room" for only one attractiveness variable). Calculation of the probabilities using the automated Huff Model is shown in Figure 8.6.

On the basis of the probabilities, the primary and secondary trade areas of Promenade and Yorkdale shopping centers, as well as Vaughan Mills Mall, are delineated and mapped (see Figure 8.4), and demographic and socioeconomic data are extracted and aggregated for

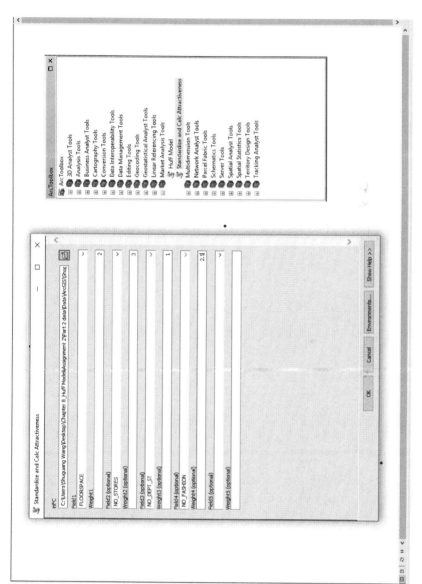

Figure 8.5 Screen Shot of Calculation of Composite Attractiveness Using the Calculator App.

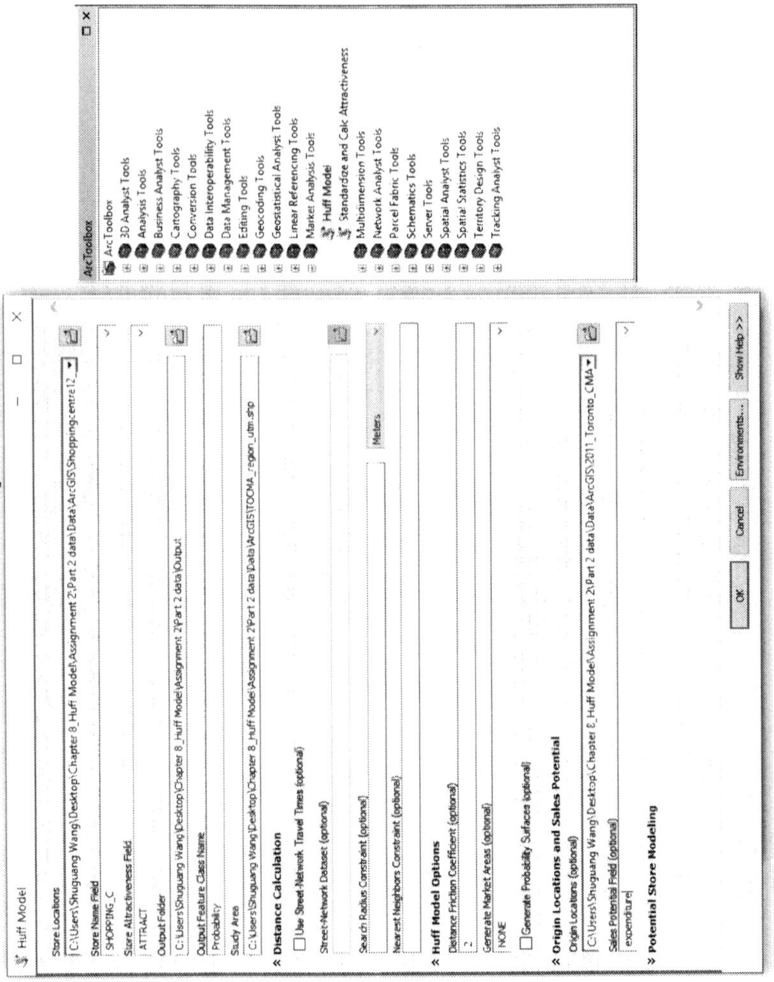

Figure 8.6 Screen Shot of Calculation of Probabilities Using the Automated Huff Model.

these trade areas. Sales potential in each census tract is calculated using the following formula:

> Sales potential = number of households * average household income * percentage of income spent on consumer goods and services typically sold in shopping centers * probability of consumers purchasing these goods and services from the shopping facility

Based on the Survey of Household Spending data, it is estimated that consumers in metropolitan Toronto spend about 20 percent of their household income on goods and services typically sold in regional shopping centers. Unlike the circular method that follows the spatial monopoly approach in defining trade area and assumes that the probability of the consumers who live in the trade area and patronize the respective shopping center is 1, the Huff Model calculates probability for each individual census tract. Using the above formula, sales potential in each census tract is calculated first; the figures are then aggregated for the primary and secondary trade areas.

The impacts of Vaughan Mills Mall on Yorkdale and Promenade shopping centers are summarized in Table 8.6. It has reduced both the size of the trade areas and the sales potentials in them for Yorkdale and Promenade. For Yorkdale, the numbers of CTs that form its primary and secondary trade areas are reduced by three and five, and sales potentials are reduced by $61.7 million and $57.6 million, respectively. For Promenade, the numbers of CTs that form its primary and secondary trade areas are reduced by three and eight, and sales potentials reduced by $169.2 million and $62.3 million respectively. As can

Table 8.6 Impacts of Vaughan Mills Mall on Yorkdale and Promenade Shopping Centers*

Trade area		Yorkdale		Promenade		Vaughan Mills
		Without VM	With VM	Without VM	With VM	
Primary	# of CT	32	29	20	17	17
	Sales potential ($ million)	864.9	803.2	652.3	483.1	465.6
Secondary	# of CT	51	46	21	13	11
	Sales potential ($ million)	861.8	804.2	313.1	250.8	237.1

Note
* calculated using 2011 Canadian census.

be seen from Table 8.6 and Figure 8.4, the Huff Model is used not only to assist in examining the impacts of a new shopping center on existing centers, but also to define the trade areas of the new shopping center—Vaughan Mills—and estimate the sales potentials in its primary and second trade areas.

While the example serves well the purpose of illustrating the operation of the Huff Model, the estimated sales potentials may not be close to the real sales. Shopping center management may not necessarily use $p \geq 0.6$ and $0.6 > p \geq 0.4$ to define their primary and secondary trade areas. As Ghosh & McLafferty (1987) emphasize and warn, all Huff Model inputs, exponents, trade area size, and results require detailed analysis by someone who is well versed in the operation of such a model. Some calibration is always required to account for other factors such as leakage. For instance, people may not buy all their goods and services (with 20 percent of their household income) from the closest shopping center, and some of that spending may leak to other trade areas. In fact, Vaughan Mills has a number of factory outlets which are not available in the other two shopping centers, which may attract a considerable number of shoppers from its tertiary trade area. Adjacent to Canada's Wonderland—a 134-hectare recreation and entertainment theme park—Vaughan Mills also attracts a large number of tourists in the summer time. It even provides a complimentary shuttle bus service between the downtown Union Station and the mall in the summer months from June 1 to September 30, then again over the holiday season from November 29 to December 26. It is difficult to incorporate these additional factors in the Huff Model. In sum, the Huff Model is better used for specific categories of retailers than for large shopping centers with diverse tenant mixes.

KEY POINTS OF THE CHAPTER

- Trade area analysis often goes hand in hand with retail location analysis, as they are complementary procedures. It is conducted as part of an evaluation of a potential store site; it is also used to monitor and manage trade areas of existing stores, track trade area changes, and measure cannibalization.
- Church & Murray (2009) distinguish two types of trade area: descriptive and prescriptive. Descriptive trade areas are defined based on data of existing customers. Prescriptive trade areas are delineated using mathematically and statistically based modeling,

and are based on assumptions or inference of shopping habits and consumption patterns of potential customers. In the modern era of "big data", the importance of descriptive trade area is expected to grow.

- There are three approaches to trade area delimitation, each of which is represented by different methods and techniques. These approaches are *spatial monopoly, market penetration,* and *dispersed market.*

- Two types of data are used in trade area analysis: primary data and secondary data. Primary data are compiled by retailers at POS or through online orders. The commonly used secondary data are from the census. Census data are useful to identify potential customers, but many of the potential customers in a trade area do not necessarily patronize the store.

- The circular trade area method is the easiest, quickest, and least expensive method of trade area delineation. This method assumes that the transport surface is uniform, and the store is equally accessible from all directions. Demographic and socioeconomic data for the trade area can be extracted from the circle for further analysis.

- Trade areas defined using the travel distance/time method are irregular-shaped polygons, often elongated along major transportation routes. Demographic and socioeconomic data for the trade area can also be extracted from these trade areas for further analysis. This method has the ability to produce more accurate trade areas than the circular method, because it takes into consideration transportation friction.

- The Thiessen Polygon works well for chain stores that sell the same types of products at the same price levels, but is not recommended for use to delineate trade areas for stores that are different in size or sell different products, because it does not take into consideration store attractiveness. This method also works well in areas with minimal physical barriers to movement and transportation, because it does not recognize the existence of barriers and ignores their effects. In addition, this method can be used to assist with store site selection (along the edges, or at the vertices, of the polygons).

- The probability-based Huff Model is useful for generating customer volume estimate for either existing stores or proposed new stores. It helps to answer such strategic questions as: (1) what would happen to my trade area if my store expanded by 50 percent?

(2) what would happen to my trade area if an existing competitor were to leave the market? (3) what would happen to my trade area if a competitor introduced a new store in the market? Operation of the Huff Model requires the use of three sets of data: (1) a list of stores with their locations and attributes; (2) a list of building block areas with associated demographic and socioeconomic data; and (3) a matrix of distance between each building block and each store.

NOTES

1 This case study is adapted from lecture materials conceptualized by Maurice Yeates of Ryerson University.
2 The calculator app is developed by Michael MacDonald of Ryerson University.

REFERENCES

Applebaum, W. (1968). *Store Location Strategy*. Boston, MA: Addison-Wesley.
Church, R. L. & Murray, A. T. (2009). *Business Site Selection, Location Analysis, and GIS*. Hoboken, NJ: John Wiley & Sons, Inc.
Converse, P. D. (1949). New law of retail gravitation. *Journal of Marketing, 14*(3), 379–384.
Davis, R. L. (1976). *Marketing Geography with Special Reference to Retailing*. London, England: Methuen.
Ghosh, A. & McLafferty, S. L. (1987). *Location Strategies for Retail and Service Firms*. Lexington, MA: Lexington Books.
Goodchild, M. (2005). GIS, spatial analysis, and modelling overview. In D. J. Maguire, M. Batty, & M. F. Goodchild (Eds.), *GIS, Spatial Analysis and Modelling* (pp. 1–18). Redlands, CA: ESRI Press.
Hernandez, T., Lea, T., & Bermingham, P. (2004). *What Is in a Trade Area?* Toronto, Canada: Center for the Study of Commercial Activity, Ryerson University.
Huff, D. (1963). A probabilistic analysis of shopping center trade areas. *Land Economics, 39*(1), 81–90.
Huff, D. (2003). Parameter estimation in the Huff Model. *ArcUser*, October–December, 34–36.
"Huff Model". (2012). www.arcgis.com/home/item.html?id=f4769668fc3f 486a992955ce55caca18.
Jones, K. & Simmons, J. (1993). *Location, Location, Location: Analyzing the Retail Environment*. Toronto, Canada: Nelson Canada.
Malczewski, J. & Rinner, C. (2015). *Multi-criteria Decision Analysis in Geographic Information Science*. New York, NY: Springer.

Matadeen, R. (2019). *An Open-Source Multi-Criteria Decision Analysis Toolkit to Calculate Retail Site Attractiveness for the Huff Model* (Major Research Paper for the degree of Master of Spatial Analysis). Toronto, Canada: Ryerson University.

Reilly, W. J. (1929). *Method for the Study of Retail Trade Relationships.* (Research Monograph No. 4). Austin, TX: University of Texas Press.

Reilly, W. J. (1931). *The Law of Retail Gravitation.* New York, NY: Knicker-bocker.

Richards, D. (1984). General sources of information within North America. In R. L. Davis and D. S. Rogers (Eds.), *Store Location and Store Assessment Research* (pp. 212–137). Chichester, England: John Wiley & Sons, Ltd.

Segal, D. B. (1998). Retail trade area analysis: concepts and new approaches. *DM Insights on Location.* www.directionsmag.com/article/4157.

9 Store Network Planning and Location-allocation Modeling

Retail chains are often concerned with selection of multiple store locations to serve a spatially dispersed population: that is, to allocate a given spatial distribution of demand to a specific number of retail outlets. This is achieved using *location-allocation* modeling, which is grounded upon the third law of location science: sites of an optimal multi-site pattern must be selected simultaneously rather than independently, one at a time (Church & Murray, 2009). In this chapter, the concepts of location-allocation are explained, and its operations in ESRI's *Network Analyst* platform are illustrated with two case studies.

LOCATION-ALLOCATION MODELING AND DATA REQUIREMENTS

Location-allocation is used to select sites for a number of facilities simultaneously, from which services/goods are provided to a spatially dispersed population. It is suitable for spatial planning of both public and private service facilities. When used in store network planning, this method assists in determining how many stores are needed in the target market, how many stores can be supported, and where the stores should be located. Location-allocation modeling combines site selection and trade area delineation in the same process. Questions to be answered include: (1) how do all the outlets of a chain work together to efficiently serve the market? (2) if one store were to be added or closed, how would that change affect the performance of the other stores? (3) if some of the outlets are to be closed, which ones should be closed and which ones should remain open? Location-allocation modeling follows the deterministic approach in defining trade areas, which is different from the Huff Model.

Grounded upon the central place theory (Beaumont, 1987), the location-allocation method was first introduced in the 1960s by Cooper (1963). Since then, it has attracted a considerable amount of academic interest, especially in the 1970s and the 1980s, when related publications proliferated. A succinct explanation of location-allocation modeling is provided by Ghosh and McLafferty in their book *Location Strategies for Retail and Service Firms*, where they define location-allocation modeling as "a method for evaluating alternative network configurations and determining the sites that are most accessible to consumers" (Ghosh & McLafferty, 1987: 129). Location-allocation is not a single method, but a modeling procedure with several solutions, each using a different mathematical algorithm. It allows systematic evaluation of a large number of possible locational configurations, while meeting a set of user-defined criteria (or allocation rules), such as maximum cover, minimum travel distance, desired travel distance and time, and desired number of facilities.

Based on the objectives of particular problem solutions, location-allocation models can be differentiated into two general classes (Narula, 1984): *cover models* and *mini-sum models*. Cover models are concerned with locating facilities to maximize the number of clients to be served by them within a desired distance/time threshold by locating a fixed number of facilities (Church & ReVelle, 1974). They are commonly, but not necessarily only, applied to services that are delivered to patrons (such as emergency services). Mini-sum models aim to minimize the distance traveled by patrons to facilities. More precisely, they aim to determine the locations of a number of facilities such that the total weighted distance to the closest facility is minimized (Kemp, 2008). Mini-sum models are typically applied to services/businesses that patrons travel to, such as retail stores.

Description and explanation of the location-allocation models in mathematical terms is beyond the scope of this chapter. Fortunately, a number of easy-to-use "apps" are built into two of the many extensions of ESRI's *ArcGIS: Network Analyst* and *Business Analyst*. Specifically, six location-allocation models are included in *Network Analyst*, of which three are included in *Business Analyst* (see Table 9.1). These apps spare the ordinary users from having to use the complex mathematical formulas to reiterate many rounds of calculations, and make computations and presentation of the results much easier and faster.

Table 9.1 Location-allocation Models in ESRI's *Network Analyst* and *Business Analyst*

Model class	Model	
	In Network Analyst	*In Business Analyst*
Cover models	Maximum coverage	Maximum coverage
	Maximum attendance	
	Maximum market share	Maximum market share
	Target market share	
Mini-sum models	Minimum impedance (*p*-median)	Minimum impedance (*p*-median)
	Minimum facility	

The *maximum coverage* model locates facilities in such a way that all demand points, or the greatest possible number of them, within a specified impedance cutoff are allocated to the chosen facilities. The *maximum attendance* model uses the location of each demand site as an indicator, and tends to locate facilities closer to the areas with the highest density of demands; the proportion of demand allocated to the nearest facility decreases with increasing distance (ESRI, 2019). With the maximum attendance model, a set of facilities that maximize the total allocated demand is chosen; the demands that are further than the specified impedance cutoff do not affect the chosen set of facilities.

While the maximum coverage and the maximum attendance methods are deterministic (or spatial monopoly) methods of choosing new locations among all candidate sites in the study area, the *maximum market share* method chooses facilities in the presence of competitors, to maximize their captured market share (Lee & O'Kelly, 2011). Gravity model concepts are followed to determine the proportion of demand allocated to each facility, and the set of facilities that maximizes the total allocated demand is chosen. The *target market share* model is a variation of the maximum market share method: instead of maximizing the market share, it determines the minimum number of facilities and locates them to reach a specified market share that the business is content to capture, in accordance with the available company resources and the existing competitive market environment.

The *minimum impedance* model, also known as the *p*-median model, chooses facility locations such that the sum of all weighted travel distance/time (i.e., the demand allocated to a facility multiplied by the distance between each demand point and the facility) is minimized for a given impedance cutoff (Gokbayrak & Kocaman, 2017). The main objective is to minimize the cost of transportation, which is an important component of the total shopping cost. In a variant method, a *P* power (or exponent) is used to amplify the effects of distance (Morrill, 1974). This calculation creates an effective distance value from each point of demand to each candidate site, and is generally used to limit the number of candidate sites with a larger distance from the given supply points. The *minimum facility* method, as its name indicates, chooses the smallest number of facilities needed to cover the greatest amount of demand within a specified impedance cutoff.

Goodchild (1984) distinguishes two types of corporate strategies that influence the choice of location-allocation models: the *conservative strategy*, and the *aggressive strategy*. The first strategy excludes from consideration the locations that are adjacent to established competitors, and favors locations in the "holes" of the existing market coverage. Associated with this strategy are market share models of location-allocation (both *maximum market share* and *target market share*). The second strategy looks for locations that are most accessible to customers, regardless of the presence of established competitors. With this strategy, the "competition-ignoring models" of location-allocation are used, and locations adjacent to competitors are also included in the list of candidate sites for consideration. If such locations are deemed "optimal", the company may attempt to obtain them through business merger and acquisition.

Finally, readers should be aware that location-allocation models are subject to the effects of the modifiable areal unit problem (MAUP) (Chakrapani et al., 2006; Sedgwick, 2015). MAUP is one of the largest sources of statistical bias that can significantly impact spatial analysis. It is a result of varying geographies at differing scales, which can represent closely, or misrepresent, a target population in the market (Dark & Bram, 2007). In location-allocation modeling, the points of demand are usually represented by the centroids of the census geographies (such as census tracts or dissemination areas) from which distance to the location of facilities is calculated. The location-allocation results may vary depending on the scale of the census geography to be used to aggregate demands, and the market shares and population characteristics in the trade area of each facility can change as well. Because the *minimum impedance* model is based on reducing the weighted travel time or distance, it is more sensitive to the issues of MAUP.

Location-allocation modeling requires the use of three types of data: (1) a list of census tracts or dissemination areas as points of demand; (2) a list of candidate sites as potential facility locations; and (3) a road network that links the points of demand with the candidate sites, and is used to calculate travel distance/time. Two case studies are presented in the rest of this chapter to illustrate the location-allocation procedure and operations in the *Network Analyst* environment.

CASE STUDY 1: SUPERMARKET LOCATION SELECTION IN THE CITY OF BRAMPTON

A retail company intends to enter the City of Brampton, the third largest city in Toronto CMA, for the first time with a plan to open six supermarkets. The location analysis team is assigned four tasks: (1) to determine the six supermarket locations such that the total weighted travel distance for the local population is minimized; (2) to estimate the sales potential for groceries in each of the six trade areas; (3) to analyze the competitive environment around each of the six proposed locations; and (4) to investigate the level of visibility and accessibility for each of the six selected locations.

One of the most important criteria that consumers take into consideration when making a store location choice is how close the store is to the consumer's home. With the exception of multipurpose trips, this behavior is particularly true for the selection of supermarkets, which are low-order routine shopping trips. People tend to shop at their closest local grocery store with everything else being held constant amongst competitors (such as price, service level, product availability, and shopping environment). So in Task 1, the *minimum impedance* model of location-allocation is used, with input of the following three sets of data:

- census tract–level demographic and socioeconomic data, along with centroid coordinates (98 census tracts in total)
- land parcels that are zoned for commercial use (110 in total), along with the size of the parcels in square footage and their centroid coordinates
- Brampton road network

The centroids of the census tracts represent the locations of demand. The level of demand associated with each point is represented by the number of households, household income, and expenditure on groceries. The use of the centroid assumes that households are concentrated at that point within each census tract. Determination of the feasible locations for the six supermarkets is based on the requirement that the sites be on land zoned for commercial use or commercial properties greater than 100,000 square feet in size (33 of the 110 parcels meet the size criterion), meaning that non-commercial lands and smaller parcels of commercial lands are excluded from consideration. Although it is possible to apply to the city for rezoning if the retailer wishes to develop a store on land not zoned for commercial use, the application process can be lengthy and costly, as it involves public consultation and may face possible appeals. (See Chapter 5 on zoning regulations.) The road network layer includes such topological information as junctions (intersections) and edges (road segments), as well as the attributes of each road segment (such as travel direction, speed limits, and type of road). These attributes make the road layer a suitable "network dataset" for modeling movement between points of demand and points of feasible sites in the *Network Analyst* environment.

It should be noted that Brampton already has other supermarkets serving its population. The existing competitors can be treated with two alternative approaches. In the first approach, the presence of the existing competitors is recognized upfront, and the six sites to be chosen should avoid these locations. This is consistent with the *conservative strategy* described by Goodchild (1984). In the second approach, the location-allocation model is run without considering the presence of competitors; instead, competition analysis is conducted afterwards. This is in line with the *aggressive strategy*. The second approach is taken in this case study because it allows for selecting six optimal locations including the ones already occupied by the existing competitors. In reality, if a highly suitable and profitable location is identified and desired, the retailer with sufficient resources and in a strong market position may take the acquisition approach in new store development and purchase a competitor outright. With the *conservative* approach, such opportunities may be lost.

A network environment is created in *ArcCatalog* first, on the basis of which travel time is calculated. Then, parameters are set up to allocate points of demand to the selected facility locations, to delineate trade areas of the six selected store locations. As is shown in Figure 9.1, the *minimum impedance* model of location-allocation is selected for **Problem Type**; the number of **Facilities to Choose** is set at 6; and **Impedance**

Cutoff (i.e., maximum distance or time that a customer is willing to travel) is set at five minutes. This means that any demand point that is more than five minutes of driving time from any of the six facilities will not be allocated. After deriving the solution, three outputs are generated: an output table showing the six selected candidate sites (Figure 9.2); an output table showing the allocation of the census tracts to each of the six selected sites (Figure 9.3); and a "spider-web" map (also known as desire-line map) connecting the six optimal locations and the centroids of the census tracts that are allocated to them (Figure 9.4). The spider-web map can be transformed to show the resulting trade areas, as shown in Figure 9.5.

In Task 2, and based on the location-allocation outputs and the associated demographic and socioeconomic profiles for their respective

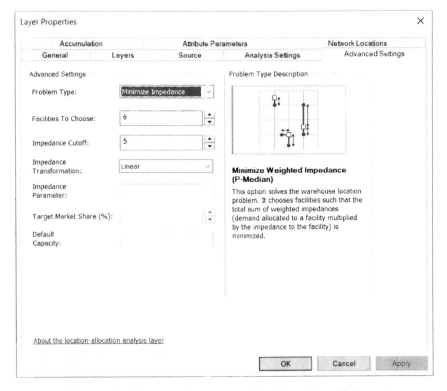

Figure 9.1 Select the Minimum Impedance Model and Specify Location-allocation Criteria in ESRI's *Network Analyst*.

Note
When the *minimum impedance* model is selected, the two boxes of *target market share* and *default capacity* are grayed and become inactive.

Table

Facilities

	ObjectID	Shape	Name	FacilityType	Weight	Capacity	DemandCount	DemandWeight
▶	1	Point Z	Location 1	Chosen	1	<Null>	6	43180
	3	Point Z	Location 3	Chosen	1	<Null>	16	85217
	10	Point Z	Location 10	Chosen	1	<Null>	11	50445
	16	Point Z	Location 16	Chosen	1	<Null>	18	109944
	31	Point Z	Location 31	Chosen	1	<Null>	13	67695
	39	Point Z	Location 39	Chosen	1	<Null>	12	90808
	2	Point Z	Location 2	Candidate	1	<Null>	0	0
	4	Point Z	Location 4	Candidate	1	<Null>	0	0
	5	Point Z	Location 5	Candidate	1	<Null>	0	0
	6	Point Z	Location 6	Candidate	1	<Null>	0	0
	7	Point Z	Location 7	Candidate	1	<Null>	0	0
	8	Point Z	Location 8	Candidate	1	<Null>	0	0
	9	Point Z	Location 9	Candidate	1	<Null>	0	0
	11	Point Z	Location 11	Candidate	1	<Null>	0	0
	12	Point Z	Location 12	Candidate	1	<Null>	0	0
	13	Point Z	Location 13	Candidate	1	<Null>	0	0
	14	Point Z	Location 14	Candidate	1	<Null>	0	0
	15	Point Z	Location 15	Candidate	1	<Null>	0	0
	17	Point Z	Location 17	Candidate	1	<Null>	0	0
	18	Point Z	Location 18	Candidate	1	<Null>	0	0
	19	Point Z	Location 19	Candidate	1	<Null>	0	0
	20	Point Z	Location 20	Candidate	1	<Null>	0	0
	21	Point Z	Location 21	Candidate	1	<Null>	0	0
	22	Point Z	Location 22	Candidate	1	<Null>	0	0
	23	Point Z	Location 23	Candidate	1	<Null>	0	0
	24	Point Z	Location 24	Candidate	1	<Null>	0	0
	25	Point Z	Location 25	Candidate	1	<Null>	0	0
	26	Point Z	Location 26	Candidate	1	<Null>	0	0
	27	Point Z	Location 27	Candidate	1	<Null>	0	0
	28	Point Z	Location 28	Candidate	1	<Null>	0	0

◄◄ ◄   1 ► ►◄ ▦ ▤ (0 out of 39 Selected)

Lines Facilities

Figure 9.2 Output Table Showing the Six Selected Candidate Sites.

trade areas, sales potential for each of the six selected sites is calculated. From the Survey of Household Spending, it is found that, on average, households in the Toronto CMA spend 9 percent of their gross income on groceries and convenience goods commonly sold in a supermarket. Because location-allocation models take the deterministic, or monopolistic, approach to trade area delineation, probability is assumed to be 1, which therefore does not affect the calculation of sales potential. The formula for estimating sales potential is simplified as the following:

> Sales potential = number of households * average household income * percentage of household income spent on food and convenience goods purchased from supermarket

In total, the six sites capture 86 percent of Brampton's population, 88 percent of the households, and 86 percent of the sales potential (see

Table

Demand Points

ObjectID	Shape	Name	Weight	FacilityID	AllocatedWeight	GroupName	Impedance Transformation
1	Point Z	5350528 20	0	<Null>	<Null>	<Null>	<Null>
2	Point Z	5350528 21	4354	39	4354	<Null>	<Null>
3	Point Z	5350528 22	6543	39	6543	<Null>	<Null>
4	Point Z	5350528 31	6332	39	6332	<Null>	<Null>
5	Point Z	5350528 36	8215	39	8215	<Null>	<Null>
6	Point Z	5350528 37	8535	39	8535	<Null>	<Null>
7	Point Z	5350560 00	6270	10	6270	<Null>	<Null>
8	Point Z	5350561 00	6447	<Null>	<Null>	<Null>	<Null>
9	Point Z	5350562 02	6494	10	6494	<Null>	<Null>
10	Point Z	5350562 03	4824	3	4824	<Null>	<Null>
11	Point Z	5350562 04	4528	3	4528	<Null>	<Null>
12	Point Z	5350562 05	5659	10	5659	<Null>	<Null>
13	Point Z	5350562 06	3036	3	3036	<Null>	<Null>
14	Point Z	5350562 07	4480	3	4480	<Null>	<Null>
15	Point Z	5350562 08	4103	3	4103	<Null>	<Null>
16	Point Z	5350562 09	3880	10	3880	<Null>	<Null>
17	Point Z	5350562 11	3030	10	3030	<Null>	<Null>
18	Point Z	5350562 12	7092	10	7092	<Null>	<Null>
19	Point Z	5350562 13	1227	10	1227	<Null>	<Null>
20	Point Z	5350562 14	3924	3	3924	<Null>	<Null>
21	Point Z	5350562 15	3724	3	3724	<Null>	<Null>
22	Point Z	5350563 01	6743	10	6743	<Null>	<Null>
23	Point Z	5350563 02	2934	10	2934	<Null>	<Null>
24	Point Z	5350564 01	2328	10	2328	<Null>	<Null>
25	Point Z	5350564 02	4788	10	4788	<Null>	<Null>
26	Point Z	5350570 01	3297	31	3297	<Null>	<Null>
27	Point Z	5350570 02	3645	31	3645	<Null>	<Null>
28	Point Z	5350571 01	3855	31	3855	<Null>	<Null>
29	Point Z	5350571 02	3998	31	3998	<Null>	<Null>
30	Point Z	5350572 01	6789	31	6789	<Null>	<Null>

1 ▶ ▶I 📖 (0 out of 98 Selected)

Lines | Facilities | Demand Points

Figure 9.3 Output Table Showing the Allocation of Census Tracts to Each of the Six Selected Sites.

Table 9.2). Twenty-two census tracts are not allocated to any of the six sites because they are beyond the cutoff impedance distance (or possibly because they are part of new subdivisions, and the local streets are not included in the road network yet). Calculations show that Sites 16, 39, 3, and 31 have much higher sales potential than the other two sites (1 and 10): all close to or over $200 million. Site 1, near the east border of Brampton has the smallest trade area (including only six census tracts) and the lowest sales potential ($89 million), partly because the study area is limited to Brampton itself. A store at that site may also serve consumers who live in the adjacent cities of Toronto and Mississauga, but they are not included in this exercise.

Because these are total sales potentials in each trade area and are to be divided among all the competing supermarkets, including the new stores, competition analysis must also be done in order for the new retail entrant to make an informed decision. This part of the analysis forms Task 3.

Data on existing supermarkets in Brampton are collected from corporate websites and from DMTI Spatial Inc.'s Enhanced Points of

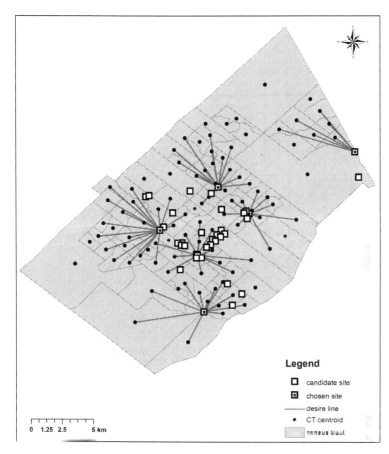

Figure 9.4 Spider-web Map with "Desire Lines" Connecting the Six Optimal
Sites and (the Centroids of) the Census Tracts That Are Allocated to Them.

Interest (EPOI) file. Competitors within 1, 2.5 and 5 km from the six
optimal sites are then identified and examined (see Figure 9.6 and
Table 9.3). They range from full-line supermarkets operated by the
major retail chains (such as the mainstream Metro and Sobeys), to discount supermarkets (such as Food Basics and FreshCo, which are also
operated by Metro and Sobeys), independent supermarkets, and
ethnic grocery stores (such as Oceans and Asian Food Center). Since
Brampton is known for having a large South Asian population, ethnic
grocery stores that cater to the taste of this market segment will be
strong competitors of any new supermarket. However, independent
and ethnic supermarkets are often also easy acquisition targets of the
large corporate retailers for their superior locations. Investigation

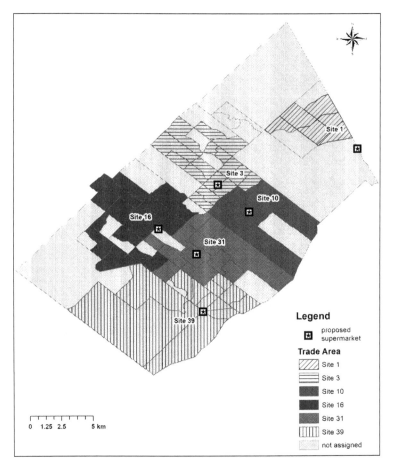

Figure 9.5 Trade Areas of the Six Optimal Sites Transformed from the "Spider-web" Map.

shows that each of Sites 3, 10, and 31 has three existing competitors within a 2.5 km distance. Site 3 has two full-line supermarkets (a Metro and a Sobeys) and one discount supermarket (a Food Basics); Site 10 has one full-line supermarket (a Metro), one discount supermarket (a FreshCo), and one ethnic supermarket (an Oceans); Site 31 has one full-line supermarket (a Metro) and two discount supermarkets (a Food Basics and a FreshCo). This needs further analysis by other departments of the supermarket company.

Finally, in Task 4, visibility and accessibility of each selected site are examined, as they influence how well the retail location can be seen from the surrounding roadways by passing traffic, and how easy it is for

Table 9.2 Trade Area Statistics for the Six Selected Supermarket Sites

Facility ID	No. of CTs in trade area	Total population		Total no. of households		Average household income ($)	Total household income ($ million)	Sales potential ($ millions)	Market share (%)
		No.	%	No.	%				
1	6	43,180	8.3	9,959	6.5	98,822	984.2	89	7.0
3	16	85,217	16.4	23,252	15.1	93,661	2,177.8	196	15.4
10	11	50,445	9.7	18,252	11.9	78,179	1,426.9	128	10.1
16	18	109,944	21.2	31,287	20.3	99,216	3,104.1	279	21.9
31	13	67,695	13.0	26,165	17.0	82,051	2,146.8	193	15.2
39	12	90,808	17.5	25,749	16.7	91,410	2,353.7	212	16.6
Not allocated	22	72,190	13.9	19,147	12.4	101,807	1,949.3	175	13.8
City total	98	519,479	100.0	153,811	100.0	91,950	14,142.9	1,273	100.0

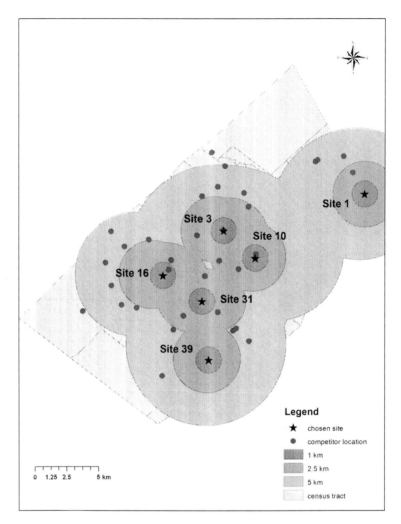

Figure 9.6 Existing Supermarkets in Brampton.

a customer to get to the store location. Number of lanes, speed limit, and adjacency to intersection all affect how easily a location can be accessed. As described in Chapter 7, retailers tend to locate their stores along major roads and at intersections to benefit from high traffic volume and increased visibility and accessibility. This can be done either through field work, or using Google Earth satellite imagery to visually examine the transportation infrastructure (see Figure 9.7). Since most customers in Brampton (a suburban municipality) travel to a supermarket by private automobile, locations adjacent to arterial

Table 9.3 Investigation of Competing Supermarkets

Selected site	1 km		2.5 km		5 km	
	No. of stores	Name of stores	No. of stores	Name of stores	No. of stores	Name
1	0	–	1	Food Basics	4	Asian Food Centre (2); Food Basics; FreshCo
3	1	Sobeys	3	Metro; Food Basics; Sobeys	13	FreshCo (3); Sobeys (2); Metro (2); Asian Food Centre (2); Fortinos; Food Basics; Oceans
10	2	Metro; FreshCo	3	Metro; FreshCo; Oceans	8	Metro (2); Food Basics; Sobeys; Foodland; FreshCo; Asian Food Centre; Oceans
16	1	Fortinos	2	Fortinos; FreshCo	13	FreshCo (3); Metro (2); Fortinos (2); Food Basics (2); Asian Food Centre (2); Foodland; Sobeys
31	0	–	3	Metro; Food Basics; FreshCo	11	Food Basics (2); FreshCo (2); Oceans (2); Metro; Longo's; Foodland; Sobeys; Fortinos
39	0	–	0	–	7	FreshCo (2); Metro; Longo's; Sobeys; Food Basics; Oceans

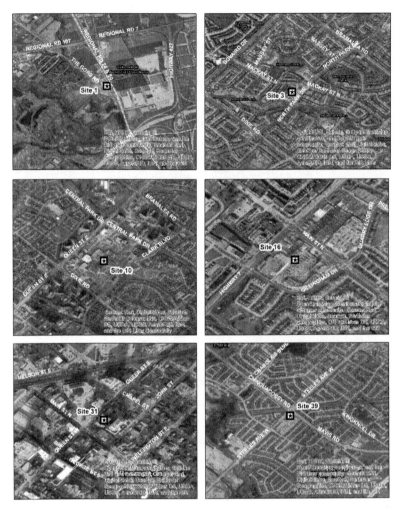

Figure 9.7 Visual Inspection of Visibility and Accessibility for the Six Selected Supermarket Sites.

roads are better than those on local residential streets, as arterial roads have a higher posted speed limit (60 km) than the local streets (40 km or lower), thus shortening driving time. Further, intersection locations are preferred to mid-block locations, as they provide access to the site from four directions, instead of only two. The examination results are summarized in Table 9.4. Sites 1, 10, 16, 31, and 39 are all located at intersections of two arterial roads, so their visibility and accessibility are both considered high. Site 3 is located at the intersection of two lower-level roads, so its accessibility is rated medium.

Table 9.4 Accessibility Characteristics of the Six Selected Sites

Site	Accessibility characteristics	Level of accessibility
1	Intersection of two arterial roads	High
3	Intersection of two lower-level roads	Medium
10	Intersection of two arterial roads	High
16	Intersection of two arterial roads	High
31	Intersection of two arterial roads	High
39	Intersection of two arterial roads	High

The location-allocation procedure is repeated with the same sets of data using three other models: *maximum coverage, maximum market share,* and *target market share* (to capture 60 percent market share). In this particular case, *maximum coverage* and *maximum market share* happen to produce the same results: the same six sites are selected, which capture the same amount of market share (86 percent). However, the compositions of their respective trade areas by census tracts are different from the allocations derived from the *minimum impedance* model. With the *target market share* model, only three sites (3, 16, and 39) are selected, meaning that only three stores are needed to capture 60 percent of the Brampton market.

To conclude, location-allocation supports exploratory study. Although it reveals a number of useful insights, post-location-allocation analysis is needed for final investment decision. In the case of Brampton, further demographic analysis, such as ethnic composition, may be needed for the trade areas of each chosen site, in order to determine a particular merchandise mix. It would also not be ideal for a supermarket to set up at a location where intense competition already exists. The barriers of entry will be much higher in these areas as the competitors will drive up the cost of leases in the area in addition to drawing away the same customers that the proposed supermarket will be targeting, unless it is possible to acquire one of the existing competitors. At sites where competition is weak, the next step is to examine the affordability of real estate, which is not an input factor in location-allocation modeling.

CASE STUDY 2: SELECT STORE LOCATIONS FOR GROCERY PICKUP[1]

Grocers are among the latest retailers to embrace e-commerce to make their products more accessible to customers and to reduce labor cost

(Sagan, 2018). Using the internet as a platform for ordering groceries, customers have two choices as to how they receive their orders: to have their orders delivered to their home (for convenience but at a cost), or to pick them up at a nearby store (to save delivery cost). All major grocery retailers in Canada are now experimenting with providing such services.

Loblaws, Canada's largest food retailer, operates more than 2,000 stores across the country, with 452 of them in the Toronto CMA. These stores are operated under different banners, including Loblaws, Valu-Mart, Fortinos, The Real Canadian Superstore, No Frills, and T&T. In 2014, it acquired the ownership of Shoppers Drug Mart—a drug store chain with many convenient locations in community and neighborhood plazas. Some Shoppers Drug Mart stores carry limited lines of frozen foods in addition to health and beauty products. After a short period of experiment with "order online and pick up in store" service in its Loblaws banner supermarkets in the Toronto CMA (Strauss, 2015), the company contemplated expanding the service by adding more pickup locations, including supermarkets of other banners and some of the Shoppers Drug Mart sites, the aim being to eventually "blanket the country" (Charlebois, 2017a, 2017b; Sagan, 2018; Shaw, 2018).

Using the *minimum impedance* model of location-allocation, this case study simulates a geographical analysis to gauge the benefit of including Shoppers Drug Mart stores as pickup locations if Loblaws wishes to "blanket" the Toronto CMA. That is, what is the gain in market coverage if Shoppers Drug Mart stores are included in the pickup network?

Three sets of data are used to carry out the analysis. The first set of data is the Canadian census at the census tract level of geography, used to establish the geographical distribution of demand for groceries in the CMA. The second dataset contains information about all Loblaw-owned stores (except T&T, which is a chain of ethnic Chinese supermarkets acquired by Loblaws in 2009). These stores are treated as candidate pickup locations, from which a subset will be selected. The third dataset is a digital road network connecting the points of demand with the candidate sites of supply.

In order to hold the online-ordered groceries for customers to pick up, the stores would need dedicated floor space, which is why store size can be a constraint (Douglas, 2014). As is commented in a *Globe and Mail* article (Mourtada, 2018), supermarkets have been seeing a shrinkage in size after the introduction of e-commerce, but they are usually at least 14,000 square feet in size. Research also found that people in U.S. cities are willing to travel up to 2.6 miles (or 4 km) for grocery shopping (Liu et al., 2015), which is equivalent to about five minutes of driving time on city streets. In consideration of the above observations and suggestions, three criteria are applied to the impedance model of location-allocation. First, five-minute driving time is chosen as the impedance cutoff. Second, only those stores that are 14,000 square feet and larger are included in the candidate list; smaller stores are excluded. Third, if two stores (usually stores of different banners) are within 1-km distance of each other, only one of them is retained in the candidate list, and the other is removed from consideration. The decision is made with the following orders of priority:

- full-line (and larger) supermarkets have the first priority to be retained, and these include the banners of Loblaw, The Real Canadian Superstore, Valu-Mart, and Fortino;
- the discount No Frills supermarkets are given the second priority, because they cater to lower-income families, who, according to the literature, are less likely to buy food online;
- the Shoppers Drug Mart stores are given the least priority to be included in the candidate list, because most of them do not have an existing "cold room" to store the orders, and there is cost involved in installing kiosks for grocery pickup.

As a result, 102 supermarkets and 35 Shopper Drug Mart are retained as pickup locations.

The *minimum impedance* model is run twice: first, with the 102 supermarkets only; second, with the 35 Shoppers Drug Mart stores as well as the 102 supermarkets. Figures 9.8 and 9.9 display the spider-web maps of the two runs. The summary statistics are shown in Table 9.5. The Shoppers Drug Mart stores take some census tracts away from the service (or trade) areas of the supermarkets because these census tracts are physically closer to a Shoppers Drug Mart store. Using supermarkets only as pickup location, the store network covers 60 percent of the 1,151 census tracts in the CMA, and 65 percent of the CMA population. By adding 35 Shoppers Drug Mart stores to the network, market coverage increases to 65 percent of the census tracts and 72 percent of the population. The gain of 5 percent in census tracts and 7 percent of population may not be significant enough to justify the cost of adding cold rooms and pickup kiosks to the

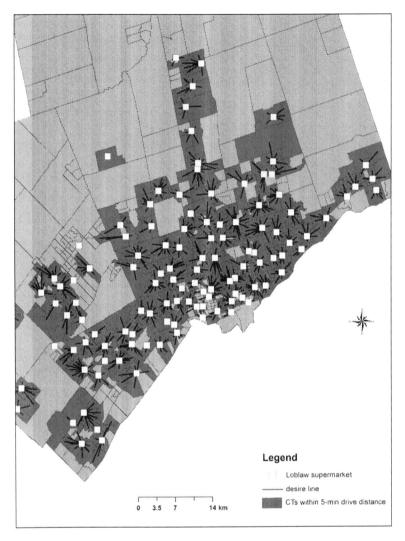

Figure 9.8 Spider-web Map with 102 Supermarkets.

35 Shoppers Drug Mart stores. Besides, many of the chosen Shoppers Drug Mart stores are located in the fringe of the City of Toronto instead of the central area, which is well served by the Loblaws supermarkets already.

At the current level of demand for "order online and pick up in store" service—only 3 percent of the Canadian population, but predicted to go up to 8 percent by 2022 (Charlebois, 2017c)—Loblaws may want to implement this long-term project in phases. A

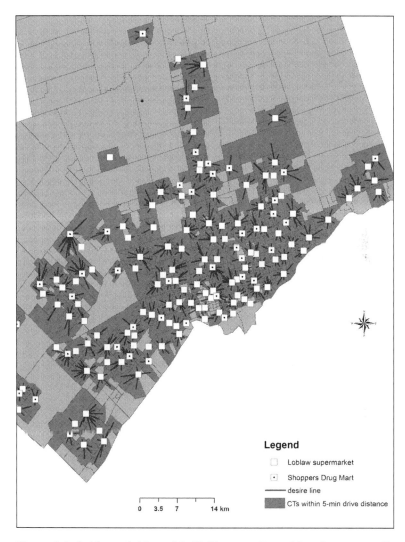

Figure 9.9 Spider-web Map with 35 Shoppers Drug Mart Stores as well as the 102 Supermarkets.

geodemographic analysis can be conducted to identify areas with high concentrations of potential online grocery shoppers and expand or roll out the service at the stores in those areas first. After its competitors—Sobeys and Metro—spread the same service in the CMA, Loblaws may need to modify or "recalibrate" its network using the *maximum market share* or the *target market share* models of location-allocation.

Table 9.5 Allocation of Demand to Each Loblaws-owned Pickup Location within 5-minute Driving Time

Store banner	Without Shoppers Drug Mart			With Shoppers Drug Mart		
	No. of stores	No. of CTs	Population	No. of stores	No. of CTs	Population
Loblaws	19	137	746,094	19	124	688,760
No Frills	62	396	2,312,081	62	324	1,852,933
The Real Canadian Superstore	8	55	330,897	8	42	242,715
Valu-Mart	4	49	232,665	4	37	178,429
Fortinos	9	51	268,547	9	46	257,497
Shoppers Drug Mart	–	–	–	35	177	1,067,984
Total	102	688	3,890,284	137	750	4,288,318
Coverage of CMA	–	60%	65%	–	65%	72%

Source: adapted from Tahir, 2018.

KEY POINTS OF THE CHAPTER

- Location-allocation modeling combines site selection and trade area delineation in the same process. It is used to select sites for a number of facilities simultaneously, from which services/goods are provided to a spatially dispersed population. It follows the deterministic approach in defining trade areas, which is different from the Huff Model.
- Location-allocation is not a single method, but a modeling procedure with several solutions, each using a different mathematical algorithm. It allows systematic evaluation of a large number of possible locational configurations, while meeting a set of user-defined criteria or allocation rules.
- Location-allocation models can be differentiated into two general classes: *cover models* and *mini-sum models*. Cover models are concerned with locating a fixed number of facilities to maximize the number of clients to be served within a desired distance/time threshold. Mini-sum models aim to determine the locations of a number of facilities such that the total weighted distance to the closest facility is minimized.
- There are two types of corporate strategies that influence the choice of location-allocation models: the *conservative strategy*, and the *aggressive strategy*. The former excludes from consideration the locations that are adjacent to established competitors. The latter looks for locations that are most accessible to customers, regardless of the presence of established competitors. Large retail corporations often use the aggressive strategy, with which the "competition-ignoring models" of location-allocation are used, and locations of, or adjacent to, competitors are also included in the list of candidate sites for consideration. If such locations are deemed "optimal", the company may attempt to obtain them through merger and acquisition.
- Location-allocation modeling requires input of three types of data: (1) a list of census tracts or dissemination areas as points of demand; (2) a list of candidate sites as potential facility locations; and (3) a road network that links the points of demand with the candidate sites, and is used to calculate travel distance/time. Use of smaller census geography is preferred, with which calculation of total weighted distance tends to be more accurate.
- The model-suggested sites should not be treated as final, and post-location-allocation analysis is also needed for final investment

decisions. The selected sites are presented to business decision makers for further consideration while competition and real estate costs are investigated and calculated.

NOTE

1 This case study is based on Zara Tahir's (2018) Major Research Paper for the degree of Master of Spatial Analysis at Ryerson University, which was supervised by the lead author of this textbook.

REFERENCES

Beaumont, J. R. (1987). Location allocation models and central place theory. In A. Ghosh & G. Rushton (Eds.), *Spatial analysis and location-allocation models* (pp. 21–55). New York, NY: Van Nostrand Reinhold Company.

Chakrapani, C., Lea, T., & Hernandez, T. (2006). *Market Segmentation: A Practitioner's Guide*. Toronto, Canada: Centre for the Study of Commercial Activity, Ryerson Polytechnic University.

Charlebois, S. (2017a). Loblaw, the latest to experience the "Amazon effect," but at least it has the foresight to act now. *Globe and Mail*, November 20. http://ezproxy.lib.ryerson.ca/login?url=https://search-proquestcom. ezproxy.lib.ryerson.ca/docview/1965994439?accountid=13631.

Charlebois, S. (2017b). A bogeyman keeps grocers up at night; Loblaw home delivery shows Amazon effect in action as retailers struggle to keep up. *Chronicle–Herald*, November 21. http://ezproxy.lib.ryerson.ca/ login?url=https://searchproquest-com.ezproxy.lib.ryerson.ca/docview/ 1966962743?accountid=13631.

Charlebois, S. (2017c). Amazon and the slow death of the traditional grocery store; the Amazon effect has Loblaws and others reimagining their businesses. *The Brooks Bulletin*, December 12. http://ezproxy.lib. ryerson.ca/login?url=https://search-proquestcom.ezproxy.lib.ryerson. ca/docview/1976068267?accountid=13631.

Church, R. L. & Murray, A. T. (2009). *Business Site Selection, Location Analysis, and GIS*. Hoboken, NJ: John Wiley & Sons, Inc.

Church, R. L. & ReVelle, C. (1974). The maximal covering location problem. *Papers of the Regional Science Association, 32*, 101–118.

Cooper, L. (1963). Location-allocation problems. *Operations Research, 11*(3), 331–343.

Dark, S. J. & Bram, D. (2007). The modifiable areal unit problem (MAUP) in physical geography. *Progress in Physical Geography, 31*(5), 471–479.

Douglas, M. (2014). New retail strategies: It's a store! It's a Site! It's a Warehouse! *Inbound Logistics*, August 8. www.inboundlogistics.com/ cms/article/new-retail-strategies-its-a-store-its-a-site-its-a-warehouse/.

ESRI. (2019). Location-allocation analysis. https://desktop.arcgis.com/en/arcmap/latest/extensions/network-analyst/location-allocation.htm.

Ghosh, A. & McLafferty, S. (1987). *Location Strategies for Retail and Service Firms.* Lexington, MA: Lexington Books.

Gokbayrak, K. & Kocaman, A. S. (2017). A distance-limited continuous location-allocation problem for spatial planning of decentralized systems. *Computers and Operations Research, 88,* 15–29.

Goodchild, M. (1984). ILACS: a location-allocation model for retail site selection. *Journal of Retailing, 60*(1), 84–100.

Kemp, K. (2008). *Encyclopedia of Geographic Information Science.* Thousand Oaks, CA: Sage Publications Inc.

Lee, G. & O'Kelly, M. E. (2011). Competitive location modelling with a rank proportional allocation. *Environment and Planning B: Planning and Design, 38*(3), 411–428.

Liu, J. L., Han B., & Cohen, D. A. (2015). Beyond neighborhood food environments: distance travelled to food establishments in 5 US Cities, 2009–2011. *Preventing Chronic Disease, 12.* (online publication with no page number). http://dx.doi.org/10.5888/pcd12.150065.

Morrill, R. L. (1974). Efficiency and equity of optimum location models. *Antipode, 6*(1), 41–46.

Mourtada, R. (2018). The incredible shrinking grocery store. *Globe and Mail,* April 29. www.theglobeandmail.com/report-on-business/industry-news/propertyreport/the-incredible-shrinking-grocery-store/article1318936/.

Narula, S. C. (1984). Hierarchical location-allocation problems: a classification scheme. *European Journal of Operational Research, 15*(1), 93–99.

Sagan, A. (2018). Grocers adding online heft as Amazon raises home delivery stakes. *National Post,* January 22. http://nationalpost.com/pmn/life-pmn/food-lifepmn/sobeys-signs-online-grocery-partnership-deal-with-british-company-ocado-group.

Sedgwick, P. (2015). Understanding the ecological fallacy. *BMJ: British Medical Journal, 351,* h4773.

Shaw, H. (2018). "Blanket the country": Loblaws plans nationwide home delivery rollout to counter Amazon. *Financial Post,* May 2. http://business.financialpost.com/news/retail-marketing/loblaw-extending-delivery-andpick-up-service-across-canada-in-battle-with-amazon.

Strauss, M. (2015). Loblaw's online ordering service helps to keep shelves full. *Globe and Mail,* June 3. www.theglobeandmail.com/report-on-business/loblawsonline-ordering-service-helps-to-keep-shelves-full/article24787579/.

Tahir, Z. (2018). *Store Network Modelling for Grocery Pick Up: A Case Study of Loblaws in the Toronto CMA.* (Major Research Paper for the degree of Master of Spatial Analysis). Toronto, Canada: Ryerson University.

10 Location Analysis and Site Selection of Distribution Centers

Spatial expansion of a store network must be supported by a network of distribution centers (DCs). For retailers operating large chains, the deployment and construction of DCs is also an important part of the retail planning process (see Box 8 in Figure 1.1), because the location of DCs affects the inventory policy (Drezner & Scott, 2013). Even e-retailing is not completely location-free because it must also be supported by distribution centers or fulfillment centers. Rooted in the pioneering work of Weber (Davis & Rogers, 1984), location analysis of DCs is a classic geographic problem, and siting of DCs has always been an explicitly geographical activity (Birkin et al., 2002). With growing transportation and operating costs, the importance of DC location decision is also growing.

There are three primary sub-problems identified in literature involving the design of a DC: location-allocation problems, vehicle routing problems, and inventory control problems (Ahmadi Javid & Azad, 2010; Helberg, 2013). Location-allocation decisions address how many DCs to locate, where to locate them, what capacity level to consider for each of them, and how to allocate the goods-receiving stores to them. Vehicle routing decisions address how to build or select vehicle routes between a DC and the stores to be served. Inventory decisions address how much and how often to re-order at a DC, and what level of safety stock to maintain. The first two sub-problems are clearly geographical in nature; yet, they are rarely dealt with in retail geography textbooks. Most papers written on DCs are the works of industrial and transportation engineers. This chapter is devoted to a discussion of location analysis and site selection of DCs from a geographic perspective.

THE ROLE OF DISTRIBUTION CENTERS

A DC operated by a corporate retailer is a specialized break-of-bulk ware-house enabling a single facility to stock a vast number of products and redistribute them for final delivery to the retail outlets in the same regional market. It is a vital part of the entire supply chain, linking pro-duction plants (or wholesalers) with retail outlets. In the retail industry, and in the relevant literature, a DC is also known as a logistics center or a consolidation center. Well placed distribution centers can simplify the delivery of products to retail outlets and reduce the cost of shipping, especially when production is not in an advantageous central location.

Most large corporate retailers own and run their own distribution networks, while smaller companies may outsource this function to ded-icated logistics firms that coordinate the distribution of products for a number of retailers. A typical retail distribution network consists of multiple DCs located in different parts of a market, with each DC serving a subset of stores. Large DCs may serve 50–100 stores.

All DCs have three main functional areas: the receiving dock, the storage area, and the shipping dock. Suppliers ship truckloads of prod-ucts to the DCs, which store the product until needed by the retail outlets and then ship the proper quantity to the retail stores. The receiving area can be specialized, based on the handling characteristics of the freight, on whether the product is going into storage or directly to a store, or on the type of vehicle delivering the product. However, not all products are stored in a DC for any period of time. Some prod-ucts arrive in the DC from an inbound semitrailer truck, and are trans-ferred directly to an outbound truck without going into the storage area of the warehouse—a practice known in the logistics industry as "cross-docking". Some DCs have dedicated dock doors for each store in their shipping area.

Usually, DCs do not interact directly with end consumers. With rapid expansion of internet retailing, consumer-oriented "order fulfill-ment centers" (also called by some researchers "express distribution centers"; see Ji et al., 2013) have emerged and are increasing in numbers. Retail orders are shipped from a fulfillment center rather than from a warehouse. Many fulfillment centers are at separate loca-tions from DCs, but some DCs combine both functions at the same facility. Fulfillment centers are bustling with activity: they are always working around the clock to process, pack, and ship orders to customers. The "pure-play" online retailer Amazon owns an extensive distribution network consisting of both warehouse DCs and order

fulfillment centers. Merchandise is delivered to consumers from fulfillment centers, and fulfillment centers are replenished by DCs.

Most retail chains operate multiple DCs due to the wide geographical dispersion of their constituent stores and to the high aggregate
volume that has to be distributed from the suppliers via the DCs to the
outlets. However, it is not favorable to assign all products to a DC as
physically close to the stores as possible because product characteristics
often vary widely. Certain products are better distributed via the DCs
that supply a larger number of stores (Holzapfel et al., 2018). For this
reason, retail chains operate a distribution network with different types
of DCs: central, regional, and local. Usually, central DCs distribute
lower-demand products to all stores; regional DCs distribute frequently
demanded products to a subset of stores; local DCs distribute to local
stores only (Nozick & Turnquist. 2001)

As of 2017, Walmart had 175 distribution centers in the United
States, differentiated into eight types (MWPVL International, 2019):

- regional general merchandise DC (42)
- grocery/perishable food DC (44)
- fashion (7)
- e-commerce fulfillment (6)
- special DC (21)
- imports/redistribution (9; consolidate inbound merchandise from
  overseas for shipment to other DCs)
- center point (19; consolidate inbound merchandise from domestic
  suppliers for shipment to other DCs)
- Sam's Club DCs (27)

Eighty-one percent of the merchandise sold at Walmart stores is
shipped through Walmart-owned and -operated DCs, with the rest
being direct store deliveries (DSD) from producers/suppliers (MWPVL
International, 2019).

In Canada, Walmart has 11 distribution facilities, located in three
cities: Calgary, Mississauga, and Cornwall (*Newswire*, 2018). Each DC supports approximately 135 stores within a 500-km distance. Goods are
moved to and from the DCs across the country through a dedicated fleet
of 180 tractors, 2,000 trailers, and more than 250 drivers. Walmart
Canada plans to invest more than $175 million to build a new state-of-the-
art fulfillment center in Surrey, British Columbia (*Newswire*, 2018). Slated
to open in 2020, the fulfillment center will provide fresh and frozen
grocery items to 60 stores within the province of British Columbia.

LOCATION FACTORS

The location decision for DCs is one of the critical concerns in retail planning for corporations operating a large number of stores. Two fundamental questions that are related to DC location decisions are "how many DCs are needed?" and "where should they be located?" The answer to the question of "where" rests on a good understanding of the location criteria and factors that are critical to the success of a distribution center.

Three general location selection criteria for DCs are commonly agreed upon (He et al., 2017; Musolino et al., 2019): economic, social, and environmental. Economic criteria include price of land, possibility of expansion, access to transportation, delivery time, tax policy, and resource availability (utilities and skilled workers, etc.). Social criteria include impact on surrounding traffic and nearby residents, and harmonization with regional economic planning. Environmental criteria include impacts on ecological landscape and protection of the environment.

Under the umbrella of these three general criteria are a number of specific factors that need to be closely examined and investigated when making a decision on geographical positioning of a DC. These are:

- proximity to the retail outlets to be served
- availability and affordability of suitable land
- adjacency to transport hubs (ports or intermodal terminals)
- closeness to major transportation routes (highway and arterial road)
- availability of reliable utilities (power and water)
- availability of skilled workers
- environmental sensitivity
- tax incentives
- community attitude

In general, the main goal in site selection is to optimize service, while minimizing the overall cost associated with the initial construction and day-to-day operation of a DC. In the spirit of this goal, the DC should be centrally located relative to the set of stores to be served, so that the total weighted travel distance is minimized. A stipulated industry standard is an average distance of approximately 200 miles (320 km) between the DC and the stores, at an average transit lead time of just over one day (Bjorson, 2005).

As described in the preceding section, DCs consist of receiving docks, storage areas, and outbound shipping areas. They also use various equipment in the handling of inventories, such as forklifts, pallet jacks, lengthy conveyors, and automated storage and retrieval systems. To meet the space need, DCs range from less than 50,000 square feet ($5,000\,m^2$) in floor area to as much as three million square feet ($300,000\,m^2$). Therefore, development of a DC requires a large parcel of land that is usually available only in suburbs or countryside, where land is also cheaper than in the densely populated central city. Order fulfillment centers are usually smaller than DCs, and smaller lots of land can meet the requirement.

In today's globalized economy, for a DC to be close to manufacturing plants is much less important than before, because a lot of merchandise is imported and shipped from overseas countries via ocean-going vessels. As such, being close to an intermodal, mass transport terminal is more cost-effective and efficient than being close to production plants.

A large DC may receive and ship more than 10,000 truckloads of goods each year. The high volume of both inbound and outbound traffic can easily cause road congestion in the surrounding area. For this reason, DCs are required to be close to highways and arterial roads. This is especially important for outbound transportation, which bridges the geographical disparity between the DCs and the stores using semitrailer trucks, instead of railway cars.

Modern DCs are essentially operation centers that manage the flow of both goods and information between retailers and suppliers through the use of sophisticated information technologies. One other location factor is the availability of skilled workers within commuting distance of the DC. It is equally important that the living environment, living cost, and local amenities in the host community are attractive for skilled workers and their families to move to. Suburban areas of metropolitan regions can easily meet these conditions. Small towns and rural areas often lack these human resources and amenities to attract skilled workers.

In addition to human resources, availability of utilities is also an important consideration. If power lines and water/sewage pipelines exist nearby, construction cost can be greatly reduced; otherwise, the retailer may be asked to contribute to the cost of extending the utility lines to the site.

A DC is a large investment on the part of the corporate retailer. Once in operation, it can make a significant economic contribution to the local economy by creating quality jobs and paying business taxes. Such development, as long as it is environmentally compatible, is welcome by local governments, which may even offer investment incentives and tax reduction to entice such development. Therefore, incentives and reduced tax rate, which may vary by municipality, should also be a location selection consideration.

The large number of both inbound and outbound trucks may cause pollution in the forms of exhaust emission and oil leaks. The environmental impact of DC development often causes community concerns and even triggers opposition. Therefore, building of DCs should avoid ecologically sensitive areas, such as areas close to sources of underground water, fertile farmland, and areas with natural disaster risks.

Figures 10.1 and 10.2 show the locations of two DCs in Canada, from which the embodiment of some location principles is evident. In Figure 10.1 is a Walmart DC located in the City of Mississauga. A suburb of metropolitan Toronto, Mississauga is the sixth-most populous municipality in Canada, with a population of 722,000 (as of the 2016 census). It is also home to Canada's busiest airport—Toronto Pearson International Airport—as well as the headquarters of many Canadian and multinational corporations. First of all, the DC is adjacent to Highway 401, via which (and the other nearby provincial-level highways: 400, 403, QEW, 407, 410, and 427), delivery trucks can reach the Walmart stores in its service area with reasonable speed. Second, being in an industrial park, the DC is separated from the residential area (to its west) by a ravine as a buffer. Figure 10.2 shows the location of a Canadian Tire DC in the city of Brampton. Canadian Tire Corporation Ltd.—the owner of the DC—is a retail company with 480 stores across the country, selling a wide range of automotive, hardware, sports and leisure, and home products. Brampton is another suburban municipality in metropolitan Toronto, immediately north of Mississauga. The ninth-most populous municipality in Canada, Brampton has a population of 593,638 (as of 2016). Its major economic sectors include advanced manufacturing, retail administration, logistics, information, and communication technologies, food and beverage, life sciences, and business services. Also located in an industrial park, the Canadian Tire DC is completely separated from residential areas by green space, major roads, and buffer zones, to minimize negative impacts on the local community. The industrial park is served by a large railway yard, which is also an intermodal transportation terminal. Both inbound and outbound trucks can be easily facilitated by the nearby highways: HWY407, HWY427, and HWY401.

Figure 10.1 A Walmart Distribution Center in Mississauga, Ontario.

Figure 10.2 A Canadian Tire Distribution Center in Brampton, Ontario.

CONTROVERSIES OF DISTRIBUTION CENTER SITING: THE CASE OF CANADIAN TIRE

As cost of land and real estate has soared in built-up areas, new DCs tend to be located towards outer suburbs. While they are welcomed by local municipalities for economic reasons, they are also confronted by local citizens for their impacts on community life. Due to the lack of land for expansion to meet its growing business needs, Canadian Tire made the decision in 2013 to close its second distribution center in Brampton and build a new and larger national DC in Bolton—a rural community in the City of Caledon. North of Brampton and mostly rural, Caledon has more land than the City of Toronto, but has only 2 percent of Toronto's population. So development potential is huge.

The building site was chosen due to its proximity to the Canadian National rail and Canadian Pacific rail intermodal facilities, as well as the 400 series of provincial highways. According to the plan, the project would convert 73 hectares (180 acres) of prime agricultural land into a major industrial development for a 1.5-million-square-foot DC—one of the largest distribution facilities in Canada. The distribution center was to be constructed in two phases, with Phase 1 providing space for 162 dock doors and Phase 2 adding an additional 69 dock doors. When completed, the distribution center was expected to handle 1.56 million cubic meters of goods per year (Gruske, 2013).

As noted by Canadian Tire's spokesperson Josœlyn Dosanjh,

> The project, which will create over 350 construction-related jobs and over $235 million in construction-related salaries and benefits, is consistent with the town and region's employment and growth objectives.... [When completed,] we expect to employ approximately 1,200 people at the facility.
>
> (Warmington, 2013)

The council was divided about the development application, but the Province of Ontario weighed in to issue a special development permit for its potential economic benefits to Bolton and Caledon. However, the citizens of Bolton strongly opposed the plan, citing negative externalities. More than 200 people turned out to public meetings on the issue, almost all of them opposed to the DC (Grewal, 2013). Most of all, local citizens were concerned that there would be huge loss of green space, changing Bolton from a rural area to an urban area. They feared that Bolton would one day end up looking like the suburban sprawl of cement and row after row of housing similar to what has happened in Brampton (Warmington, 2013). Moreover, local citizens feared that traffic gridlock and environmental pollution would be caused by delivery trucks (projected to be 350 truck trips a day). The transportation of hazardous material was another issue that the public had not been told about (Grewal, 2014). Some protesters cited studies that have shown a high risk of lung cancer to the general population in areas with high levels of diesel exhaust. Those who live nearby were also strongly concerned about the property value depreciation due to construction of the distribution center. To the opposition group, the number of new jobs to be created for Caledon residents would be much smaller than Canadian Tire had claimed, because most of the workers would be transferred from the Brampton facility: they would still live in Brampton and commute to the new warehouse. To add legitimacy to their opposition, local residents even argued that the development application violated the province's smart growth planning rules, and the permit was issued without adequate consultation with the citizens.

Caledon City Council submitted the matter to Ontario Municipal Affairs and Housing Ministry. Minister Linda Jeffrey granted a "Ministerial Zoning Order" in favor of the application. With power derived from the Ontario Planning Act, a Ministerial Zoning Order (MZO) is the province saying to a municipality that this is important to all of us, so we are supporting it. It is a quick and decisive instrument to combat perceived NIMBYism, a necessary power to protect provincial interests and end the process on an application they deem too important to be a subject of further discussion, including the public's right to appeal to the Ontario Municipal Board (Strader, 2013). One of the reasons the Ontario government approved the plan was that Canadian Tire told Caledon councilors that it had also purchased land in Montreal and could use that land to build a distribution center there. If the company did decide to move operations into the Province of Québec, it would mean the loss of a large number of jobs for Ontario (Gruske, 2013).

As soon as the MZO was issued, Canadian Tire quickly sent bulldozers to the construction site. Local residents continued to protest, citing procedural errors. Due to the strong opposition and protests, Minister Linda Jeffery hit the pause button on the MZO and sent the decision to the Ontario Municipal Board (OMB). As described in Chapter 5, OMB is an appeal body that could stop the project and even cancel it. If that happened, there could be a possibility of legal action on the part of Canadian Tire, which could leave taxpayers responsible for the costs already incurred on the project. Eventually, the OMB made an arbitration decision also in favor of Canadian Tire, and the distribution center was completed and went into operation in July 2017 (see Figure 10.3).

Amazon also built a one-million-square-foot fulfillment center in Bolton, Caledon (adjacent to the Canadian Tire DC), but did it differently and quietly, after learning the Canadian Tire lesson. The site plan and development application were made by the owner and developer of the land, Blackwood Properties, not by Amazon itself, to avoid loud community opposition. The city councilors were even kept out of the loop until a public announcement was made in July of 2018. By the account of Caledon Mayor Thompson, it was necessary to "respect the non-disclosure request to protect the 800-plus good paying, stable and long-term jobs that Amazon would bring to our community" (Strader, 2018). Two city councilors complained about the lack of consultation and expressed concern about turning Bolton into a "freight village" (a term the mayor used in his announcement of the fulfillment center); but it was possible that the no-consultation decision was a way

Figure 10.3 The New Canadian Tire Distribution Center in Caledon, Ontario.

to protect the councilors from being blamed by their constituents. The fulfillment center was completed as planned and on time in August 2019 (Strader, 2019).

LOCATION ANALYSIS AND SITE SELECTION

A DC site selection process, as suggested by BCI Global—a business management consulting firm specializing in project management in the areas of supply chain strategy and location search/site selection— consists of the following steps (BCI Global, 2019):

- compile a list of possible locations for review
- quickly scan 20 or so of them
- conduct detailed analysis of ten or so
- pay site visits to the top three to five
- make final location decisions
- implement the development plan

Industrial and transportation engineers have used complex mathematical methods in determining warehouse locations including a simplex algorithm with branch and bound (Maharjan & Hanaoka, 2017), a genetic algorithm in a linear model (Wang et al., 2014), a non-linear program based on the load distance technique (Monthatipkul, 2016), and artificial intelligence techniques called particle swarm optimization (Hua et al., 2016). In this chapter, three methods which are familiar to retail geographers and have already featured in preceding chapters are described. These are cluster analysis, multi criteria ranking, and location-allocation.

Cluster Analysis

Widaningrum et al. (2017) used the method of cluster analysis to determine the location of DCs for a fast food restaurant chain in Jakarta, Indonesia. The restaurant chain has 96 retail locations served by one distribution center. In the context of DCs, avoiding back order and delivery lead time is the main goal of increasing the number of warehouses apart from decreasing transportation costs and environmental requirements in terms of emission reduction. The research is done to find out if service efficiency can be improved by setting up additional DCs, and where the additional DCs should be located.

The study is implemented in three stages. In the first stage, spatial data are collected, including geocoded restaurant locations, road networks, and boundary lines. In the second stage, a cluster analysis is performed to determine natural groupings of the 96 restaurants by adjacency. The results are used to consider the location of additional DCs. The third stage is a network analysis, to observe the difference between the current condition (with only one distribution center) and the altered conditions (with proposed additional distribution centers). The analysis is done in the *ArcGIS* environment.

The Grouping Analysis tool in *ArcGIS* is used to compute the mean, standard deviation, minimum and maximum values for each restaurant location's X and Y (or longitude and latitude), as the clustering factor in the case study is based on the proximity of location of one point to another. R^2 value is also computed to analyze the appropriateness of variables for separating the points. In this case, R^2 values for X and Y are 0.608 and 0.55, respectively.

The cluster analysis results in three representative spatial clusters of restaurants. The first cluster has eight restaurants, the second cluster has 19, and third cluster, also the largest, consists of 69 restaurants. The first two clusters exhibit a directional dimension in an elliptical shape. Based on the orientations of location distribution, Widaningrum et al. (2017) conclude that adding two new DCs is the most reasonable decision. This conclusion is supported by their network analysis, which shows that the total distance that must be traveled in the distribution process becomes shorter with the addition of two new DCs.

While reducing total weighted travel distance has the benefit of saving energy and reducing pollution, this study stops short of addressing if land or real estate for the additional DCs is available and affordable near the center of the restaurant clusters.

Multi Criteria Evaluation

In a case study of Chongqing City of China, He et al. (2017) proposed and tested a multiple criteria decision-making method for selecting an optimal location of a single DC. The purpose of the research is to select an optimal site among four potential locations. This real-world example is also an application of the ranking method described in Chapter 7.

Thirteen site evaluation criteria are selected in three dimensions: economic, social, and environmental. These are:

Economic:
1 price of land
2 possibility of expansion
3 access to transportation
4 delivery timeline
5 resource availability
6 tax policy

Social:
7 impact on traffic congestion
8 impacts on nearby residents
9 role of promoting development of leading industry
10 harmonization with regional economic planning

Environmental:
11 impact on ecological landscape
12 environmental projection level
13 natural conditions

Four possible locations are compared and evaluated on the basis of their relative superiority. Five expert panels (each of which consists of three experts with background in academia, industry, and government, with 15 experts in total) are invited to, first, rate the 13 evaluation criteria by their relative importance, and then rank the four alternative locations. The linguistic terms of the ratings for the 13 criteria are as the following:

- of little importance (LI)
- moderately important (MI)
- important (I)
- very important (VI)
- absolutely important (AI)

The linguistic terms of rankings of the four alternative locations are:

- very low in superiority (VL)
- low in superiority (L)
- medium in superiority (M)
- high in superiority (H)
- very high in superiority (VH)

The method involves decision makers using linguistic terms to establish an evaluation matrix for the weights of the criteria, and a relative-performance matrix for the four alternative locations with respect to each criterion. Table 10.1 shows the linguistic ratings given by the five expert panels for the 13 evaluation criteria. Table 10.2 shows the linguistic rankings of the four alternative locations using the 13 criteria and the weights established in Table 10.1.

After obtaining the linguistic ratings for the four alternative locations with respect to the 13 criteria, the linguistic preferences, or subjective criteria weights, are translated into triangular fuzzy numbers or objective criteria weights, using the method of *fuzzy analytic hierarchy process* (AHP). The AHP method undertakes a hierarchical representation of the elements involved in the process, to better visualize the decision-making context. The approach consists of (1) defining the objective, (2) determining which criteria and sub-criteria are influencing decision making, (3) identifying which alternatives make it possible to achieve the objective, (4) comparing pairs among the criteria to define priorities, and (5) calculating the consistency index for all criteria (Szeremeta-Spak & Colmenero, 2015). Through normalization, the fuzzy AHP method is considered to permit a more stable ranking order to be established compared to the traditional method of fuzzy *TOPSIS* (technique for order of preference by similarity to ideal solution), which uses Euclidean distance (He et al., 2017). Based on the fuzzy numbers or fuzzy scores, the ranking order of the four alternative locations by their relative superiority is established as L2>L1>L3>L4.

The fuzzy AHP equation is bound to be too complex for undergraduate students to comprehend. For a more intuitive illustration, the

Table 10.1 Linguistic Ratings of the 13 Criteria by Expert Panels

	C1	C2	C3	C4	C5	C6	C7	C8	C9	C10	C11	C12	C13
EP1	AI	I	VI	VI	I	VI	I	AI	I	I	VI	AI	AI
EP2	AI	VI	VI	AI	VI	I	MI	VI	VI	VI	I	AI	VI
EP3	VI	VI	AI	AI	MI	LI	VI	I	LI	VI	VI	VI	AI
EP4	I	MI	AI	I	MI	MI	VI	VI	MI	VI	MI	VI	AI
EP5	AI	I	VI	AI	LI	VI	AI	I	MI	VI	VI	AI	AI

Source: He et al., 2017.

Notes
1 EP1 … EP5 represent the five expert panels
2 C1 … C13 represent the 13 evaluation criteria
3 AI, VI, I, MI, LI represent linguistic ratings of the 13 criteria by their relative importance.

Table 10.2 Linguistic Ratings of the Four Alternative Locations Using the 13 Criteria by Expert Panels

		C1	C2	C3	C4	C5	C6	C7	C8	C9	C10	C11	C12	C13
EP1	L1	VH	H	H	M	VH	H	H	H	H	H	VH	H	H
	L2	VL	VH	VH	H	H	VH	L	H	VH	M	L	H	VH
	L3	L	M	H	H	H	H	H	M	H	M	M	VH	H
	L4	M	VH	M	M	M	VH	L	M	VH	H	M	H	VH
EP2	L1	H	H	VH	H	VH	H	M	H	H	H	H	H	H
	L2	H	VH	VH	VH	H	VH	VL	VH	VH	L	L	H	VH
	L3	M	M	M	H	M	H	L	H	H	H	M	H	H
	L4	M	VH	M	M	M	M	L	M	VH	M	L	M	M
EP3	L1	VH	VH	H	VH	VH	VH	M	H	M	VH	H	VH	M
	L2	L	VH	H	VH	H	VH	L	VH	H	L	VL	VH	H
	L3	M	H	M	H	VH	H	L	M	H	H	M	H	VH
	L4	L	VH	H	H	M	H	L	H	VH	L	M	H	H
EP4	L1	VH	VH	VH	H	H	VH	VH	VH	M	VH	H	M	H
	L2	M	VH	VH	H	VH	H	M	VH	H	M	VL	VH	H
	L3	L	M	H	VH	H	H	L	H	M	H	L	H	VH
	L4	L	H	M	H	H	VH	L	M	H	M	L	M	M
EP5	L1	VH	H	H	H	VH	H	H	H	M	H	M	M	H
	L2	L	VH	VH	VH	H	VH	L	VH	M	M	L	VH	H
	L3	M	H	H	M	H	H	L	H	H	VH	M	H	M
	L4	M	H	H	M	M	H	M	VH	VH	M	L	M	M

Source: He et al., 2017.

Notes
1　EP1 … EP5 represent the five expert panels
2　C1 … C13 represent the 13 evaluation criteria
3　L1 … L4 represent the four alternative locations,
4　VH, H, M, L and VL represent the relative superiority of the four candidate locations.

translation of the linguistic preferences, or subjective criteria weights, is re-done using the following simple numeric ratings:

For criteria weight:

1　for of little importance (LI)
2　for moderately important (MI)
3　for important (I)
4　for very important (VI)
5　for absolutely important (AI)

For rankings of the four alternative locations:

1　for very low in superiority (VL)
2　for low in superiority (L)

3 for medium in superiority (M)
4 for high in superiority (H)
5 for very high in superiority (VH)

The simple numeric ratings of the 13 criteria are shown in Table 10.3. The weighted ratings of the four candidate locations are shown in Table 10.4. For example, by Criterion 1, Location 1 is rated by the Expert Panel 1 as VH (very high in superiority, see Table 10.2). This is translated into a numeric value of 5. The numeric value of 5 is then multiplied by 4.4, which is the average weight of Criterion 1 from all five expert panels, as shown in the last row of Table 10.3. This translates into a score of 22 for Location 1 by Expert Panel 1. The weighted scores for all four candidate locations from the five respective expert panels are calculated in the same way. Total weighted scores for all four candidate locations are then calculated, and their ranks are established, as shown in Table 10.5. The resulting order of superiority is L1 > L2 > L3 > L4, which is only slightly different from the order established with the complex fuzzy AHP method.

This method has two limitations. First, in contrast to the cluster analysis method, this method considers candidate sites only, but not the retail outlets to be served. As the authors themselves acknowledged, this method is more suitable for site selection of fulfillment centers for pure-play online retailers. Second, the effects of possible interactions between criteria are not considered.

Location-allocation Modeling

Location-allocation modeling can also be used for site selection of DCs. As described in Chapter 9, location-allocation modeling requires the use of three sets of data: a list of candidate sites (i.e., feasible sites for DCs), a list of demand points (retail stores to be served by a DC),

Table 10.3 Numeric Weights for the 13 Criteria (Transformed from Table 10.1)

	C1	C2	C3	C4	C5	C6	C7	C8	C9	C10	C11	C12	C13
EP1	5	3	4	4	3	4	3	5	3	3	4	5	5
EP2	5	4	4	5	4	3	2	4	4	4	3	5	4
EP3	4	4	5	5	2	1	4	3	1	4	4	4	5
EP4	3	2	5	3	2	2	4	4	2	4	2	4	5
EP5	5	3	4	5	1	4	5	3	2	4	4	5	5
Average weight	4.4	3.2	4.4	4.4	2.4	2.8	3.6	3.8	2.4	3.8	3.4	4.6	4.8

Table 10.4 Weighted Scores for the Four Candidate Locations given by the Five Expert Panels (Transformed from Tables 10.2 and 10.3)

Expert panel	Location	C1	C2	C3	C4	C5	C6	C7	C8	C9	C10	C11	C12	C13	total score
EP1	L1	22	12.8	17.6	13.2	12	11.2	14.4	15.2	9.6	15.2	17	18.4	19.2	197.8
	L2	4.4	16	22	17.6	9.6	14	7.2	15.2	12	11.4	6.8	18.4	24	178.6
	L3	8.8	9.6	17.6	17.6	9.6	11.2	14.4	11.4	9.6	11.4	10.2	23	19.2	173.6
	L4	13.2	16	13.2	13.2	7.2	14	7.2	11.4	12	15.2	10.2	18.4	24	175.2
EP2	L1	17.6	12.8	22	17.6	12	11.2	10.8	15.2	9.6	15.2	13.6	18.4	19.2	195.2
	L2	17.6	16	22	22	9.6	14	3.6	19	12	7.6	6.8	18.4	24	192.6
	L3	13.2	9.6	13.2	17.6	7.2	11.2	7.2	15.2	9.6	15.2	10.2	18.4	19.2	167.0
	L4	13.2	16	13.2	13.2	7.2	8.4	7.2	11.4	12	11.4	6.8	13.8	14.4	148.2
EP3	L1	22	16	17.6	22	12	14	10.8	15.2	7.2	19	13.6	23	14.4	206.8
	L2	8.8	16	17.6	22	9.6	14	7.2	19	9.6	7.6	3.4	23	19.2	177.0
	L3	13.2	12.8	13.2	17.6	12	11.2	7.2	11.4	9.6	15.2	10.2	18.4	24	176.0
	L4	8.8	16	17.6	17.6	7.2	11.2	7.2	15.2	12	7.6	10.2	18.4	19.2	168.2
EP4	L1	22	16	22	17.6	9.6	14	18	19	7.2	19	13.6	13.8	19.2	211.0
	L2	13.2	16	22	17.6	12	11.2	10.8	19	9.6	11.4	3.4	23	19.2	188.4
	L3	8.8	9.6	17.6	22	9.6	11.2	7.2	15.2	7.2	15.2	6.8	18.4	24	172.8
	L4	8.8	12.8	13.2	17.6	9.6	14	7.2	11.4	9.6	11.4	6.8	13.8	14.4	150.6
EP5	L1	22	12.8	22	22	12	11.2	14.4	15.2	7.2	15.2	10.2	23	19.2	188.4
	L2	8.8	16	22	22	9.6	14	7.2	19	7.2	11.4	6.8	13.8	19.2	186.2
	L3	13.2	12.8	17.6	13.2	9.6	11.2	7.2	15.2	9.6	19	10.2	18.4	14.4	171.6
	L4	13.2	12.8	17.6	13.2	7.2	11.2	10.8	19	12	11.4	6.8	13.8	14.4	163.4

Notes
1 EP1 ... EP5 represent the five expert panels
2 C1 ... C13 represent the 13 evaluation criteria
3 L1 ... L4 represent the four alternative locations.

Table 10.5 Total Weighted Scores for the Four Candidate Locations and Ranks (Derived from Table 10.4)

Location	Total scores	Rank
L1	**999.2** (197.8 + 195.2 + 206.8 + 211.0 + 188.4)	1
L2	**922.8** (178.6 + 192.6 + 177.0 + 188.4 + 186.2)	2
L3	**861.0** (173.6 + 167.0 + 176.0 + 172.8 + 171.6)	3
L4	**805.6** (175.2 + 148.2 + 168.2 + 150.6 + 163.4)	4

and a road network that connects the candidate sites with the retail stores for routing analysis. This means that the locations of the retail stores are known or have already been determined, and the candidate sites have been evaluated and assessed as similarly feasible with regard to the economic, social, and environmental criteria. Competition is not an issue because those DCs that are operated by other retail chains would have nothing to do with the stores to be served by the planned DCs. The operation procedure is the same as the one described in Chapter 9. Through the location-allocation procedure, one or more sites will be selected, depending on the number of distribution centers that the retail corporation plans to build, to minimize the total weighted outbound travel distance.

This method is less frequently used by the retail industry, especially in a new market. When a retailer enters a new market taking the organic growth approach, opening of stores is progressive and the locations of new stores may not be known in the early stages of development. Due to the restrictions posed by some of the location factors, the number of feasible candidate sites may be small, rendering the use of location-allocation modeling unnecessary.

KEY POINTS OF THE CHAPTER

- Spatial expansion of a store network must be supported by a network of distribution centers (DCs). For retailers operating large chains, the deployment and construction of DCs is also an important part of the retail planning process.
- There are three primary sub-problems in the design of DCs: location-allocation problems, vehicle routing problems, and inventory control problems. Location-allocation decisions address how many DCs to locate, where to locate them, what capacity level to consider for each of them, and how to allocate the

goods-receiving stores to them. Vehicle routing decisions address how to build or select vehicle routes between a DC and the stores to be served. Inventory decisions address how much and how often to re-order at a DC, and what level of safety stock to maintain.

- Large retail chains operate a distribution network with different types of DCs, which have different location and space requirements. With rapid expansion of internet retailing, consumer-oriented *order fulfillment centers* (also called *express distribution centers*) have emerged and are increasing in number.

- There are three general location selection criteria for DCs: economic, social, and environmental. Under the umbrella of those criteria are a number of specific factors that need to be closely examined and investigated when making a decision on geographical positioning of a DC.

- A suggested DC site selection process consists of the following steps:

  - compile a list of possible locations for review
  - quickly scan 20 or so of them
  - conduct detailed analysis of ten or so
  - pay site visits to the top three to five
  - make final location decisions
  - implement the development plan

- Industrial and transportation engineers have used complex mathematical methods in determining DC locations. The methods that are familiar to retail geographers are cluster analysis, multi criteria ranking, and location-allocation.

REFERENCES

Ahmadi Javid, A. & Azad, N. (2010). Incorporating location, routing and inventory decisions in supply chain network design. *Transportation Research Part E: Logistics and Transportation Review, 46*(5), 582–597.

BCI Global. (2019). Distribution center site selection. https://bciglobal.com/en/distribution-center-site-selection.

Birkin, M., Clarke, G., & Clarke, M. (2002). *Retail Geography and Intelligent Network Planning.* Chichester, England: John Wiley & Sons, Ltd.

Bjorson, K. D. (2005). Retail distribution center site selection. *Trade and Industry Development.* www.tradeandindustrydev.com/industry/retail/retail-distribution-center-site-selection-362.

Davis, R. L. & Rogers, D. S. (1984). *Store Location and Store Assessment Research*. Chichester, England: John Wiley & Sons, Ltd.

Drezner, Z. & Scott, C. H. (2013). Location of a distribution center for a perishable product. *Mathematical Methods of Operations Research*, *78*(3), 301–314.

Grewal, S. (2013). Canadian Tire to build huge warehouse in Caledon under ministerial zoning order. *Toronto Star*, July 22. www.thestar.com/news/gta/2013/07/22/canadian_tire_to_build_huge_warehouse_in_caledon_under_ministerial_zoning_order.html.

Grewal, S. (2014). Caledon officials lobbied for Canadian Tire facility before public was consulted, documents show. *Toronto Star*, June 24. www.thestar.com/news/gta/2014/06/24/caledon_officials_lobbied_for_canadian_tire_facility_before_public_was_consulted_documents_show.html.

Gruske, C. (2013). Controversial Canadian Tire DC approved: Ontario Ministry of Municipal Affairs and Housing steps in. *Inside Logistics*, July 22. www.insidelogistics.ca/dc-and-warehouse-operations/controversial-canadian-tire-dc-approved-111299/.

He, Y., Wang, X., Lin, Y., Zhou, F., & Zhou, L. (2017). Sustainable decision making for joint distribution center location choice. *Transportation Research Part D*, *55*, 202–216.

Helberg, M. N. (2013). *Location-allocation Optimization of Supply Chain Distribution Networks: A Case Study*. (Master Thesis). Provo, UT: Brigham Young University.

Holzapfel, A., Kuhn, H., & Sternbeck, M. G. (2018). Product allocation to different types of distribution center in retail logistics networks. *European Journal of Operational Research*, *264*(3), 948–966.

Hua, X., Hu, X., & Yuan, W. (2016). Research optimization on logistics distribution center location based on adaptive particle swarm algorithm. *International Journal for Light and Electron Optics*, *127*(20), 8461 8468.

Ji, Y., Yang, H., Zhang Y., & Zhong, W. (2013). Location optimization model of regional express distribution center. *Procedia—Social and Behavioral Sciences*, *96*, 1008–1013.

Maharjan, R. & Hanaoka, S. (2017). Warehouse location determination for humanitarian relief distribution in Nepal. *World Conference on Transport Research, Shanghai, 2017*, 1151–1163.

Monthatipkul, C. (2016). A non-linear program to find an approximate location of a second warehouse: a case study. *Kasetsart Journal of Social Sciences*, *37*(3), 190–201.

Musolino, G., Rindone, C., Polimeni, A., & Vitetta, A. (2019). Planning urban distribution center location with variable restocking demand scenarios: general methodology and testing in a medium-size town. *Transport Policy*, *80*(August), 157–166.

MWPVL International. (2019). The Walmart Distribution Center Network in the United States. www.MWPVL.com/html/walmart.html.

Newswire. (2018). Walmart Canada to invest more than $175 million to build new sustainable, state-of-the-art fulfillment centre in Surrey, British Columbia. www.newswire.ca/news-releases/walmart-canada-to-invest-more-than-175-million-to-build-new-sustainable-state-of-the-art-fulfillment-centre-in-surrey-british-columbia-689221811.html.

Nozick, L. K. & Turnquist, M. A. (2001). A two-echelon inventory allocation and distribution center location analysis. *Transportation Research Part E: Logistics and Transportation Review, 37*(6), 425–441.

Strader, M. (2013). What is a ministerial zoning order? *Caledon Enterprise,* August 7. www.caledonenterprise.com/news-story/3925473-what-is-a-ministerial-zoning-order-/.

Strader, M. (2018). Amazon warehouse a shock to 2 Caledon councilors. *Caledon Enterprise,* July 27. www.caledonenterprise.com/news-story/8765797-amazon-warehouse-a-shock-to-2-caledon-councillors/.

Strader, M. (2019). Video: a behind the scenes tour of Caledon's new Amazon warehouse. *Caledon Enterprise,* August 13. www.caledonenterprise.com/news-story/9548017-video-a-behind-the-scenes-tour-of-caledon-s-new-amazon-warehouse/.

Szeremeta-Spak, M. D. & Colmenero, J. C. (2015). A two-stage decision support model for a retail distribution center location. *Medellín,* 74(March): 177–187. (Paraná, Brazil: Revista Facultad de Ingeniería, Universidad de Antioquia).

Wang, B., Fu, X., Chen, T., & Zhou, G. (2014). Modeling supply chain facility location problem and its solution using a genetic algorithm. *Journal of Software, 9,* 2335–2341.

Warmington, J. (2013). Canadian Tire warehouse project divides Bolton. *Toronto Sun,* September 19. https://torontosun.com/2013/09/19/canadian-tire-warehouse-project-divides-bolton/wcm/83e8227d-3fc4-432d-aee7-8ac9d231b228.

Widaningrum, D. L., Andika, A. & Murphiyanto, R. D. J. (2017). Cluster analysis for determining distribution center location. *IOP Conference Series: Earth and Environmental Science, Volume 109, Conference 1.* IOP Publishing Ltd. https://iopscience.iop.org/article/10.1088/1755-1315/109/1/012021.

11 Conclusions

To reiterate, the retail sector is an integral part of a national economy. From the political economy point of view, all consumer goods have surplus values locked up in them, and the surplus values are not realized until the consumer goods are purchased by consumers through various distribution channels (Blomley, 1996). As such, retailing is the essential link between production and consumption.

The retail industry has always been evolving, both in response to socioeconomic changes and prompted by technological innovations. In the last three decades, the retail industry has undergone several revolutionary changes, almost simultaneously, which have given rise to new retail formats and new delivery channels, and resulted in significant industry wide restructuring and reshuffling. These include retail capital concentration and spatial switching of retail capital (Wrigley, 1993); waning popularity (or even demise) of department stores and emergence of big box stores and power centers as new leading retail formats; intensification of retail internationalization; and the more recent retail disruptions caused by e-commerce. Combining forces, these changes have led to a so-called "retail apocalypse", referring to unprecedented, disruptive and accelerating changes in the retail industry (ProShares, 2019). They have also made store location research more challenging and opened new avenues of research.

These industry changes have been accompanied by more pronounced market differentiation/segmentation, and shifting consumer preference and shopping behaviors. In general, today's consumers want greater choice, comfort of shopping, lower prices, and fast delivery. They also interact with retailers through multiple intervention points, including mobile devices, social media, e-commerce sites, as well as physical stores. This in turn has altered the way retailers operate. Most corporate retailers nowadays reach their customers through omnichannel—an integrated retail distribution model in which online and physical stores are integrated to provide a seamless customer experience.

Despite e-commerce continuing to make massive gains, online retailing is not expected to exceed physical stores in sales and market share. On the one hand, store network rationalization has been made necessary; on the other hand, e-retailers (including Amazon) are opening smaller footprint stores with little or no inventory to showcase merchandise. Sales are generated at these locations but are fulfilled online. Shopping also forms a part of social interactions, and many shoppers look for treasure hunt excitement and unexpected bargains, which happen only in shopping malls and other physical stores.

So, it is still true that the success of a retail business depends on two general factors: the location of the retail outlets, and management of the business. Both factors are equally important, and geography indeed matters. A long-established subject of study, retail geography is concerned primarily with store location research and trade area analysis. The major paradigm shift in the study of retail geography in the early 1990s has led to the emergence of a new geography of retailing. Taking a political economy approach, the new geography of retailing extends the scope of study to include the changing (vertical) relations between retailers and suppliers and the grounding of retail capital in emerging markets. More importantly, it calls for serious treatment of regulations because the regulatory state is an important force influencing both corporate strategies and geographical market structures.

In the views of Birkin et al. (2002: 30), "the location issues in retailing have never faded away and ... have never been as important as they are today". Breheny (1988) shares this view for several reasons: the pressure (mainly from stakeholders) to invest in new outlets is mounting, but easy sites have been developed; experience has become a much less reliable location search guide because the sunk cost of mistakes in location decisions is formidable. Retail geographers with training in spatial analysis are equipped with the skillset to play an important role in market condition analysis and location research in the holistic planning process, as discussed in Chapter 1. While these tasks reflect the typical concerns of the orthodox retail geography, their conceptualization is now informed and improved by the re-theorization in the new geography of retailing. Over the last two decades, new models and computer-based geotechnologies have been developed progressively to advance the study of retail geography, and location research has been strengthened with the emergence of versatile commercial modeling software packages, particularly GIS (Church & Murray, 2009). Most long-standing and time-tested models are computerized and incorporated in the GIS environment, and they are being used more widely by more people. Many computerized models also have the capability of generating summary reports in numeric and graphic forms.

Because neighborhoods are stratified by social class, economic status, and ethnicity, demand for consumer goods varies across the surface of a city or region. All retailers want to ascertain which demographics are most likely to shop at their stores, and place their stores as close to them as possible in order to increase shopping convenience and frequency. Understanding the geography of demand through market segmentation research is therefore the first step in market condition analysis—a topic of discussion in Chapter 2. Market segmentation is based on the "science" of geodemographics, which is well established as a data-driven analysis tool for the study of the geography of demand, and is now widely embedded in customer databases and GIS (Leventhal, 2016). Several leading business consulting firms offer off-the-shelf commercial segmentation systems, such as Claritas' *PRIZM Premier*; Environics Analytics' *PRIZM5*; ESRI's *Tapestry*; MapInfo's *PSYTE*; and Applied Geographic Solutions' *MOSAIC*. Researchers who do not have access to (or cannot afford) these commercial systems can create their segments for a localized market from the census and using the technique of cluster analysis, though a lack of retailer data could be a deficiency.

For planning of large retail facilities, population projection is always an important part of market condition analysis. In general, population projection works better for shorter periods of time and for larger areas of geography. The longer the projection period and the smaller the geographic area, the less accurate the projection tends to be. In all methods of population projection, the challenge is to determine the optimum level of geography.

On the supply side in market condition analysis, retail structure analysis helps business owners to gauge the level of market saturation, the strengths and weaknesses of the competitors, and the market space or gaps left for them to fill. Municipal planners also conduct retail structure analysis to determine if there is an over-supply of certain types of stores, which therefore should be controlled, and if there is an under-supply of other types of businesses, which should be encouraged, through denying or issuing of new business licenses and building permits. Retail structure of a market is by no means static; it changes and evolves over time. A multi-year comprehensive database that includes both location information and store/trade area attributes is required to analyze business structure and reveal changes.

Store location research and trade area analysis are at the heart of retail geography. Retail location analysis is conducted in two stages and at two spatial scales. In the first stage and at macro scale, the analyst focuses on screening of the local market to identify areas with a concentration of target consumers. In the second stage and at micro scale, potential sites are selected and evaluated. K-means cluster analysis is a useful method for market screening. However, it does not always produce a straightforward and clear-cut classification of submarkets. Often, several trial runs are needed for experiment, and some degree of "human intervention" is necessary, to combine several natural clusters into a single submarket, as illustrated in the China case study in Chapter 7. Some form of visualization on the cluster map is also needed to narrow down the location search, as shown in the T&T case study, also in Chapter 7. Indeed, retail location research is a combination of science and "arts".

In site evaluation, two methods are commonly used by corporate retailers: multi criteria ranking, and regression analysis. Since the relative importance of the selection criteria often differs, weighted ranking with varying weights assigned to different criteria is highly recommended, as demonstrated in Chapters 7 and 10. A sophisticated locational modeling system should at its heart have a sales forecasting model of spatial interaction form (Wrigley, 1988). Multivariate regression is such a model. In order to build a robust regression model, several conditions must be met: there should be reasonable grounds to believe that the selected independent variables (including both store attributes and demographic characteristics) influence merchandise demand and sales volume explicitly; the selected independent variables should be as uncorrelated with each other as possible to minimize the effects of multicollinearity; and the set of sample stores should have similar trade area characteristics, and the sample size should meet minimum requirements as well ($n \geq 30$). The statistically derived regression model is then assessed against two critical indicators: the R-squared (R^2), and the significance level (α).

Trade area analysis is conducted not only to evaluate potential sites for new stores, but also to monitor and manage trade areas of existing stores, track trade area changes, and measure cannibalization. Retail geographers have developed a variety of methods to delineate trade areas for analysis, which are based on different assumptions and follow different approaches. The circular buffer, driving distance/time and Thiessen Polygon methods, which follow the deterministic approach, are still widely used by some retailers, because they have the ability to produce results fast with low costs. The probability-based Huff Model is conceptually more robust and defines more "realistic" trade areas; yet, it also requires the use of an extensive amount of data as well as personnel with a high level of computer literacy.

Location-allocation modeling combines site selection and trade area delineation uniquely in the same process. It is especially suitable for selecting sites for a number of retail stores simultaneously, or selecting new sites while also gauging the impacts on the existing stores. The various location-allocation techniques are powerful weapons in the hands of experienced analysts, who can use them to simulate a variety of future scenarios (Jones & Simmons, 1993). In retail location research, the *mini-sum models* are often used, because such models are designed on the principle that the locations of a number of stores are determined such that the total weighted distance to the closest store is minimized. To achieve this goal, use of smaller census geography is preferred because calculation of total weighted distance using smaller census geography tends to be more accurate. Users must be aware that the model-suggested sites should not be treated as final. They are presented to business decision makers for further consideration. Post-location-allocation analysis is also necessary for final investment decisions, including the results of real estate acquisition, lease negotiation, and pro forma financial calculations.

For retailers operating large chains, the deployment of distribution centers is also a necessary part of the retail planning process. Siting of distribution centers has been a classic geographic problem; yet, this topic has rarely been dealt with in retail geography textbooks. Three general location selection criteria guide distribution center research: economic, social, and environmental. Under the umbrella of these three criteria are a number of specific factors that need to be closely examined and investigated when making a decision on geographical positioning of a distribution center.

Large retail chains operate a distribution network with different types of distribution centers, which have different location and space requirements. With rapid expansion of internet retailing, consumer-oriented *order fulfillment centers* (also called *express distribution centers*) have emerged and are increasing in number to meet the need of the e-retailers to reduce logistic costs and serve customers more efficiently.

In the new era of omnichannel retailing, customers want faster ship-
ments at low cost. This means that inventory has to be located closer to
the consumer. The existing model of shipping from a limited number
of distribution centers or fulfillment centers may not always be agile
enough to meet customer demands. Some retailers are converting
some retail stores that are already close to where customers live into
mini-fulfillment centers as a more cost-effective way to expand the distribution network. The Loblaws case study in Chapter 9 is an example
of such analysis.

It should be emphasized that more than one method may be used
to solve a single location problem. Students are also reminded that
the retail planning process is complex. It requires the participation
of experts with different professional backgrounds. Retail geographers are not location decision makers. What they contribute to
the retail planning process is to provide decision support to the high-
level corporate management team. In the eyes of corporate management, store location analysis transforms data into relevant and useful
information to assist them in serious business decision making.
Through communication of results, retail geographers serve as
liaison between management and the new technology, methods, and
data (Beaumont, 1988). As liaison people, retail geographers need to
understand the business and strategic problems that the management team faces. In the past, investigation of the regulatory environment and selection of corporate growth strategies were not tasks
performed by retail geographers, but they are today, as advocated in
the new geography of retailing. This is because regulation is a significant force shaping competition between firms and the governance
of investment, and the regulatory environment varies greatly from
country to country, and even within a country. Land use zoning is the
basic form of location regulation, but foreign investment policies,
business tax law, and anti-competition law all also pose geographical
constraints. It is particularly important to investigate the various regulations when planning for an entry into a foreign market. Spatial
growth strategies also have explicit geographical implication. Need-
less to say, opening a new store always requires screening of local
market and detailed location research. In some cases of merger and
acquisition, location analysis is also needed for such corporate decisions as which existing stores should be acquired and retained, and
which ones should be excluded or closed, as was the case with Target
acquiring the leaseholds of Zellers when entering Canada (as
reported in Chapter 6).

All methods have limitations, and many limitations of their applications result from the lack of appropriate data. Today's retail corporations are collecting vast amounts of data from all aspects of their operations via omnichannel. Big data are better capable of correlating customer purchase history with profit information. The insights derived from intelligent analysis of these big data are valuable for businesses to know better their consumers and their consumers' shopping behaviors. Retailers are already using the big data to lower customer acquisition costs and, in a limited way, to guide their retail location research. In the big-data era, the importance of descriptive trade areas (defined based on data of existing customers) is expected to grow, relative to prescriptive trade areas (delineated by mathematically and statistically based modeling). Some online brands are tapping the big data to identify high-value customers. It is reported that Reset—a U.S.-based digitally native retailer—is using the vast amount of data that it has collected about customers (including customer age, ZIP code location, purchasing history, and sales) to decide where to open popup stores that stay open only for several months or several weeks, depending on lease agreements (Kitchens, 2019).

E-commerce will not mean the death of the importance of distance and geography, and big data do not necessarily make the existing location research methods obsolete. However, they will lead to better choice of variables (especially variables concerning consumer behavior, shopping preference, and residential location) to improve simulation and prediction accuracy through model calibration. In the meantime, retail geographers do need to develop more sophisticated and intelligent spatial analysis techniques, capable of dealing with omnichannel networks. A recent survey of retail location decision makers by Aversa (2018) found that the majority of the respondents still frequently rely on the traditional methods, but they also feel an urgent need for new techniques to make use of the big data for rigorous location decision making. The emerging techniques that have been identified in literature include *log analytics, predictive analytics, machine learning, advanced search relevance ranking, social media analytics, real-time data visualization,* and *NoSQL database.* Yet, no publications are found that illustrate how these methods and techniques are operated with input of big spatial data, to perform "customer journey", or "path-to-purchase", analysis as new location selection and trade area delineation models. The big data indeed offer an opportunity for revamping the traditional theories that typically are normatively based approaches; however, because they contain commercially sensitive transaction information and private information on shoppers' identity, big data are hard to obtain by university-based researchers for

both teaching and research. Collaboration between academic researchers, company in-house practitioners, and data scientists is most likely to
lead to breakthroughs in searching for improved or innovative methodology. Hopefully, the next generation of retail geography textbooks will
feature and incorporate such techniques.

REFERENCES

Aversa, J. (2018). *Spatial Big Data Analytics: The New Boundaries of Retail
    Location Decision-Making* (Doctoral Dissertation). Wilfrid Laurier Univer-
    sity, Canada: Department of Geography and Environmental Studies.
Beaumont, M. J. (1988). Store location analysis: problems and progress. In
    Neil Wrigley (Ed.), *Store Choice, Store Location and Market Analysis*
    (pp. 87–105). London, England: Routledge.
Birkin, M., Clarke, G., & Clarke, M. (2002). *Retail Geography and Intelligent
    Network Planning.* Chichester, England: John Wiley & Sons, Ltd.
Blomley, N. (1996). "I'd like to dress her all over": masculinity, power and
    retail space. In N. Wrigley and M. Lowe (Eds.), *Retailing, Consumption
    and Capital: towards the New Retail Geography* (pp. 238–256). Essex,
    England: Longman Group Ltd.
Breheny, M. (1988). Practical methods of retail location analysis: a review.
    In N. Wrigley (Ed.), *Store Choice, Store Location and Market Analysis*
    (pp. 39–86). London, England: Routledge.
Church, R. L. & Murray, A. T. (2009). *Business Site Selection, Location Ana-
    lysis, and GIS.* Hoboken, NJ: John Wiley & Sons, Inc.
Jones, K. & Simmons, J. (1993). *Location, Location, Location: Analyzing the
    Retail Environment.* Toronto, Canada: Nelson Canada.
Kitchens, S. (2019). Online brands tap customer data to create pop-up
    shops. *Wall Street Journal,* December 2. www.thestar.com/business/
    technology/2019/12/02/online-brands-tap-customer-data-to-create-pop-
    up-shops.html?source=newsletter&utm_source=ts_nl&utm_medium=
    email&utm_email=845F0D24BA4D1E55855D3A5156D46E8E&utm_
    campaign=sbj_18313&utm_content=a10.
Leventhal, B. (2016). *Geodemographics for Marketers: Using Location Analysis
    for Marketers.* London, England: Kogan Page Ltd.
ProShares. (2019). Understanding retail disruption. www.proshares.com/
    media/documents/understanding_retail_disruption.pdf.
Wrigley, N. (1988). Retail restructuring and retail analysis. In Neil Wrigley
    (Ed.), *Store Choice, Store Location and Market Analysis* (pp. 3–38). London,
    England: Routledge.
Wrigley, N. (1993). Retail concentration and the internationalization of
    British grocery retailing. In R. D. F. Bromley & C. J. Thomas (Eds.),
    Retail Change: Contemporary Issues (pp. 41–68). London, England: UCL
    Press Ltd.

Index